Onondaga
Community
College
Library
ONONDAGA COMMUNITY COLLEGE
1962

Passport to UTOPIA

BOOKS BY ARTHUR WEINBERG

Attorney for the Damned

BOOKS BY ARTHUR AND LILA WEINBERG

The Muckrakers

Verdicts Out of Court

Instead of Violence

PASSPORT TO

Great Panaceas

EDITED WITH AN INTRODUCTION BY

CHICAGO | QUADRANGLE BOOKS

in American History

ARTHUR AND LILA WEINBERG

1968

 For information, address: Quadrangle Books, Inc., 12 East Delaware Place, Chicago 60611. Manufactured in the United States of America. Published simultaneously in Canada by Burns and MacEachern Ltd., Toronto.

Library of Congress Catalog Card Number: 68-10836

Designed by Lawrence Levy

TO DREAMS:

wild and imaginative;
to the men and women
who dared to dream them.

ACKNOWLEDGMENTS

WE THANK THE MANY INDIVIDUALS who have helped in preparing this book. We have talked with historians, political scientists, social scientists, psychiatrists, businessmen, and newspapermen, as well as some persons who took part in some of the movements discussed. All have been most cooperative and encouraging.

Among those who helped us are Daniel J. Boorstin, University of Chicago; Stanley Chyet, Hebrew Union College; Morton Frisch, Northern Illinois University; Oscar Handlin, Harvard University; Richard Hofstadter, Columbia University; Sophia McDowell, Howard University; Arthur Mann, University of Chicago; Milton Rakov, University of Illinois, Chicago Circle; David Shannon, University of Maryland; and Irvin G. Wyllie, University of Wisconsin. Also helpful were Louis Zara, James K. Senior, Sidney Lens, Francis Coughlin, Robert Galvin, Upton

Sinclair, and our editor and friend, Ivan Dee. The interpretations and conclusions expressed herein are ours alone.

We are grateful to the staff of the Newberry Library in Chicago which was, as always, most cooperative in providing the facilities that made our task easier; to the archives of the Hebrew Union College which was generous in opening its files to us; to Harper, Swift, and the Business and Economics libraries of the University of Chicago; and to the Chicago Public Library and the New York Public Library.

Our thanks, too, to our daughters: Anita, who not only did much of the typing of the manuscript but helped to prepare the bibliography; Hedy, who assisted in the preparation of the bibliography; and Wendy, who could always be counted on to locate a misplaced book and to file references.

All possible care has been taken to obtain necessary permission to reprint copyrighted material; any errors or omissions are unintentional and will be rectified in future printings upon notification to the editors. We wish to express our gratitude for permission to reprint material from the following sources:

Congressional Digest for "Is the Townsend Plan for 'Old Age Pensions' Sound?" by F. E. Townsend, M.D. (March 1935 issue).

A. Jacques Garvey for "An Appeal to the Soul of White America" by Marcus Garvey, published originally in the *Negro World*, October 1923.

Mrs. Benjamin Lindsey for "The Companionate Marriage" which appeared as the introduction to Judge Lindsey's book *The Companionate Marriage*.

National Education Association for "Thrift: An Educational Necessity" by S. W. Straus, which appeared in the 1916 volume of the NEA Addresses and Proceedings.

Dr. Grant Sanger for portions of *Woman and the New Race* by Margaret Sanger.

Howard Scott for *Science vs. Chaos*.

Upton Sinclair for portions of *I, Governor of California, and How I Ended Poverty*.

CONTENTS

Passport to UTOPIA

INTRODUCTION

THIS BOOK IS THE STORY of a nation in search of a dream, told through the lives, ideas, words, and determinations of single-minded men and women and the movements they fostered. It is a story of promise, anticipation, hope, disappointment, fulfill-ment, the drive for security, plenty, happiness, leisure, and power. It is a study of prefabricated solutions to problems that have con-fronted the nation and the individual—from economic insecurity to sexual frustrations and maladjustments, from social irritations to political uncertainties, from the inequities of race to the degrada-tion of women.

Panaceas are cure-alls. In our political, social, and economic history they have been passports to utopia. They are evangelical responses to crises, answers to disjunctions caused by industrial advances and technological developments, solutions for human frustrations and exasperations. They are based on history, philosophy, sociology, psychology, economics, ambition, and myth.

"One characteristic of man," writes Hadley Cantril in *The Psychology of Social Movements*, "is his capacity to dream and scheme when all is not so perfect as it might be in what he regards as his world. Sometimes the dreams drive him to the ruthless conquest of his neighbors, sometimes they send him across oceans in search of unknown treasure, sometimes they lead him to revolt and to set up a new social order. Sometimes man knows his schemes are only imaginative creations impossible of realization; sometimes they are carefully calculated to meet the contingencies of contemporary life; sometimes they are uncritically accepted as immediate panaceas."

Some of the panaceas in this book were conceived by experimental minds, some by obsessive minds. The individuals who led these movements were monomaniacs. Some were geniuses, some fanatics and charlatans; some were sincere, others mountebanks. Most believed that they—and only they—had the wisdom to lead the way to utopia. Here, now, no waiting for tomorrow. Many considered themselves above the mores of their time and had their own morality, a new code of ethics which they flaunted at contemporary society. Some were malcontents. All were mavericks. Many were vainglorious, their schemes grandiose.

The panaceists were not only dreamers or visionaries; they were doers. They saw their programs as meaningful to their times, and they worked to institute them. They were, therefore, disturbers of the peace in that they challenged the status quo for the benefit of all mankind, or for a specific group or class. They dared to upset the equilibrium of society.

Definitions are important in a book of this nature, as are its scope, limitations, and time period. Let us therefore define our terms:

Mention the words "political or economic panacea" and specific individuals and movements come immediately to mind. "Oh, you mean Townsend, Huey Long, Single Tax, Free Silver." Someone else will add: "Father Coughlin, Technocracy, Prohibition, the utopian communities of the nineteenth century." Others will ask: "How about the New Deal? Socialism? Communism? What about the KKK, the Populists, the Great Society, the John Birchers, civil rights, Ayn Rand, Paul Goodman?"

In the broadest sense, all of these might be considered panaceas. Throughout history, beginning at least with Plato if not earlier, man has been offered political, social, and economic panaceas as well as dietary and medical nostrums. Phrenology, mesmerism, and spiritualism were only a few of the cure-alls cults.

Because of the wide variety of remedies we discovered throughout the course of American history, we had to establish limiting criteria for the selection of those which appear in the pages to follow. First, we have included only schemes designed to alleviate political, social, economic, and racial ills *of the United States*. Thus we have ignored such international movements as socialism, communism, anarchism, Nazism, Zionism, syndicalism, and fascism. Except for William Jennings Bryan and Free Silver, Upton Sinclair and End Poverty in California, and Huey Long and Every Man a King, we have not included major political party platforms or third-party proposals. (Bryan, Sinclair, and Long brought more of the aura of panacea to their political platforms than did other candidates.)

Second, we have drawn from the period 1825 to 1935, excluding earlier and later ideologies. In the revolutionary and early national years of the republic, some millennial proposals did arise; but the main concern in the late eighteenth century was whether the colonies could separate themselves from England and establish an enduring nation. It was not until 1825 that "complete" solutions caught the imagination of the people. This is our starting point.

We stopped in 1935 because with the emergence of the New Deal government began to implement its own panaceas in an attempt to pull the country out of the Great Depression. With such programs as the National Recovery Act, the Works Progress Administration, the Agricultural Adjustment Act, Social Security, and unemployment compensation, many schemes that had formerly been the product of American individualism and eccentricity now became public property. And during World War II there was no time for utopian proposals.

Our third criterion for selection was that the proposals included here generally offered unique and usually unorthodox solutions to specific or general ills of the time. They provoked an emotional fervor which surrounded the leader and his ideas, and led followers to expect even more from the panacea than was originally intended. The schemes made newspaper headlines and captured the imagination of the public.

In making these selections, the most difficult factor has been to bear in mind the radical nature of a panacea *within the context of its own times;* for it is intriguing to see how some panaceas have been incorporated into the fabric of a latter-day society and are now taken for granted. Who today would scoff at the eight-hour day or an old-age pension? True, it took years of struggle by militant labor, helped by industrial automation—the two sometimes mutually opposed to each other—to achieve a semblance of what Ira Steward, the philosopher of the eight-hour day, believed would be the "pleasure society." And while Francis Townsend's concept of helping the aged was different from the old-age pension in effect today, it was a beginning.

Fanny Wright, Henry Clay, and the Abolitionists saw themselves as the harbingers of Negro freedom, but it took a Civil War to finally free the slaves and a civil rights movement to give the Negro his dignity.

The Pill has liberated more women than John Humphrey Noyes and his coitus interruptus or Margaret Sanger and her birth-control clinics. But each was a necessary step to this phase of woman's freedom.

The point is that the fulfillment of a seemingly utopian idea has not necessarily come within its proponent's lifetime. Sometimes panaceas have been starting points for change; sometimes they have merely acted as vehicles for debates, as shakers of complacency, as catalysts for social action. Some panaceas have become chapters in history books, while others remain mere footnotes;

some faded away or, as with Carry Nation and Prohibition, were tried and discarded.

Throughout American history the advocates of change have generally operated at the left of the political, social, and economic spectrums. Right of center have been the "anti" movements, such as the Know-Nothing party and the Ku Klux Klan—conservative ideologies which have no confidence in particular solutions and are antagonistic to change, especially if the change involves a radical deviation from the institutions of the past or present. These people want utopia, too, but utopia to them is either the status quo or a return to the past. They live with the terrible fear of being displaced.

While every panaceist embraces reform, he has something grander in mind. The reformer is usually more limited in his objectives: he does not believe his scheme will solve the total problem. It may not even solve the specific problem, but it will alleviate it; it will soothe, it will make life a little more bearable. The panaceist, on the other hand, is all-inclusive, dogmatic. He is an absolutist, bold and opinionated. His is the only way: Follow me—mine is the road to the millennium. Follow me and utopia is yours. The panaceist is convinced that his fellowmen need him because their lives are empty, dreary, desperate.

The scope of proposals for bringing the United States to the perfect society is astonishing. Contrast the Populists' simple remedy of crushing the money barons and business kings to Emerson's "There will dawn ere long on our politics, on our modes of living, a nobler morning . . . in the sentiment of love. This is the one remedy for all ills, the panacea of nature. We must be lovers, and at once the impossible becomes possible." The same idea of love is found in the philosophy of the late Martin Luther King, Jr., and his nonviolent civil rights movement, and in the hippy's belief in a "spiritual oneness of all men." "Love" is one of the few panaceas of the mid-twentieth century.

At the other extreme, hate is the panacea offered specifically for the Negro by some Black Nationalists and Black Power advocates. These extremists want a utopia which will revenge the hundreds of years the Negro has spent as the underdog; their means to achieve it are not dissimilar from those of the Know-Nothings and the KKK of yesterday and today.

Education has frequently been put forward as a panacea—as the one sure means for perfecting democracy. Jefferson and Franklin thought it so, as did the Knights of Labor, Josiah Holbrook and the Lyceum movement, the Chautauqua movement, and the "better-school" advocates. In 1894 the Committee on Education of the National Grange asserted: "The subject of education underlies all other subjects, and not only in the fundamental principle of our Order, but it is the fundamental principle of progress and advancement in all classes of society and all industries relating to human welfare."

Andrew Carnegie was similarly enchanted: "Educate man and his shackles fall." He proposed education as the "true panacea for all the ills of the body politic. . . . Free education may be trusted to burst every constriction which stands in the path of democracy towards its goal, the equality of the citizen, and this it will reach quietly and without violence." Horace Mann, who initiated a new era in American public-school education, saw it as "a great equalizer of the condition of men"; it "gives each man the independence and the means by which he can resist the selfishness of other men."

Labor unions and cooperatives were conceived as vehicles through which the worker would gain his just share of economic well-being. The good-government advocates believed that politics could be cleansed and crookedness and political machines eliminated through such panaceas as the initiative, the referendum, and the recall. The eugenics cult enjoyed a vogue in the 1920's; it claimed that in "less than four generations," with the control of mating and birth, nine-tenths of the crime, insanity, and sickness of the "present generation in our land, asylums, prisons . . . indigent old age and hopeless degenerates would cease to trouble civilization."

Generally, economic crises in American history have been

"breeders of panaceas" and "panacea mongers." The Panic of 1837 brought on a variety of monetary and banking schemes; the Panic of 1893 was followed by Jacob Coxey and his army of unemployed, and a demand for "public improvements" and money reform; the depression of the 1930's gave birth to scores of panaceas—from Ham 'n Eggs, to Mankind United, to the I AM movement, to Psychiana, as well as those included in this book.

Where are the panaceas today? Surprisingly, many of the old prefabricated solutions are still around—perhaps revised and restated—or, as noted before, they have become part of our social, economic, and political structure. Certainly Upton Sinclair's EPIC was a miniature of Lyndon Johnson's anti-poverty program. The "complex marriage" of John Humphrey Noyes and the "companionate marriage" of Judge Ben B. Lindsey were but steps to the sexual morality of the later twentieth century. (In fact, Noyes, stripped of religious justification, *is* twentieth century.) The evangelism of Billy Graham has the same fervency and promise as that of Billy Sunday; Robert Theobald's proposal for a guaranteed minimum income, which might be called "Vote Yourself a Wage," echoes Henry George Evans' "Vote Yourself a Farm" proposal for an agrarian society. The Know-Nothings who saw America being "corrupted" by Catholic immigrants would no doubt recognize the John Birch Society's invocation of the "communist conspiracy"—both offer "anti" solutions.

Despite the various movements of post–World War II America—from the John Birch Society to the powerful civil rights movement, from Barry Goldwater to the hippies, Billy Graham, "Soul Power," and Timothy Leary—our present age has not been an era of panaceas. It is too existential: it doesn't project or care to. It moves from day to day. Perhaps it is so because issues are more complex, perhaps because we have become preoccupied as never before with international affairs—Berlin, Korea, NATO, the Middle East, Vietnam—perhaps because government has engaged in modest reforms. Or perhaps we are so filled with disillusionment—Watts and Buchenwald, Detroit and Hiroshima,

Bolshevism and the Cold War, computers and automation, Medgar Evers and John Kennedy, Martin Luther King, Jr., and Robert Kennedy—that we are no longer capable of dreaming.

To start a search for utopia, there must be a dream—and not only a lack of faith in the present but a kind of adoring faith in the future.

Is this all missing today? Or is some of the discontent so visible in the late 1960's the beginning of the search for a new dream?

Part I

ANTE-BELLUM

[IMAGES: 1825–1864]

MUCH IS TO BE DONE *in the five decades after the American Revolution. Independence means establishing a government, working out relationships with European countries. America, in the process of remaking itself, questions special privileges, worries about developing manufacturing so it will not have to depend upon imports. Frontiers expand, a culture develops.*

The quarter of a century that follows is the era of Andrew Jackson and Ralph Waldo Emerson; of the "spoils system" and Transcendentalism; of utopian colonies and religious revivals; of Henry David Thoreau, William Lloyd Garrison, Frances Wright, and Stephen Foster, of Horace Mann, John Smith, Cyrus McCormick, John Humphrey Noyes, and Robert Owen.

Emerson writes: "We are all a little bit wild here with numberless projects of social reform. No reading man but has a draft of a new community in his waistcoat pockets." New Harmony, Brook Farm, Nashoba, Hopedale, Yellow Springs, Modern Times, the Shaker villages, Sylvania Associates, North American Phalanxes—these colonies represent answers to problems created by industrialization.

It is an age of religious revivals, the founding of the Workingmen's party, the American Peace Society, the Mormon Church. Josiah Holbrook establishes the first American Lyceum whose object is the "immediate improvement of its members in useful knowledge and the advancement of popular education." The Seneca Falls Convention passes women's rights resolutions.

P. T. Barnum perpetrates his first hoax; the American Moral Reform Society pledges "to practice and sustain the principles of Moral reform in the United States, especially Education, Temperance, Economy, and Universal Liberty." Phrenology comes to America as a "science" that claims to evaluate man's moral character as well as his intellectual being by the shape of his cranium; William Miller prophesizes the second coming of Christ.

It is the age of nativism with its anti-Catholic, anti-foreign feeling. It is the time of the Free Soil party, of the Know-Nothings, of Manifest Destiny. Harriet Beecher Stowe writes a bestseller, Uncle Tom's Cabin. *The U.S. Supreme Court rules that Dred Scott is a slave.*

Agitation for the abolition of slavery reaches fever pitch: William Lloyd Garrison founds the Liberator, *proclaiming: "I will not retreat a single inch, and I will be heard." Nat Turner's insurrection; Wendell Phillips' first abolitionist speech; the murder of Abolitionist Elijah Lovejoy; the Lincoln-Douglas debates; John Brown's raid.*

Civil War.

FRANCES WRIGHT, 1795–1852

☆ Nashoba and the Gradual Abolition of Slavery

"THE SIGHT OF SLAVERY is revolting everywhere," wrote Frances Wright, "but to inhale the impure breath of its pestilence in the free winds of America is odious beyond all that the imagination can conceive."

During a visit to the United States, Miss Wright, a native of Scotland, saw a vessel headed for the slave market. It was overloaded with Negro slaves chained together. The sight revolted her. To free the Negro from slavery became one of her chief determinations. This and the freedom of American women, who she felt were caught in a legal system which made them virtual slaves, became her major life's work.

Frances Wright, born in Dundee, Scotland, was the daughter of a wealthy tradesman who sympathized with Thomas Paine and helped to circulate a reprint of *The Rights of Man* throughout

Scotland. Her mother was the beautiful daughter of General Duncan Campbell. Both parents died when Frances was two years old, and she and her younger sister Camilla were brought up by maternal relatives in London for whom raising the high-spirited Fanny was difficult. She became progressively more devoted to many humanitarian causes and frequently rebuked her well-to-do relatives for their comfortable way of living when there were so many other humans in need.

When Fanny was twenty-three, her relatives suggested that she and Camilla make the conventional Grand Tour of Europe, visiting Greece and Italy. But Frances was more interested in seeing young, free America.

So in the spring of 1819 the Wright sisters began their journey through the northern and eastern parts of the United States. When they returned to England, Fanny wrote *Views of Society and Manners in America,* the book which catapulted her to relative fame and led to her lifelong friendship with General Lafayette.

From her talks with both slave owners and abolitionists, with Robert Owen, James Madison, Thomas Jefferson, and Chief Justice Marshall, grew her proposal for "A Plan for the Gradual Abolition of Slavery in the United States, Without Danger of Loss to the Citizens of the South." This first appeared as a pamphlet published in September 1825.

That same month Frances started to put her plan into effect. She bought three hundred acres of land along the Wolf River in western Tennessee; eventually this preserve was increased to almost two thousand acres. The new community was named Nashoba, the Chickasaw Indian name for Wolf.

Here she intended to establish her utopia—a white cooperative community where the Negro slaves would work out the terms of their emancipation and eventually colonize outside the United States. She gave a public pledge not to set her Negroes free in this country.

Within three months the community had built housing for its immediate needs and planted vegetable gardens and cotton.

But Frances Wright was not equipped for such physical labor and soon fell ill. To regain her health she visited Robert Owen's colony at New Harmony, Indiana. Her absence necessitated a change in the control of Nashoba, which Frances turned from a personal property to a trust which was to hold the estate "in perpetual trust for the benefit of the Negro race."

The slaves of the colony were also deeded to the trustees on the condition that when their labor "shall have paid, to the institution of Nashoba a clear capital of $6,000, with six per cent interest on that capital, from the first of January, 1827; and also a sum sufficient to defray the expenses of colonization, these slaves shall be emancipated and colonized."

From New Harmony, Fanny Wright went directly to Europe. While she was there, one of the trustees of Nashoba published a diary which created a violent national reaction against the colony. "Brothel" became the descriptive term for Nashoba in the furor that followed. Some excerpts from the diary may suggest its controversial flavor.

> *Friday, June 1, 1827:* Met the slaves at dinner time—Isabel had laid a complaint against Redrick, for coming during the night of Wednesday to her bedroom, uninvited, and endeavoring, without her consent, to take liberties with her person. Our views of the sexual relations had been repeatedly given to the slaves; Camilla Wright again stated it, and informed the slaves that, as the conduct of Redrick, which he did not deny, was a gross infringement of that view, a repetition of such conduct, by him, or by any other of the men, ought in her opinion, to be punished by flogging. She repeated that we consider the proper basis of the sexual intercourse to be the unconstrained and unrestrained choice of *both* parties. . . .
>
> *Sunday evening, June 17, 1827:* Met the slaves—James Richardson * informed them that, last night, Mamselle

* A white trustee of Nashoba.

> Josephine † and he began to live together; and he took this occasion of repeating to them our views on color, and on the sexual relation.

Frances made plans to return from Europe immediately. En route to Nashoba, she wrote "Explanatory Notes, Respecting the Name and Object of the Institution at Nashoba, and of the Principals upon Which It Is Founded." Here she expounded her ideas: she believed in complete freedom and happiness—political, social, sexual. She believed that with emancipation would come amalgamation.

Her views created still further scandal and alienated many of her supporters. The colony which she had planned to mark the start of the abolition of slavery began to disintegrate. In 1830 Frances gave up her dream and sailed for Haiti with Nashoba's thirty slaves. There she placed them under the protection of Haiti's President Boyer.

On her return to the United States, Frances Wright joined Robert Dale Owen in founding the *Free Enquirer,* which they used to expound their views on social reform. The unconventional Fanny already had a reputation as a radical orator from her lectures at New Harmony; this led her to the lecture platform in New York where she was a popular speaker discussing labor and women's rights.

In 1831 she married Phiquepal d'Arusmont, a fellow reformer sixteen years her senior who had long admired her. Since both felt strongly that the marriage institution detracted from woman's natural rights and individuality, Fanny and d'Arusmont did not legalize their relationship until they found they were to be parents. After a stormy life together, they were divorced in 1850. Fanny died two years later.

Despite Horace Greeley's reference to her reform activities as "belchings," Frances Wright managed to capture the enthu-

---

† Quadroon daughter of a free colored woman in the Nashoba community.

siasm and support of many of the intellectual minds of her day.

★ A PLAN FOR THE GRADUAL ABOLITION OF SLAVERY IN THE UNITED STATES, WITHOUT DANGER OF LOSS TO THE CITIZENS OF THE SOUTH

It appears superfluous, in proposing a plan for the general abolition of slavery in the United States, to observe upon the immensity of the evil, and the gloomy prospect of dangers it presents to the American people—disunion, bloodshed, servile wars of extermination, horrible in their nature and consequences, and disgraceful in the eyes of the civilized world.

It is conceived that any plan of emancipation, to be effectual, must consult at once the pecuniary interests and prevailing opinions of the southern planters and bend itself to the existing laws of the southern states. In consequence it appears indispensable that emancipation be connected with colonization, and that it demand no pecuniary sacrifice from existing slaveholders, and entail no loss of property on their children. The following plan is believed to embrace all these objects, and is presented to some southern and northern philanthropists in the hope that, if meeting with their approbation, it will also meet with their support. It was originally suggested by the consideration of the German society, lately conducted by Mr. Rapp, at Harmony, Indiana, and (since the purchase of that property by Mr. Owen) at Economy, Pennsylvania.

The great advantages of united, over individual labor, have been evinced by the practice of several religious communities—Moravians, Shaking Quakers, and Harmonites. The latter people furnish a most striking evidence in favor of this system. Ten years since, after the purchase of the congress lands in Indiana, Mr. Rapp's society had to struggle with all the inconveniences

---

From *The New Harmony Gazette*, October 1, 1825.

arising from a total deficit of monied capital. The society now is in possession of superabundant wealth, and comprises within itself all the varieties of human industry.

In directing the attention to the advantages of a co-operative system of labor, as practised in the above-named societies, it is necessary at the same time, to compare those advantages with the disadvantages of existing slave labor.

It is conceived to be an admitted truth that slave labor, considered in itself, independent of the nature of the produce it is employed in raising, is profitless. In Maryland and Virginia, and in other states and districts, where slave labor is brought in direct competition with the free labor of the north, agriculture yields indifferent profit. It is only where the produce raised by slave labor is secured from such competition that its value is certain. This is the case with respect to the four great staples of the more southern states—cotton, sugar, rice, and tobacco; which articles are, as yet, produced by free labor in no part of the world in sufficient quantities to interfere with the gains of the American and West Indian planters. It is probable that the proposed investment of British capital, with a view of raising tropical productions, by free labor, in the East Indies and South America will, at no distant period, affect the present value of southern property. This effect, whenever and by whatever produced, will tend towards the adoption of some other mode of labor, even in that section of the Union where reform may at present appear the least practicable. It is thought, however, that if a more humane and profitable system should be brought to bear in any one state, the example must gradually extend through all.

To render these advantages more immediately apparent, and to bring the first experiment within the reach of a small capital, it is proposed:

To purchase two sections of congress lands, within the good southwestern cotton line—say in some tract bordering on Tennessee, either in Alabama, or Mississippi, unless within Tennessee itself, or elsewhere, some suitable and advantageous purchase of improved property should present itself.

To place on this land from fifty to one hundred Negroes (the greater the number the more will the advantages of a system of united labor be apparent), and to introduce a system of co-operative labor, conducted, as far as shall be advisable in the given case, on the plan of the German and other communities above mentioned, holding out, as the great stimulus to exertion, the prospect of liberty together with the liberty and education of the children.

To open a school of industry which, on the Lancasterian plan, shall carry order and co-operation from the schoolroom into the field, the children working, under the direction of their monitors, with such intermission as shall keep their minds cheerful and their bodies vigorous. It is believed that on a cotton plantation, such a system will raise the value of youthful to nearly that of mature labor. The same may apply, also, to such establishments as shall hereafter combine manufactures with agriculture.

It appears unnecessary to enlarge on the probable effect which a mild but steady system of order and economy, together with the improved condition and future destinies of the children, and an induced personal and family interest in the thriving of the establishment, will produce on the dispositions and exertions of the parents. The better to insure those effects, the parents will be gradually brought to understand, in weekly evening meetings, the object of the establishment and taught orally (in simple language) the necessity of industry, first for the procuring of liberty, and afterwards the value of industry when liberty shall be procured. Any deficiency of exertions or other misconduct may also be explained to them as charged to their account, and binding them to a further term of service.

The duration of the term of service must be somewhat decided by experience. It must cover the first purchase money; the rearing of infancy, and loss by sickness or other accidents;

and bring replacing labor into the community, according to the estimate subjoined. To prevent the separation of families, it would be proposed to value the labor, not by heads, but by families, retaining the parents for an additional number of years rather than manumitting them, and retaining the children to a certain age. It would be advisable also, to continue the labor for an additional year or years, the profits of which should defray the expenses of removal, and supply implements of husbandry and other necessaries to the colonists.

The term of five years has been chosen as an average term in which a good laborer will return his first purchase money with interest. On sugar, rice, and some cotton lands, the term is now esteemed much shorter—from one to three; on other cotton lands, from four to five; in Kentucky, from six to ten; in Virginia, it is difficult to arrive at any estimate, so completely is the value of slave labor depressed. But as the proposed system admits of all kinds of industry, agricultural and manufacturing, it may be expected to raise the value of labor in Virginia, Maryland, and Kentucky, to meet the term of five years; in which case, supposing an improvement in the labor of all the slave states, the average will not be taken too favorably. It should be observed, further, that so long as colonization shall be connected with emancipation, it may always relieve every establishment from the support of age; moving the parents usually, before the period of infirmity, in company with a vigorous youth, sufficient for their support.

It is hoped that, after one successful experiment, a similar establishment will be placed in each state; and that when the advantages of the system shall be ascertained, many planters will lease out their property, to be worked in the same way, receiving an interest equal or superior to that returned at present, while the extra profits may be devoted to the general system.

The experiment farm, which it is proposed to establish by subscription, will, as it is hoped, among other advantages, offer an asylum and school of industry for the slaves of benevolent masters, anxious to manumit their people, but apprehensive of throwing them unprepared into the world.

It may not be superfluous to observe, that due care shall be taken to prevent all communication between the people on the proposed establishment, and laborers on the plantations. And to prevent this more effectually, it may be advisable that the property shall be somewhat isolated: of course every possible facility to be afforded to planters and other strangers for examination of the property and the principles on which it shall be conducted.

Should it be objected that the price of laborers will rise in proportion to their scarcity it may be answered that, supposing the success of the emancipating system of labor to have reached the point at which the rise in the price of people would be anticipated, the supposition involves the competition of valuable with valueless or inferior labor; and that, consequently, the price of the old laborers could not rise. In general, however, these anticipations look too far ahead to admit of accuracy, either in objection or answer.

It remains to meet a difficulty, frequently stated at a first view of the plan. In removing the old laborers, how do you supply their place? It must, in general, be answered that in all cases the supply is soon found to meet the demand. It is presumed, however, that a very large portion of the southern states is perfectly suited to white labor; and that this could, in a great measure, be furnished from the class of poor whites, throughout that section of the Union depressed by the slave system and excluded from industry, to their loss and ruin.

It must be remembered, also, that with the same facility that the door of colonization is opened, so also can it be closed. Whenever and wherever the improved system of black labor shall appear of value, it may be continued by retaining (on the footing of tenants, removable at will) as many as the property can employ, and *no more*. The internal slave trade, which now paralyzes the industry and disgraces the character of Virginia, Maryland, and Kentucky, may thus gradually decline, until the legislatures of those states, and of other states, see proper to check it entirely.

It is thought unnecessary, at present, to specify any place, or country, for the reception of the colonists. Many ideas prevail on this subject; and all perhaps may be consulted. Independent of Haiti, there is the Mexican territory of Texas, touching the line of the United States, free to all colors, with a climate suited to the complexion of the Negro race, and a fine region beyond the Rocky Mountains, within the jurisdiction of the United States.

This plan, proposed in a spirit of equal good will to master and slave, is intended to consult the interests of both. To prepare the latter for liberty, before it is granted, and in no case to grant liberty but in accordance with the laws of the state, by removal out of the state. To remove, by gradual and gentle means, a system fraught with danger as well as crime. To turn labor to account, which is in many places, worse than profitless, and everywhere to heighten its value. To assimilate the industry of the south to that of the north, and enable it to multiply its productions, and improve all the rich advantages of the southern soil and climate. To open also the field of industry to free white labor, now in a great measure closed throughout a large portion of this magnificent country.

Estimate of the First Cost of the Proposed Establishment.

	Dr.	
100	Slaves, averaging $300	$30,000
2	Sections of government land	1,600
	Provisions, clothing, medicines, $35 each	3,500
40	Axes $80	
60	Hoes $30	
40	Grub Hoes $70	300
15	Ploughs $120	
18	Horses $40 each	720
	Harness	150
	Horse-keeping for the first year	1,548
30	Cows at $15	450
20	Hogs	100
	Cotton gin and mill	1,000

Overseer's wages	300
Incidental expenses	1,500
	$41,168

CR.

Allowing 1,000 lbs. of cotton to each hand (200 lbs. less than the statements furnished by southern planters) at 12½ cents	$12,500
Deduct interest of money at 6 percent.	2,520
Net Profit	$ 9,980

Taking this low estimate, both as to price and quantity, it will be seen that hands (between nine and fifty years of age) will repay the purchase money, with interest, in less than four years. But allowing deductions for sickness and deaths, the average term is stated at five years.

The above estimate is based upon the actual gains of southern slave labor, without any calculation as to expected advantages to arise from an improved system of labor.

This estimate shows how advantageous an investment of capital might be found in the proposed establishment. One experiment may suffice to convince the southern planters of its safety and its efficacy, and lead them to attract within their borders a portion of that floating capital, foreign and domestic, which is now employed in developing the resources of Mexico, Colombia, and Peru.

The location, as above stated, will in the first instance be preferred in a good upland cotton country, as demanding less capital. If, however, an establishment shall be attempted in Virginia, Maryland, or generally within that section of the country where existing labor is valueless, all the advantages of the improved system may be yet more forcibly developed.

★ CALCULATION

Shewing at What Period the Labor of One Hundred People (Doubling Itself Every Five Years) Might Redeem the Whole Slave Population of the United States.

A *Plan*

Years	Slave population at present.	Persons on the Establishment doubling their number every five years from their earnings.	
	2,000,000	Begin with 100	Begin with 800
5		200	1,600
10		400	3,200
15		800	6,400
20		1,600	12,800
25	}	3,200	25,600
30	} 3,920,000	6,400	51,200
35	} (natural increase)	12,800	102,400
40		25,600	204,800
45		51,200	409,600
50		102,400	819,200
55		204,800	1,638,400
60		409,600	3,276,800
65	7,840,000 (natural increase)	819,200	6,553,600
70		1,638,400	
75		3,276,800	
80		6,553,600	
85		13,107,200	

It is not supposed that the end is to be obtained in the manner above shown. The calculation is only presented to evince the general redeeming power of labor, if all its earnings be preserved and applied to one purpose. Numerous establishments must be required to embrace a large population. To form any calculation with accuracy, it would be necessary, on one side, to subtract the people as sent off from the establishments, and on the other side, that is to say, from the sum of the slave population, the people who enter the establishments, together with their natural increase.

NOTE: It may be necessary to state more distinctly that masters desirous of emancipating their people, but withheld from so doing by inability to meet the expenses usually attendant on manumission, and anxious to procure for them some preparatory instruction, will find free access to the society. It will be necessary first to send a statement of the age, sex, number, and previous employment of such slaves, to some agent for the establishment who will, in return, supply any information that may be required.

ROBERT OWEN, 1771–1858

☆ New Harmony: A System of Society

ROBERT OWEN SAW NEW HARMONY as a steppingstone to a new social order. The New Harmony community, he explained to its colonists, "is the best halfway house I could procure for those who are going to travel this extraordinary journey with me," a journey which would lead members into "the new state of existence" and show the world that man could live successfully and happily in a cooperative society.

Robert Owen was the son of a North Wales saddler and ironmonger. At the age of seven he was already so proficient in reading, writing, and the simple rules of arithmetic that he spent the next two years as a teacher's assistant. Of these years, Owen later wrote, they "were lost to me, except that I thus early acquired the habit of teaching others what I knew."

Religion was one of Owen's major interests. "The more I

heard, read, and reflected, the more I became dissatisfied with Christian, Jew, Mahomedan, Hindoo, Chinese, and Pagan." He lost "all belief in every religion which had been taught to man. But," he continued, "my religious feelings were immediately replaced by the spirit of universal charity—not for a sect or a party, or for a country or a color—but for the human race, and with a real and ardent desire to do them good."

By the time he was nineteen Owen was employed as the manager of a Manchester cotton mill which he developed into one of the most efficient in Great Britain. He became part owner. He experimented with building a model town. Although profits were increasing, his partners in the Lanark Mill did not approve of Owen's activities. When they forced the sale of the mill at auction, Owen formed another company with new partners who agreed to give him a free hand.

New Lanark became the mecca for social reform. But Owen was still not satisfied. He started to agitate for factory reform throughout England. Child labor was his particular concern. He called a meeting of factory owners with a twofold purpose: to repeal the revenue tariff on raw cotton, and to improve the conditions of the workers. The manufacturers agreed to the first recommendation but would give him no support for the second. Owen continued to agitate. He believed that if the environment were healthy, the individual would be strong. Hence, he concentrated on perfecting the community.

He turned to the United States for his experiment in communal living. The land of the Rappite colony on the banks of the Wabash River in New Harmony, Indiana, was for sale, and Owen bought it. He felt that the new nation had fewer vested interests and less tradition, and was less dominated by commercialism; his experiment would therefore have a better chance of success here.

Owen asked the Congress of the United States for permission to address a session: "I have to propose . . . measures so new and extensive," he said, "that to bring them under immediate beneficial consideration of the proper parties requires, not ordinary, but extraordinary means."

On February 25 and March 7, 1825, Robert Owen spoke in the Hall of the House of Representatives. Among those present were President James Monroe and President-elect John Quincy Adams. The "father of American socialism" addressed himself to the country at large and invited "the industrious and well-disposed" to come to his community at New Harmony and join in creating the new society.

Hundreds answered his call. There was no selection of members as had been Owen's original intention. William Owen, writing to his father, who was on a lecture tour in October 1825, worried: "We have been much puzzled to know what to do with those who profess to do anything and everything: they are perfect drones, and can never be satisfied here. We have gotten rid of a good many such, although we still have a few left."

Earlier, Robert Owen had impressed on the members of the community the fact that change from an individualistic society to the new society was an evolutionary process. Time, patience, and faith in the new social state were needed. There would be some inequities at first, but these would be only temporary, he explained.

The proposed constitution of the Preliminary Society announced as its goal: "To promote the happiness of the world . . . improve the character and conditions of its own members, and to prepare them to become associates in independent communities, having common property."

Owen planned that New Harmony would remain under his personal control for the first three years. At the end of that time the members should be prepared to live as a "Community of Equality" and "so forever bury all the evils of the old selfish individual system."

Although New Harmony was suffering from a shortage of skilled labor and housing, progress was being made in the education of the children and in the area of recreational needs. More than 125 children were boarded and educated in the school. There were band concerts, dancing, public meetings, and discussions. Many of the members were agnostics, yet each Sunday ministers of various denominations preached at the colony.

Robert Owen sailed for Europe to bring back the professionals and skilled labor which the community lacked. He returned in January 1826 with his "boatload of knowledge"—his son Robert; the educator William Maclure; Thomas Say, a zoologist; Charles Lesueur, French naturalist and draftsman; Gerard Troost, Dutch chemist and geologist; and Phiquepal d'Arusmont, another educator, later the husband of Frances Wright.

While the community was still working to establish a firm foothold, Robert Owen, on July 4, 1826, announced his own Declaration of Mental Independence: "I now declare to you and to the world, that man up to this hour has been in all parts of the earth a slave to a trinity of the most monstrous evils that could be combined to inflict mental and physical evil upon the whole race. I refer to private or individual property, absurd and irrational systems of religion and marriage founded upon individual property, combined with some of these irrational systems of religion."

Criticism was immediately leveled at the promising colony by a young America not prepared for such unorthodoxy.

Now, dissenting elements arose within the community itself. Conflicting theories regarding New Harmony's organization and a desire for more religious activity were among the major causes of friction. Some of the dissenters formed new societies which adopted a common constitution based on that of New Harmony. Owen cooperated with them. He turned over acres of land to these new colonies as well as to other groups which became offshoots of the parent community.

Robert Owen was ready to admit that unless people were specifically trained in community living, the project could not succeed. He observed sadly that his attempt was "premature to unite a number of strangers not previously educated for the purpose, who should carry on extensive operations for their common interest and live together as a common family."

He then proposed that his land be returned to him. He offered those who wanted to remain a choice of keeping the land on a long-term lease or buying acreage at a low price. He was willing to take a financial loss. Some men took advantage of Owen's offer and remained in the area as small farmers or craftsmen. The rest of his holdings Owen left to his sons, including Robert Dale, who became a member of the U.S. House of Representatives from Indiana. By 1830 the New Harmony movement had disintegrated.

Returning to England, Robert Owen continued his former career as a philanthropist and social reformer until he died at the age of eighty-seven. On his tombstone are inscribed his own words: "It is the one great and universal interest of the human race to be cordially united, and to aid each other to the full extent of their capacities."

★ MR. OWEN'S DISCOURSE ON A NEW SYSTEM OF SOCIETY

THE SUBJECT which I shall now endeavor to explain is, without exception, the most important that can be presented to the human mind. And, if I have been enabled to take a right view of it, then are changes at hand greater than all the changes which have hitherto occurred in the affairs of mankind.

But if, on the contrary, I have been deceived in my ardent and earnest and honest endeavors to discover truth, for the benefit of my fellow men, then it behooves those distinguished individuals now before me and all, indeed, who are interested in the improvement of our species to take the most effectual means to show wherein I am wrong.

For, believing, as I do, most conscientiously that the principles which I am about to explain are founded in fact, are in unison with all nature, and are abundantly competent to relieve society from its errors and evils, I must, while this conviction so remains, adopt every measure that my faculties and experience can suggest, to enable all men to receive the same impressions, and to act upon them.

It is, therefore, no light duty that is about to devolve on those who are to direct the affairs of this extensive empire. For the time is come when they will have to decide whether ignorance and pov-

---

Delivered in the U.S. House of Representatives, February 25, 1825.

erty, and disunion, and counteraction, and deception, and imbecility, shall continue to inflict their miseries upon its subjects, or whether affluence, and intelligence, and union, and good feeling, and the most open sincerity in all things shall change the condition of this population and give continually increasing prosperity to all the states, and secure happiness to every individual within them. And this is but a part, and a small part, of the responsibility with which they cannot avoid being invested: for it is not merely the ten or twelve millions who are now in these states who will be injured or essentially benefitted by their decisions; but their neighbors in the Canadas, in the West Indies, and over the whole continent of South America will be almost immediately affected by the measures that shall be adopted here. Nor will their responsibility be limited within this new western world. The influence of their proceedings will speedily operate most powerfully upon the governments and people of the old world.

If, upon a fair and full examination of the principles which I am to present to you, they shall be found true and most beneficial for practice, those who are appointed to administer the general affairs of the union and of the respective states of which it is composed will have to decide upon the adoption of measures to enable the people of this continent to enjoy the advantages which those principles and practices can secure to them and to their posterity. . . .

And, through long experience, I am prepared to say that the advantages to be derived from these principles and practices will be so superior to any now possessed by any people that, if the governments of the old world do not gradually alter their institutions so as to permit the subjects of their respective states to partake of similar benefits, then will the population of the old world come to the new; for, within its limits, from north to south, there is an abundance of capacity to sustain and support, in high comfort, much more than all the present population of the old world. Therefore, the rulers of these states, in coming to a decision on this subject, will have to decide upon the destinies of the human race, both in this and in future generations. . . .

My desire now is to introduce into these states, and through them to the world at large, a new social system, formed in practice of an entire new combination of circumstances, all of them having a direct moral, intellectual, and beneficial tendency, fully adequate to effect the most important improvements throughout society. This system has been solely derived from the facts relative to our common nature, which I have previously explained.

In this new social arrangement, a much more perfect system of liberty and equality will be introduced than has yet any where existed or been deemed attainable in practice. Within it, there will be no privileged thoughts or belief; every one will be at full liberty to express the genuine impressions which the circumstances around them have made on their minds, as well as their own undisguised reflections thereon, and then no motive will exist for deception or insincerity of any kind.

Every one will be instructed in the outline of all the real knowledge which experience has yet discovered. This will be effected on a plan in unison with our nature and by which the quality of the mental faculties will be rendered more perfect, and by which all will be elevated much above what any can attain under the existing despotism of mind; and by these arrangements the general intellect of society will be enabled to make greater advances in a year, than it has been hitherto allowed to attain in a century. The innumerable and incalculable evils and absurdities which have arisen from the inequality of wealth will be effectually overcome and avoided throughout all the future. By arrangements as simple and desirable as they will be beneficial for every one, all will possess, at all times, a full supply of the best of every thing for human nature, as far as present experience on these matters can direct our knowledge.

The degrading and pernicious practice in which we are now trained, of buying cheap and selling dear, will be rendered wholly unnecessary; for, so long as this principle shall govern the transactions of men, nothing really great or noble can be expected from mankind.

The whole trading system is one of deception; one by which

each engaged in it is necessarily trained to endeavor to obtain advantages over others, and in which the interest of all is opposed to each, and, in consequence, not one can attain the advantages that, under another and a better system, might be, with far less labor and without risk, secured in perpetuity to all.

The consequence of this inferior trading system is to give a very injurious surplus of wealth and power to the few and to inflict poverty and subjection on the many.

In the new system, union and co-operation will supersede individual interest and the universal counteraction of each other's objects; and, by the change, the powers of one man will obtain for him the advantages of many, and all will become rich as they will desire. The very imperfect experiments of the Moravians, Shakers, and Harmonites give sure proof of the gigantic superiority of union over division, for the creation of wealth. But these associations have been hitherto subject to many disadvantages and their progress and success have been materially counteracted by many obstacles which will not exist under a system founded on a correct knowledge of the constitution of our nature.

We cannot fail to be alive to the superiority of combined over individual efforts, when applied to destroy. We all know the increased power acquired by a small army, united and acting as one body, over the same number of men acting singly and alone—and if such advantages can be gained by union to destroy, why should it not be applied to our benefit for civil purposes?

The new combinations proposed will be associations of men possessing real religious and mental liberty, with every means for obtaining great mental acquirements, and these, it is expected, will rapidly increase among all the members.

Under this system, real wealth will be too easily obtained in perpetuity and full security to be much longer valued as it now is by society, for the distinctions which it makes between the poor and rich. For when the new arrangements shall be regularly organized and completed, a few hours daily of healthy and desirable employment, chiefly applied to direct modern mechanical and other scientific improvements, will be amply sufficient to create a full supply, at all times, of the best of everything for every one, and then all things will be valued according to their intrinsic worth, will be used beneficially, and nothing will be wasted or abused. I did expect, before this time, to have received from Europe models upon a large scale of these new combinations and without which it is difficult to comprehend that which is so wholly new in principle and practice to you. I have here drawings of some of them; they are, however, upon too small a scale to be seen by the whole assembly, but I shall have pleasure in opening them after the meeting for the inspection of any parties who may wish to examine them.

Well knowing the great extent of these advantages, my wish now is to give them in the shortest time to the greatest number of my fellow creatures, and that the change from the present erroneous practices should be effected, if possible, without injury to a human being.

With this view, I am prepared to commence the system on my own private responsibility, or with partners having the same principles and feelings with myself; or by joint stock companies, under an act of incorporation from the state governments of Indiana and Illinois, in which the new properties which I have purchased, with a view to these establishments, are situated—or, by a general incorporated company, formed of the leading persons in each state, who could easily form arrangements by which the benefit of the system might be obtained with the least loss of time by all the inhabitants within each government belonging to the Union. Improbable and impracticable as I well know it must appear to you and to the mass of the public, I do not hesitate to state confidently from this chair, from which you have been accustomed to hear so many important truths, that the system which I am about to introduce into your states is fully competent to form them into countries of palaces, gardens, and pleasure grounds, and, in one generation, to make the inhabitants a race of very superior beings.

When the principles on which this new system is founded, and the practices to which they will necessarily lead, shall be so investigated as to be fully understood, it will be discovered that the present system of society must almost immediately give way before it.

The principles of human nature, on which its morals are founded, will render union and co-operation, to any extent, not only easy but delightful in practice. The pecuniary effects which will be produced by union and co-operation, will make the division and combination of labor, in the same persons and interest, complete, and, in consequence, all individual competition must prove unavailing and cause loss of time and capital. . . .

★ A NEW SOCIETY IS ABOUT TO BE COMMENCED AT HARMONY, IN INDIANA

The direct object of this association is to give and secure happiness to all its members.

This object will be obtained by the adoption of a system of union and co-operation, founded on a spirit of universal charity, derived from a correct knowledge of the constitution of human nature.

The knowledge thus derived, will be found abundantly sufficient to reconcile all religious and other differences.

But, to insure success in practice, a preliminary society will be organized and directed by those who understand the principles of this system, and who have already proved them by a partial yet extensive practice.

Into this preliminary society respectable families and individuals, with capital, and industrious and well disposed families and individuals, without capital, will be received.

Those who possess capital and who do not wish to be employed, may partake of the benefits of this society on paying a sum annually, sufficient to recompense the society for their expenditure.

Those without capital will be employed according to their abilities and inclinations, in building, in agriculture, in gardening, in manufactures, in mechanical trades, in giving instruction in elementary or scientific knowledge, or in some one useful occupation, beneficial to the society.

In return for which, they will be provided with the best lodging, food, and clothing that the circumstances of the establishment will afford; they will experience every attention during sickness and old age. All the children will be brought up together, as members of the same family, and will receive a good and superior education.

At the end of every year, a certain amount in value will be placed to the credit of each family, and each individual not being a member of a family, in proportion to their expenditure, and to the services rendered by them to the society.

Any one may leave the society at any time and take with them, in the production of the establishment, as much in value as shall be placed to their credit at the annual balance immediately preceding the time when they cease to become members of the society.

During the continuance of the preliminary society, any family or individual whose conduct may be injurious to the well being and happiness of the association, and obstruct its progress, will be removed; but it is expected that the spirit of charity, justice, forbearance, and kindness which will direct the whole proceedings of the society, and which will be soon diffused through all its members, will speedily render the dismissal of anyone unnecessary.

As soon as circumstances will permit, it is intended that a society will be formed, consistent in all respects with the constitution of human nature, the general principles and practices of which are explained in the prefixed paper, entitled "An Outline of a New System of Society, Recommended for Immediate and General Practice, by Robert Owen, of New Lanark," and in this society all will be equal in rights and property, and the only distinction will be that of age and experience.

Members of the preliminary society who shall acquire such a knowledge of the principles of the new system as to enable and induce them to apply them to practice, may become members of this more perfect association, in which, it is anticipated, from experiments already tried, during thirty-five years, that almost, if not all, the causes which have hitherto produced evil in the world will be gradually removed.

MORDECAI MANUEL NOAH, 1785–1851

☆ Ararat: City of Refuge for the Jews

BECAUSE OF HIS ATTEMPT to establish a Jewish enclave on American soil—at Grand Island in the Niagara River—Mordecai Manuel Noah has been called both a visionary and a charlatan.

Noah—playwright, journalist, politician, diplomat—was born in Philadelphia, the son of a soldier in the American Revolution. Orphaned at an early age, the young Noah was apprenticed as a carver and gilder. But the trades did not interest him, and he spent his leisure time at the theater or in the library.

In 1808 he wrote his first play, *The Fortress of Sorrento*. During the nineteenth century, Noah was considered in some quarters one of the important American dramatists.

But his major interest was in politics and political writing. Under the pen name of Muly Malak he wrote a series of political letters which resulted in his being challenged to three duels, two of which were called off by his opponents just before they were to take place. The third challenge was fought, with Noah the victor, wounding his adversary.

During the war of 1812, which Noah strongly favored, President Madison appointed him consul to Tunis. He left for his new post in 1813. The ship, however, was captured by the British, and Noah was detained for several days before being released. It took him a year to reach Tunis overland. As he traveled, he observed the sad conditions of many of the Jews in various parts of Europe.

When he finally reached his destination, he was confronted with the problem of liberating Americans who were being held captives of Algiers. His government had given him secret instructions to pay the ransom demanded by the captors, but to do so indirectly and not involve the U.S. government. This he accomplished through an intermediary.

And then—with no warning—in July 1815 Noah received word from James Monroe, Secretary of State, that his commission as consul had been revoked. The abruptness of Noah's recall has never been satisfactorily explained. The government charged that there had been irregularities in his financial accounting. But there were undertones of anti-Semitism. He was eventually vindicated of the charges of mishandling the government funds.

Noah returned to New York and became active in Tammany politics as an editor of the *National Advocate* and other publications. He also held various political offices, including that of sheriff of New York.

As early as 1820 Noah had petitioned the state of New York for a grant of land on Grand Island in the Niagara River where Jewish immigrants might settle. Though the committee of the legislature reported favorably on the project, the bill did not pass.

It was in 1825 that Noah startled the world with his proclamation urging Jews everywhere to join him in establishing "Ararat—the City of Refuge." Samuel Legett of New York City, Noah's friend, purchased 2,555 acres of land on Grand Island which were to be the nucleus of the Jewish city. Noah, at this time probably the "most distinguished Jewish resident of America," invited rabbis from many countries as well as Jewish laymen to serve as commissioners of the project. He had not thought it necessary to consult these candidates beforehand; before he heard from them he announced plans for cornerstone-laying ceremonies at Ararat. He planned to act as judge of the city until officials could be democratically elected.

Because there were not enough boats to bring the crowds to Grand Island, dedication ceremonies were held in Buffalo, New York, in September 1825. The ceremonies opened with a salute fired in front of the courthouse. The procession started with the grand marshal on horseback followed by a number of Tammany political leaders, a military escort, clergy, members of the Masonic order, and others, including Noah, who was dressed in an ermine robe.

The dedication was held in the local Episcopal church with the Rev. Mr. Addison Searle, a friend of Noah's, presiding. Transcribed on the cornerstone was:

Hear, O Israel, the Lord Our God, the Lord Is One
ARARAT,
A City of Refuge for the Jews,
Founded by Mordecai Manuel Noah, in the month Tishri
Sept. 1825, in the 50th year of American Independence.

The proclamation was read at the ceremony.

Throughout Noah's agitation for the establishment of Ararat he received little encouragement. The proposed commissioners refused the appointments and disassociated themselves from the project. Western and Central European Jews did not believe they needed a city of refuge; Eastern European Jews were not aware of the proclamation, since it was suppressed in both the Russian and Austro-Hungarian empires.

Reportedly, Noah himself never set foot on Grand Island.

A day or two after the dedication ceremony in Buffalo, Noah

returned to New York. The cornerstone was left outside the church. For the next forty years the stone was transferred from place to place, and, finally, in 1866, it was deposited in the Buffalo Historical Society building.

The failure of Ararat did not affect Noah's activities. He continued to follow a political career. In 1829 he was named surveyor of the Port of New York; in 1834 he founded the *New York Evening Star* to support the Whig party; in 1841 he was appointed associate judge of the New York Court of Sessions, but resigned the following year. He remained active in Jewish life until he died at the age of sixty-six.

★ PROCLAMATION TO THE JEWS [SEPTEMBER 15, 1825]

Whereas, it has pleased Almighty God to manifest to his chosen people the approach of that period, when, in fulfillment of the promises made to the race of Jacob and as a reward for their pious constancy and triumphant fidelity, they are to be gathered from the four quarters of the globe and to resume their rank and character among the governments of the earth;

And Whereas, the peace which now prevails among civilized nations, the progress of learning throughout the world, and the general spirit of liberality and toleration which exists together with other changes favorable to light and to liberty, mark in an especial manner the approach of that time when "peace on earth and good will to man" are to prevail with a benign and extended influence, and the ancient people of God, the first to proclaim His unity and omnipotence, are to be restored to their inheritance and enjoy the rights of a sovereign independent people;

Therefore, I, Mordecai Manuel Noah, citizen of the United States of America, late Consul of said States to the City and Kingdom of Tunis, High Sheriff of New York, Counselor at Law, and by the grace of God, Governor and Judge of Israel, have issued this my Proclamation, announcing to the Jews throughout the

---

From *Publications of the American Jewish Historical Society*, Vol. VIII.

world that an asylum is prepared and hereby offered to them where they can enjoy that peace, comfort, and happiness which have been denied them through the intolerance and misgovernment of former ages; an asylum in a free and powerful country, where ample protection is secured to their persons, their property, and religious rights; an asylum in a country remarkable for its vast resources, the richness of its soil, and the salubrity of its climate; where industry is encouraged, education promoted, and good faith rewarded; "a land of milk and honey," where Israel may repose in peace, under his "vine and fig tree," and where our people may so familiarize themselves with the science of government and the lights of learning and civilization as may qualify them for that great and final restoration to their ancient heritage, which the times so powerfully indicate.

The asylum referred to is in the State of New York, the greatest state in the American confederacy. New York contains forty-three thousand, two hundred and fourteen square miles, divided into fifty-five counties, and having six thousand and eighty-seven post-towns and cities, containing one million, five hundred thousand inhabitants, together with six million acres of cultivated land, improvements in agriculture and manufactures, in trade and commerce, which include a valuation of three hundred millions of dollars of taxable property; one hundred and fifty thousand militia, armed and equipped; a constitution founded upon an equality of rights, having no test-oaths and recognizing no religious distinctions, and seven thousand free schools and colleges, affording the blessings of education to four hundred thousand children. Such is the great and increasing state to which the emigration of the Jews is directed.

The desired spot in the State of New York, to which I hereby invite my beloved people throughout the world, in common with those of every religious denomination, is called Grand Island, and on which I shall lay the foundation of a City of Refuge, to be called Ararat.

Grand Island in the Niagara river is bounded by Ontario on the north, and Erie on the south, and within a few miles of each of those great commercial lakes. The island is nearly twelve miles in length, and varying from three to seven miles in breadth, and contains upwards of seventeen thousand acres of remarkably rich and fertile land. Lake Erie is about two hundred and seventy miles in length, and borders on the states of New York, Pennsylvania, and Ohio; and westwardly, by the possessions of our friends and neighbors, the British subjects of Upper Canada. This splendid lake unites itself by means of navigable rivers with Lakes St. Clair, Huron, Michigan, and Superior, embracing a lake shore of nearly three thousand miles; and by short canals those vast sheets of water will be connected with the Illinois and Mississippi rivers, thereby establishing a great and valuable internal trade to New Orleans and the Gulf of Mexico. Lake Ontario, on the north, is one hundred and ninety miles in length, and empties into the St. Lawrence, which, passing through the Province of Lower Canada, carries the commerce of Quebec and Montreal to the Atlantic Ocean.

Thus fortified to the right and left by the extensive commercial resources of the Great Lakes and their tributary streams, within four miles of the sublime Falls of Niagara, affording the greatest water-power in the world for manufacturing purposes—directly opposite the mouth of the Grand Canal of three hundred and sixty miles inland navigation to the Hudson river and city of New York, having the fur trade of Upper Canada to the west, and also of the great territories towards the Rocky Mountains and the Pacific Ocean; likewise the trade of the Western States of America—Grand Island may be considered as surrounded by every commercial, manufacturing and agricultural advantage and from its location is preeminently calculated to become, in time, the greatest trading and commercial depot in the new and better world. To men of worth and industry it has every substantial attraction; the capitalist will be enabled to enjoy his resources with undoubted profit, and the merchant cannot fail to reap the reward of enterprise in a great and growing republic; but to the industrious mechanic, manufacturer, and agriculturist it holds forth great and improving advantages.

Deprived as our people have been for centuries of a right in the soil, they will learn with peculiar satisfaction that here they can till the soil, reap the harvest, and raise the flocks which are unquestionably their own; and in the full and unmolested enjoyment of their religious rights and of every civil immunity, together with peace and plenty, they can lift up their voice in gratitude to Him who sustained our fathers in the wilderness and brought us in triumph out of the land of Egypt; who assigned to us the safekeeping of his oracles, who proclaimed us his people, and who has ever walked before us like a "cloud by day and a pillar of fire by night."

In His name do I revive, renew, and re-establish the government of the Jewish Nation, under the auspices and protection of the constitution and laws of the United States of America; confirming and perpetuating all our rights and privileges—our name, our rank, and our power among the nations of the earth—as they existed and were recognized under the government of the Judges. And I hereby enjoin it upon all our pious and venerable Rabbis, our Presidents and Elders of Synagogues, Chiefs of Colleges and brethren in authority throughout the world, to circulate and make known this, my Proclamation, and give to it full publicity, credence, and effect.

It is my will that a census of the Jews throughout the world be taken and returns of persons, together with their age and occupations be registered in the archives of the Synagogues where they are accustomed to worship, designating such, in particular, as have been and are distinguished in the useful arts, in science, or in knowledge.

Those of our people who, from age, local attachment, or from any other cause, prefer remaining in the several parts of the world which they now respectively inhabit, and who are treated with liberality by the public authorities, are permitted to do so, and are specially recommended to be faithful to the governments which protect them. It is, however, expected that they will aid and encourage the emigration of the young and enterprising and endeavor to send to this country such as will add to our national strength and character, by their industry, honor and patriotism.

Those Jews who are in the military employment of the different sovereigns of Europe are enjoined to keep in their ranks until further orders and conduct themselves with bravery and fidelity.

I command that a strict neutrality be observed in the pending wars between the Greeks and the Turks, enjoined by considerations of safety towards a numerous population of Jews now under the oppressive dominion of the Ottoman Porte.

The annual gifts which, for many centuries, have been afforded to our pious brethren in our holy City of Jerusalem (to which may God speedily restore us) are to continue with unabated liberality; our seminaries of learning and institutions of charity in every part of the world are to be increased, in order that wisdom and virtue may permanently prevail among the chosen people.

I abolish forever polygamy among the Jews, which, without religious warrant, still exists in Asia and Africa. I prohibit marriages or giving Keduchin without both parties are of a suitable age and can read and write the language of the country which they respectively inhabit, and which I trust will ensure for their offspring the blessings of education and probably the lights of science.

Prayers shall forever be said in the Hebrew language, but it is recommended that occasional discourses on the principles of the Jewish faith and the doctrines of morality generally, be delivered in the language of the country; together with such reforms, which, without departing from the ancient faith, may add greater solemnity to our worship.

The Caraite and Samaritan Jews, together with the black Jews of India and Africa, and likewise those in Cochin China, and the sect on the coast of Malabar, are entitled to an equality of rights and religious privileges, as are all who may partake of the great covenant and obey and respect the Mosaical laws.

The Indians of the American continent, in their admitted Asiatic origin—in their worship of God; in their dialect and language; in their sacrifices, marriages, divorces, burials, fastings, purifications, punishments, cities of refuge, divisions of tribes; in their High Priests; in their wars and in their victories—being in all probability, the descendants of the lost tribes of Israel, which were carried captive by the King of Assyria, measures will be adopted to make them sensible of their condition and finally re-unite them with their brethren, the chosen people.

A capitation tax of three shekels in silver, per annum, or one Spanish dollar, is hereby levied upon each Jew throughout the world, to be collected by the treasurer of the different congregations, for the purpose of defraying the various expenses of re-organizing the government, of aiding emigrants in the purchase of agricultural implements, providing for their immediate wants and comforts, and assisting their families in making their first settlements, together with such free-will offerings as may be generously made in the furtherance of the laudable objects connected with the restoration of the people and the glory of the Jewish nation. A Judge of Israel shall be chosen once in every four years by the Consistory at Paris, at which time proxies from every congregation shall be received.

I do hereby name as Commissioners, the most learned and pious Abraham de Cologna, Knight of the Iron Crown of Lombardy, Grand Rabbi of the Jews and President of the Consistory at Paris; likewise the Grand Rabbi Andrade of Bordeaux; and also our learned and esteemed Grand Rabbis of the German and Portugal Jews; in London, Rabbis Herschell and Meldola; together with the Honorable Aaron Nuñez Cordoza, of Gibraltar, Abraham Busnac, of Leghorn, Benjamin Gradis, of Bordeaux; Dr. E. Gans and Professor Zunz, of Berlin, and Dr. Leo Woolf of Hamburg to aid and assist in carrying into effect the provisions of this my proclamation, with powers to appoint the necessary agents in the several parts of the world and to establish emigration societies, in order that the Jews may be concentrated and capacitated to act as a distinct body, having at the head of each kingdom or republic such presiding officers as I shall upon their recommendation appoint. Instructions to these my commissioners shall be forthwith transmitted; and a more enlarged and general view of plan, motives, and objects will be detailed in the address to the nation. The Consistory at Paris is hereby authorized and empowered to name three discreet persons of competent abilities to visit the United States and make such reports to the nation as the actual condition of this country shall warrant.

I do appoint Roshhodesh Adar, February 7, 1826, to be observed with suitable demonstrations as a day of Thanksgiving to the Lord God of Israel for the manifold blessings and signal protection which he has deigned to extend to his people, and in order that, on that great occasion, our prayers may be offered for the continuance of His divine mercy and the fulfillment of all the promises and pledges made to the race of Jacob.

I recommend peace and union among us; charity and good-will to all; toleration and liberality to our brethren of every religious denomination, enjoined by the mild and just precepts of our holy religion; honor and good faith in the fulfillment of all our contracts, together with temperance, economy, and industry in our habits.

I humbly entreat to be remembered in your prayers; and lastly and most earnestly I do enjoin you to "keep the charge of the Holy God," to walk in His ways, to keep His statutes and His commandments, and His judgments and His testimonies, as it is written in the laws of Moses—"that thou mayest prosper in all thou doest, and whithersoever thou turnest thyself."

Given at Buffalo, in the State of New York, this second day Tishri, in the year of the world 5586, corresponding with the fifteenth day of September 1825, and in the fiftieth year of American independence.

HENRY CLAY, 1777–1852

☆ Negro Colonization of Africa

HENRY CLAY was one of the founders of the American Colonization Society. He was present at its initial meeting, presiding officer at the second, and elected a vice-president at the third, when the society was officially founded in 1816. He continued to be a zealous supporter of the organization from its inception until his death.

The object of the society was "to promote and execute a plan for colonization (with their consent) of the Free People of Color residing in our country, in Africa, or such other place as Congress shall deem most expedient. And the Society shall act to effect this object, in cooperation with the general government, and such of the states as may adopt regulations upon the subject."

The idea of shipping free Negroes from the United States back to Africa was not a new one. In 1811 Thomas Jefferson had indicated he believed it desirable for free Negroes to colonize. As early as 1787 the free Negroes of Newport, Rhode Island, had such an aim, too, when they organized the Free African Society.

The principal founder of the American Colonization Society, however, came from New Jersey: the Rev. Robert Finley, who was encouraged and supported by many prominent men. Through federal and state governments and individuals, the society endeavored to raise money for the establishment of a Negro colony in Africa. This activity resulted in the collection of thousands of dollars for the purchase and charter of ships to be used to transport the Negroes. President Monroe cooperated in the society's aims. Congress, in 1819, appropriated $100,000 as aid for the return of African Negroes who had been brought illegally into the United States. Many states had local colonization societies, and more than a dozen state legislatures officially approved the society, including such slaveholding states as Maryland, Virginia, and Kentucky.

By 1830 the society had settled about 1,420 Negroes in Liberia, whose capital, Monrovia, was named in honor of President Monroe. Joseph Jenkins Roberts, an ex-slave who came to the colony in 1829, was appointed governor in 1841, becoming Liberia's first president when the colony became a republic in 1847.

Opposition to the society came from various sources. The slaveholders, generally, were not willing to release their slaves. The free Negro, on the other hand, felt he was part of the American scene, that he was rooted to the country, and he did not want to leave.

Most abolitionists opposed the plan. They felt it strengthened slavery because it removed the free Negro from the scene. William Lloyd Garrison pointed out that at the time the society was most active, more slaves were brought into the country than the society ever returned to Africa in all its years of existence.

All the while, there were pro-slavery men in favor of the plan because they believed that the free Negro was a dangerous element in a slaveholding community; and there were philanthropists who believed that such a program would ultimately lead to the abolition of slavery.

Henry Clay was among those who believed that colonization was the road to gradual emancipation. In his initial remarks to the society, he stressed that it was not the intention of the society to affect "the tenure by which a certain species of property is held." He himself was a slaveholder. He opposed encroachment upon slave property, he said, as he did upon any other property he held. He did not think the society's aim was "impractical and utopian."

Born in Hanover County, Virginia, Henry Clay was four years old when his father died. Although his formal schooling was limited, Clay, through his stepfather, obtained an appointment as clerk in the Virginia High Court of Chancery when he was only fifteen. He read law and was licensed to practice by the time he was twenty. A member of the Kentucky legislature, professor of law, U.S. Congressman and Senator, Henry Clay was Secretary of State under John Quincy Adams and several times candidate for the presidency of the United States.

Clay, the "great compromiser," helped strengthen the fugitive slave law and opposed the exclusion of slavery from new states. Yet, at the same time, he asserted himself in favor of gradual emancipation.

The decline of the American Colonization Society began about 1840. By 1912 it was dissolved. But not many years later Marcus Garvey appeared on the scene with his own special program for returning the Negro to Africa.

★ ON AFRICAN COLONIZATION

The object of the Society was the colonization of the free colored people, not the slaves, of the country. Voluntary in its institution, voluntary in its continuance, voluntary in all its ramifications, all its means, purposes, and instruments, are also voluntary. But it was said that no free colored persons could be prevailed upon to abandon the comforts of civilized life and expose themselves to

---

Speech at the annual meeting of the American Colonization Society, Washington, January 20, 1827.

all the perils of settlement in a distant, inhospitable, and savage country; that, if they could be induced to go on such a quixotic expedition, no territory could be procured for their establishment as a colony; that the plan was altogether incompetent to effectuate its professed object; and that it ought to be rejected as the idle dream of visionary enthusiasts. The Society has outlived, thank God, all these disastrous predictions. It has survived to swell the list of false prophets. It is no longer a question of speculation whether a colony can or can not be planted from the United States of free persons of color on the shores of Africa. It is a matter demonstrated; such a colony, in fact, exists, prospers, has made successful war, and honorable peace, and transacts all the multiplied business of a civilized and Christian community. It now has about five hundred souls, disciplined troops, forts, and other means of defense, sovereignty over an extensive territory, and exerts a powerful and salutary influence over the neighboring clans.

Numbers of the free African race among us are willing to go to Africa. The Society has never experienced any difficulty on that subject, except that its means of comfortable transportation have been inadequate to accommodate all who have been anxious to migrate. Why should they not go? Here they are in the lowest state of social gradation; aliens—political, moral, social aliens—strangers, though natives. There, they would be in the midst of their friends and their kindred, at home, though born in a foreign land, and elevated above the natives of the country, as much as they are degraded here below the other classes of the community. But on this matter, I am happy to have it in my power to furnish indisputable evidence from the most authentic source, that of large numbers of free persons of color themselves. Numerous meetings have been held in several churches in Baltimore, of the free people of color, in which, after being organized as deliberative assemblies, by the appointment of a chairman (if not of the same complexion) presiding as you, Mr. Vice-president, do, and secretaries, they have voted memorials addressed to the white people, in which they have argued the question with an ability, moderation, and temper surpassing any that I can command, and emphatically recommended the colony of Liberia to favorable consideration, as the most desirable and practicable scheme ever yet presented on this interesting subject. . . .

The Society has experienced no difficulty in the acquisition of a territory upon reasonable terms, abundantly sufficient for a most extensive colony. And land in ample quantities, it has ascertained, can be procured in Africa, together with all rights of sovereignty, upon conditions as favorable as those on which the United States extinguish the Indian title to territory within their own limits. . . .

This Society is well aware, I repeat, that they can not touch the subject of slavery. But it is no objection to their scheme, limited, as it is, exclusively to those free people of color who are willing to migrate, that it admits of indefinite extension and application, by those who alone, having the competent authority, may choose to adopt and apply it. Our object has been to point out the way, to show that colonization is practicable, and to leave it to those states or individuals who may be pleased to engage in the object, to prosecute it. We have demonstrated that a colony may be planted in Africa, by the fact that an American colony there exists. The problem which has so long and so deeply interested the thoughts of good and patriotic men, is solved; a country and a home have been found, to which the African race may be sent, to the promotion of their happiness and our own. . . .

The aim of the Society is, to establish in Africa a colony of the free African population of the United States, to an extent which shall be beneficial both to Africa and America. . . .

Limited as the project is, by the Society, to a colony to be formed by the free and unconstrained consent of free persons of color, it is no objection, but, on the contrary, a great recommendation of the plan that it admits of being taken up and applied on a scale of much more comprehensive utility. The Society knows, and it affords just cause of felicitation, that all, or any one of the states which tolerate slavery, may carry the scheme of colonization into effect in regard to the slaves within their respective limits and thus ultimately rid themselves of a universally acknowledged curse. A reference to the results of the several enumerations of the population of the United States will incontestably prove the practicability of its application on the more extensive scale. The slave population of the United States amounted, in 1790, to 697,697; in 1800, to 896,849; in 1810, to 1,191,364; and in 1820, to 1,538,128. The rate of annual increase (rejecting fractions and taking the integer to which they made the nearest approach), during the first term of ten years, was not quite three per centum per annum; during the second, a little more than three per centum per annum; and during the third a little less than three per centum. The mean ratio of increase for the whole period of thirty years was very little more than three per centum per annum. During the first two periods, the native stock was augmented by importations from Africa in those states which continued to tolerate them, and by the acquisition of Louisiana. Virginia, to her eternal honor, abolished the abominable traffic among the earliest acts of her self-government. The last term alone presents the natural increase of the capital unaffected by any extraneous causes. That authorizes, as a safe assumption, that the future increase will not exceed three per centum per annum. As our population increases the value of slave-labor will diminish, in consequence of the superior advantages in the employment of free labor. And when the value of slave-labor shall be materially lessened, either by the multiplication of the supply of slaves beyond the demand, or by the competition between slave and free labor, the annual increase of slaves will be reduced, in consequence of the abatement of the motives to provide for and rear the offspring.

Assuming the future increase to be at the rate of three per centum per annum, the annual addition to the number of slaves in the United States, calculated upon the return of the last census (1,538,128), is 46,000. Applying the data which have been already stated and explained, in relation to the colonization of free persons of color from the United States to Africa, to the aggregate annual increase, both bond and free, of the African race, the result will be found most encouraging. The total number of the annual increase of both descriptions is 52,000. The total expense of transporting that number to Africa (supposing no reduction of present price), would be $1,040,000, and the requisite amount of tonnage would be only 130,000 tons of shipping—about one ninth part of the mercantile marine of the United States. Upon the supposition of a vessel's making two voyages in the year, it would be reduced to one half, 65,000. And this quantity would be still further reduced, by embracing opportunities of incidental employment of vessels belonging both to the mercantile and military marines.

But, is the annual application of $1,040,000, and the employment of 65,000 or even 130,000 tons of shipping, considering the magnitude of the object, beyond the ability of this country? Is there a patriot, looking forward to its domestic quiet, its happiness, and its glory, that would not cheerfully contribute his proportion of the burden, to accomplish a purpose so great and so humane? During the general continuance of the African slave-trade, hundreds of thousands of slaves have been, in a single year, imported into the several countries whose laws authorized their admission. Notwithstanding the vigilance of the powers now engaged to suppress the slave-trade, I have received information, that in a single year, in the single island of Cuba, slaves equal in amount to one half of the above number of 52,000 have been illicitly introduced. Is it possible that those who are concerned in infamous traffic can effect more than the States of this Union, if they were seriously to engage in the good work? Is it credible, is it not a libel upon human nature to suppose, that the triumphs of fraud, and violence, and iniquity, can surpass those of virtue, and benevolence, and humanity?

The population of the United States being, at this time, estimated at about ten millions of the European race, and two of the African, on the supposition of the annual colonization of a number of the latter, equal to the annual increase, of both of its classes, during the whole period necessary to the process of duplication of our numbers, they would, at the end of that period, relatively stand twenty millions for the white and two for the black portion. But an annual exportation of a number equal to the annual increase, at the beginning of the term, and persevered in to the end of it, would accomplish more than to keep the parent stock stationary. The colonists would comprehend more than an equal proportion of those of the prolific ages. Few of those who had passed that age would migrate. So that the annual increase of those left behind, would continue gradually, but at first insensibly, to diminish; and by the expiration of the period of duplication, it would be found to have materially abated. But it is not merely the greater relative safety and happiness which would, at the termination of that period, be the condition of the whites. Their ability to give further stimulus to the cause of colonization will have been doubled, while the subjects on which it would have to operate will have decreased or remained stationary. If the business of colonization should be regularly continued during two periods of duplication, at the end of the second, the whites would stand to the blacks, as forty millions to not more than two, while the same ability will have been quadrupled. Even if colonization should then altogether cease, the proportion of the African to the European race will be so small, that the most timid may then, forever, dismiss all ideas of danger from within or without, on account of that incongruous and perilous element in our population.

Further; by the annual withdrawal of 52,000 persons of color, there would be annual space created for an equal number of the white race. The period, therefore, of the duplication of the whites, by the laws which govern population, would be accelerated. . . .

There is a moral fitness in the idea of returning to Africa her children, whose ancestors have been torn from her by the ruthless hand of fraud and violence. Transplanted in a foreign land, they will carry back to their soil the rich fruits of religion, civilization, law, and liberty. May it not be one of the great designs of the Ruler of the universe (whose ways are often inscrutable by short-sighted mortals) thus to transform an original crime into a signal blessing, to that most unfortunate portion of the globe? Of all classes of our population, the most vicious is that of the free colored. It is the inevitable result of their moral, political, and civil degradation. Contaminated themselves, they extend their vices to all around them, to the slaves and to the whites. If the principle of colonization should be confined to them; if a colony can be firmly established and successfully continued in Africa which should draw off annually an amount of that portion of our population equal to its annual increase, much good will be done. If the principle be adopted and applied by the states whose laws sanction the existence of slavery, to an extent equal to the annual increase of slaves, still greater good will be done. This good will be felt by the Africans who go, and by the Africans who remain, by the white population of our country, by Africa, and by America. It is a project which recommends itself to favor in all the aspects in which it can be contemplated. It will do good in every and any extent in which it may be executed. It is a circle of philanthropy, every segment of which tells and testifies to the beneficence of the whole.

Every emigrant to Africa is a missionary carrying with him credentials in the holy cause of civilization, religion, and free institutions. Why is it that the degree of success of missionary exertions is so limited and so discouraging to those whose piety and benevolence prompt them? Is it not because the missionary is generally an alien and a stranger, perhaps of a different color and from a different tribe? There is a sort of instinctive feeling of jealousy and distrust toward foreigners which repels and rejects them in all countries; and this feeling is in proportion to the degree of ignorance and barbarism which prevail. But the African colonists whom we send to convert the heathen are of the same color, the same family, the same physical constitution. When the purposes of the colony shall be fully understood, they will be received as long-lost brethren restored to the embraces of their friends and their kindred by the dispensation of a wise Providence.

The Society is reproached for agitating this question. It should be recollected that the existence of free people of color is not limited to the States only which tolerate slavery. The evil extends itself to all the States, and some of those which do not allow of slavery (their cities especially) experience the evil in an extent even greater than it exists in slave States. A common evil confers a right to consider and apply a common remedy. Nor is it a valid objection that this remedy is partial in its operation or distant in its efficacy. A patient, writhing under the tortures of excruciating disease, asks of his physician to cure him if he can and, if he can not, to mitigate his sufferings. But the remedy proposed, if generally adopted and perseveringly applied, for a sufficient length of time, should it not entirely eradicate the disease, will enable the body politic to bear it without danger and without suffering.

We are reproached with doing mischief by the agitation of this question. The Society goes into no household to disturb its domestic tranquillity; it addresses itself to no slaves to weaken their obligation of obedience. It seeks to affect no man's property. It neither has the power nor the will to affect the property of any one contrary to his consent. The execution of its scheme would augment instead of diminishing the value of the property left behind. The Society, composed of free men, concerns itself only with the free. *Collateral consequences we are not responsible for. It is not this Society which has produced the great moral revolution which the age exhibits. What would they who thus reproach us have done? If they would repress all tendencies toward liberty and ultimate emancipation, they must do more than put down the benevolent efforts of this Society. They must go back to the era of our liberty and independence and muzzle the cannon which thunder its annual joyous return. They must revive the slave-trade, with all its train of atrocities. They must suppress the workings of British philanthropy, seeking to meliorate the condition of the unfortunate West Indian slaves. They must arrest the career of South American deliverance from thralldom. They must blow out the moral lights around us, and extinguish that greatest torch of all which America presents to a benighted world, pointing the way to their rights, their liberties, and their happiness. And when they have achieved all these purposes, their work will be yet incomplete. They must penetrate the human soul, and eradicate the light of reason and the love of liberty. Then, and not till then, when universal darkness and despair prevail, can you perpetuate slavery, and repress all sympathies, and all humane and benevolent efforts among freemen, in behalf of the unhappy portion of our race doomed to bondage.*

Our friends, who are cursed with this greatest of human evils, deserve the kindest attention and consideration. Their property and their safety are both involved. But the liberal and candid among them will not, can not, expect that every project to deliver our country from it is to be crushed because of a possible and ideal danger. Animated by the encouragement of the past, let us proceed under the cheering prospects which lie before us. Let us continue to appeal to the pious, the liberal, and the wise. Let us bear in mind the condition of our forefathers, when, collected on the beach in England, they embarked, amid the scoffings and the false predictions of the assembled multitude, for this distant land; and here, in spite of all the perils of forest and ocean which they encountered, successfully laid the foundation of this glorious republic. Undismayed by the prophecies of the presumptuous, let us supplicate the aid of the American representatives of the people, and redoubling our labors, and invoking the blessings of an all-wise Providence, I boldly and confidently anticipate success.

JOSIAH WARREN, *ca.* 1798–1874

☆ Equity Commerce and the Time Store

JOSIAH WARREN, founder of the principle of "Equity Commerce," was born in Boston. Some sources list him as the son of General Joseph Warren, famed hero of the Revolutionary War, but others say that the relationship was more distant. Little is known of Josiah's early life, except that he was an accomplished musician. He married at the age of twenty and moved west. The young couple settled in Cincinnati, where Warren taught music and played in a band.

During this period he devoted his leisure hours to mechanical inventions. One of his first accomplishments was a lard-burning lamp which made possible cheaper and better light than that provided by lamps using tallow. Warren patented his discovery and soon opened a lamp factory.

Perhaps Warren would have continued in his life as a musician and manufacturer if he had not heard Robert Owen speak and detail his ideal society. Warren was captivated by Owen and his ideal community.

The colony in New Harmony, Indiana, had already been established. Warren sold his lamp factory and moved to New Harmony with his family; filled with enthusiasm, he was determined to help usher in the millennium of brotherhood and plenty, first for the community and then for the world.

Warren remained for two years at New Harmony, where he worked and studied philosophies of government, property, communism, and individualism. Although he left Owen's colony still convinced of the inherent goodness and perfectibility of man, he had decided that true happiness would be realized by the differences in man rather than by the uniformity.

Out of his experiences at New Harmony, Warren evolved his philosophy of the sovereignty of the individual: the freedom to dispose of his time, his person, his property as he saw fit, at his own cost.

So came into effect Warren's Time Store, opened in Cincinnati May 18, 1827, at the corner of Fifth and Elm Streets. It was the first Equity store.

William Baile, Warren's biographer, illustrated the Time Store's operation: "A clock hangs in a conspicuous place in the store. In comes the customer to make his purchases. All goods are marked with the price in plain figures, which is their cost price, plus a nominal percentage to cover freight, shrinkage, rent, etc., usually about four cents on the dollar. The purchaser selects what he needs, with not overmuch assistance or prompting from the salesman, and pays for the same in lawful money. The time spent by the merchant in waiting upon him is now calculated by reference to the convenient clock, and in payment for this service the customer gives his labor note, something after this form: 'Due to Josiah Warren, on demand, thirty minutes in carpenter work—John Smith.' Or, 'Due to Josiah Warren, on demand, ten minutes in needlework—Mary Brown.' "

The store also acted as an exchange for goods or for Warren's labor notes.

Equitable Commerce, Warren's first written description of

his Time Store, was published two decades after the experiment began.

In his "Introduction," Warren gave some account of how his theory evolved.

> The public are here presented with the results of about twenty-five years of investigations and experiments, with a view to a great and radical, yet peaceful change in the character of society, by one who felt a deep and absorbing interest, and took an active part in the experiments of communities at New Harmony, during the two years of 1825 and 1826, and who, after the total defeat of every modification of those plans, which the purest philanthropy and the greatest stretch of ingenuity could devise, was on the point of abandoning all such enterprises, when a new train of thought seemed to throw a sudden flash of light upon our past errors and to show plainly the path to be pursued. But this led directly in the opposite direction to that which we had just traveled! It led to new principles, to new modes of action. So new and so startling were these principles and the natural conclusion from them, that the discoverer . . . dare not attempt to communicate them to his most intimate friends, for fear of being accounted 'insane'; nor would he trust his own reasonings for their accuracy, but resolved to work them practically out, step by step, silently watching and studying their operations, and trust to *results* for making an impression upon the public mind, thinking that *one* successful example, at any one point, might extend itself to the circumference of society.

At the end of two years, Warren was convinced of the practicability of the Equity principles. He founded several Equity villages: first, at Tuscarawas County, Ohio (1835–1837), then "Utopia" at Claremont, Ohio (1847–1851), and, finally his most successful, "Modern Times," at Brentwood, Long Island (1850–1862).

Warren in later years revised the basis for "labor exchange." In addition to "time" as a basis for the exchange, the "repugnance" to the work was also a factor to be considered. Therefore, he gave to the most "disagreeable" work the highest reward.

His labor-cost principle opposed high rates of interest and proposed that the interest on a loan should be determined by the length of time taken by negotiations, a practice which he followed in his own transactions. With labor exchange as the basis of an economic society, Warren added individual sovereignty. Everyone is a law unto himself, Warren believed, but in exercising his liberty one must respect the equal rights of others.

"Modern Times" could be reached "by railroad or rainbow," wrote Moncure D. Conway. In his book, *Where Angels Dare to Tread,* V. F. Calverton said, "It was closer to the rainbow than to the railroad . . . it belonged to the rainbow division of humanity" where man would reach his uniqueness as an individual.

The rainbow, however, faded away, and "Modern Times" with it. The Panic of 1857 shattered a manufacturing enterprise of the colony; the Civil War gave it the final death blow.

Warren, the man whom history calls "the first American anarchist," died quietly in Boston in April, 1874.

★ EQUITY COMMERCE: THE TIME STORE

The *value* of a loaf of bread to a starving man, is equivalent to the value of his life, and if the "price of a thing" should be "what it will bring," then one might properly demand of the starving man, his whole future life in servitude as the price of the loaf! But, any one who should make such a demand would be looked upon as insane, a cannibal, and one simultaneous voice would denounce the outrageous injustice and cry aloud for retribution! Why? What is it that constitutes the cannibalism in this case? Is it not setting a price upon the bread according to its VALUE instead of its COST? If the producers and venders of the bread had bestowed one hour's labor upon its production and in passing it

---

From Josiah Warren, *True Civilization* (Princeton, Mass., 1875).

to the starving man, then some other articles which *cost* its producer and vender an hour's *equivalent* labor, would be a natural and just compensation for the loaf. I have placed emphasis on the idea of *equivalent* labor, because it appears that we must *discriminate* between different kinds of labor, some being more disagreeable, more repugnant, requiring a more COSTLY draft upon our ease or health than others. The idea of *cost* extends to and embraces this difference. The most repugnant labor being considered the most COSTLY. The idea of cost is also extended to all contingent expenses in production or vending.

A *watch* has a *cost* and a value. The COST consists of the amount of labor bestowed on the mineral or natural wealth, in converting it into metal, the labor bestowed by the workmen in constructing the watch, the wear of tools, the rent, firewood, insurance, taxes, clerkship, and various other contingent expenses of its manufacturer, together with the labor expended in its transmission from him to its vender; and the labor and contingent expenses of the vender in passing it to the one who uses it. In some of these departments the labor is more disagreeable, or more deleterious to health than in others, but all these items, or more, constitute the COSTS of the watch. The *value* of a well-made watch, depends upon the natural qualities of the metals or minerals employed, upon the natural qualities or principles of its mechanism, upon the uses to which it is applied, and upon the fancy or wants of the purchaser. It would be different with every different watch, with every purchaser, and would change every day in the hands of the same purchaser, and with every different use to which he applied it.

Now, among this multitude of *values*, which one should be selected to set a price upon? or, should the price be made to vary and fluctuate according to these fluctuating *values!* and never be completely sold, but only from hour to hour? Common sense answers NEITHER, but, that these *values*, like those of sunshine and air, are of right, the equal property of all; no one having a right to set any price whatever upon them. COST, then, is the only rational ground of price, even in the most complicated transactions;

yet, *value* is made almost entirely the governing principle in almost all the commerce of *what is called civilized society!*

One may inform another that his house is on fire. The information may be of great value to him and his family, but as it costs nothing, there is no ground of price. Conversation, and all other intercourse of mind with mind, by which each may be infinitely benefited, may prove of inconceivable value to all; where the cost is nothing, or too trifling to notice, it constitutes what is here distinguished as purely *intellectual commerce.*

The performance of a piece of music for the gratification of oneself and others, in which the performer feels pleasure but no pain, and which is attended with no contingent cost, may be said to cost nothing; there is, therefore, no ground of price. It may, however, be of great value to all within hearing.

This intercourse of the feelings, which is not addressed to the intellect, and has no pecuniary feature, is here distinguished as our *moral commerce.*

A word of sympathy to the distressed may be of great value to them; and to make this value the ground and limit of a price, would be but to follow out the principle that a "thing should bring its *value!*" Mercenary as we are, even now, this is no where done except by the priesthood.

A man has a lawsuit pending, upon which hangs his property, his security, his personal liberty, or his life. The lawyer who undertakes his case may ask ten, twenty, fifty, five hundred, or five thousand dollars, for a few hours attendance or labor in the case. This charge would be based chiefly on the value of his services to his client. Now, there is nothing in this statement that *sounds* wrong, but it is because our ears are familiarized with wrong. . . . The cost to the lawyer might be, say twenty hours' labor, and allowing a portion for his apprenticeship, say twenty-one hours in all, with all contingent expenses would constitute a legitimate, a just ground of price; but the very next step beyond this rests upon *value,* and is the first step in cannibalism. The laborer, when he comes to dig the lawyer's cellar, never thinks of setting a price upon its future *value* to the owner; he only considers how long it will take him, how hard the ground is, what will be the weather to which he will be exposed, what will be the wear and tear of teams, tools, clothes, etc.; and in all these items, he considers nothing but the different items of COST to himself.

The doctor demands of the woodcutter the proceeds of five, ten, or twenty days' labor for a visit of an hour, and asks, in excuse, if the sick man would not prefer this rather than continuous disease or death. This again, is basing a price on an assumed value of his attendance instead of its cost. It is common to plead the difference of talents required: without waiting to prove this plea false, it is, perhaps, sufficient to show that the talents required, either in cutting wood, or in cutting off a leg or an arm, so far as they *cost* the possessor, are a legitimate ground of estimate and of price; but talents which *cost* nothing, are *natural wealth*, and like the water, land and sunshine, should be accessible to all without price. . . .

All patents give to the inventor or discoverer the power to command a price based upon the *value* of the thing patented; instead of which, his legitimate compensation would be an equivalent for the *cost* of his physical and mental labor, added to that of his materials, and the contingent expenses of experiments. . . .

★ THE GREATEST PRACTICABLE AMOUNT OF LIBERTY TO EACH INDIVIDUAL

Liberty! Freedom! Right! The vital principle of happiness! The one perfect law! The soul of every thing that exalts and refines us! The one sacred sound that touches a sympathetic cord in every living breast! The watchword of every revolution in the holy cause of suffering humanity! Freedom! The last lingering word whispered from the dying martyr's quivering lips! The one precious boon—the atmosphere of heaven. The "one mighty breath, which shall, like a whirlwind, scatter in its breeze the whole dark pile of human mockeries." When is LIBERTY to take up its abode on earth?

What is liberty? WHO WILL ALLOW ME TO DEFINE IT FOR HIM, AND AGREE BEFOREHAND TO SQUARE HIS LIFE BY MY DEFINI-

TION? Who does not wish to see it first, and sit in judgment on it, and *decide for himself* as to its propriety? and who does not see that it is his *own individual* interpretation of the word that he adopts? And who will agree to square his whole life by any rule, which, although good at present, may not prove applicable to all cases? Who does not wish to preserve his *liberty* to act according to the peculiarities or INDIVIDUALITIES of future cases, and to sit in judgment on the merits of each, and to change or vary from time to time with new developments and increasing knowledge? Each individual being thus at liberty at all times, would be SOVEREIGN OF HIMSELF. *No greater amount of liberty can be conceived—any less would not be liberty!* Liberty defined and limited by others is slavery! LIBERTY, then, is the sovereignty of the individual; and never shall man know liberty until each and every individual is acknowledged to be *the only legitimate sovereign of his or her person, time and property, each living and acting at his own cost;* and not until we live in society where each can exercise this inalienable right of sovereignty at all times without clashing with, or violating that of others. This is impracticable just in proportion as we or our interests are *united or combined with others*. The only ground upon which man can know liberty, is that of DISCONNECTION, DISUNION, INDIVIDUALITY.

You and I may associate together as the best of friends, as long as our interests are not too closely connected; but let our domestic arrangements be too closely *connected;* let me become responsible for your debts, or let me, by joining a society of which you are a member, become responsible for your sentiments, and the discordant effects of too close connection will immediately appear. Harmonious society can be erected on no other ground than the strictest INDIVIDUALITY of interests and responsibilities, nor can the liberty of mankind be restored upon any other principle or mode of action. How can it be otherwise?

GEORGE HENRY EVANS, 1805–1856

☆ Free Land as a Natural Right

TO GEORGE HENRY EVANS the land, like air and sunshine, was a natural right and therefore in the public domain. "If a man has a right on the earth," he wrote, "he has a right enough to raise a habitation." And there was place enough, certainly, in the United States to do this.

George Henry Evans was born in Bromeyard, Hereford, England. He came to the United States fifteen years later with his father and younger brother, Frederick. Both boys had been influenced by the theological and political writings of Thomas Paine. But Frederick, after a visit to a Shaker colony, turned to the Shakers' religious communism. He joined their community, where he remained a member for sixty years, eventually becoming the presiding elder. George, on the other hand, remained an avowed infidel. He continued to deny revealed religion and discarded the idea of a supernatural. To him, Nature was the Supreme Power. Of the days in which the brothers shared a common philosophy, Frederick wrote: "We were radicals in civil government, and in religion, we were Materialists."

George became active in the labor union movement in New York City. In 1829, with the cooperation of his brother, he started to publish the *Working Man's Advocate,* the official periodical of the newly formed Working Man's party, and one of the earliest labor papers to be published in the United States. Its motto was: "All children are entitled to equal education; all adults to equal property; and all mankind to equal privileges."

After the Panic of 1837, George Henry Evans moved to a farm in New Jersey, where he began to publish the *Radical.* Here, also, he put his ideas on agrarianism into perspective and started his land-reform agitation which was epitomized by the slogan "Vote Yourself a Farm."

It was not until he returned to New York City in the early 1840's and resumed publication of the *Working Man's Advocate,* later *Young America,* that Evans' theories on agrarianism, based on the doctrine of natural rights, received a national platform. His ideas can be traced to Thomas Jefferson's principle that "the land belongs to man, *in usufruct* only."

George Henry Evans' agrarianism was proclaimed in *Young America*:

"THE RIGHT OF MAN TO THE SOIL. VOTE YOURSELF A FARM."

"FREEDOM OF THE PUBLIC LANDS."

"HOMESTEADS MADE INALIENABLE."

To attain these goals, Evans formulated a plan of political action. He promised the support of the working class to those political candidates who would advocate agrarianism. A candidate who did not endorse this philosophy might find an independent nominated to run against him "as a warning to future candidates." Evans insisted there had to be a national policy to distribute unoccupied lands to the settlers instead of to the land speculators.

This was the beginning of the Agrarian League, later the

National Reform Association, which pledged: "We, whose names are annexed, desirous of restoring to man his Natural Right to Land, do solemnly agree that we will not vote for any man, for any legislative office, who will not pledge himself, in writing, to use all the influence of his station, if elected, to prevent all further traffic in the Public Lands of the states and of the United States, and to cause them to be laid out in Farms and Lots for the free and exclusive use of actual settlers."

This group printed pamphlets as part of the agitation. One of these—presumably written by Evans—was circulated by the hundreds of thousands. It was titled: "Vote Yourself a Farm."

Land reform was so important as a basis for Evans' panacea that he could not see abolition as the solution to slavery unless freedom of land was provided for the liberated slaves.

"I was formerly, like yourself, sir," he wrote to one abolitionist, "a very warm advocate of the abolition of slavery. This was before I saw that there was white slavery. Since I saw this, I have materially changed my views as to the means of abolishing Negro slavery. I now see, clearly, I think, that to give the landless black the privilege of changing masters now possessed by the landless white, would hardly be a benefit to him in exchange for his surety of support in sickness and old age, although he is in a favorable climate."

By the time Evans died he had seen the establishment of a national movement on land reform. Other forces lent their voices to the agrarian agitation of Evans' working class, and in 1862 the Congress of the United States passed the Homestead Law. From a land policy which considered public lands only as a source of revenue, the United States government now offered 160 acres of land free to any citizen after five years' residence and cultivation of that land.

Twenty-three years after Evans' death, the doctrine of natural rights was propounded in *Progress and Poverty* by Henry George, who proposed that all land should become common property by a method which would "appropriate rent by taxation."

★ "VOTE YOURSELF A FARM"

Are you an American citizen? Then you are a joint-owner of the public lands. Why not take enough of your property to provide yourself a home? Why not vote yourself a farm?

Remember poor Richard's saying: "Now I have a sheep and a cow, every one bids me 'good morrow.'" If a man have a house and a home of his own, though it be a thousand miles off, he is well received in other people's houses; while the homeless wretch is turned away. The bare right to a farm, though you should never go near it, would save you from many an insult. Therefore, Vote yourself a farm.

Are you a party follower? Then you have long enough employed your vote to benefit scheming office-seekers; use it for once to benefit yourself—Vote yourself a farm.

Are you tired of slavery—of drudging for others—of poverty and its attendant miseries? Then, vote yourself a farm.

Are you endowed with reason? Then you must know that your right to life hereby includes the right to a place to live in—the right to a home. Assert this right, so long denied mankind by feudal robbers and their attorneys. Vote yourself a farm.

Are you a believer in the Scriptures? Then assert that the land is the Lord's, because He made it. Resist then the blasphemers who exact money for His work, even as you would resist them should they claim to be worshipped for His holiness. Emancipate the poor from the necessity of encouraging such blasphemy—Vote the freedom of the public lands.

Are you a man? Then assert the sacred rights of man—especially your right to stand upon God's earth, and to till it for your own profit. Vote yourself a farm.

Would you free your country, and the sons of toil everywhere, from the heartless, irresponsible mastery of the aristocracy of avarice? Would you disarm this aristocracy of its chief weapon,

---

Circular attributed to George Henry Evans and distributed in 1846.

the fearful power of banishment from God's earth? Then join with your neighbors to form a true American party, having for its guidance the principles of the American revolution, and whose chief measures shall be: 1) to limit the quantity of land that any one man may henceforth monopolize or inherit; and 2) to make the public lands free to actual settlers only, each having the right to sell his improvements to any man not possessed of other land. These great measures once carried, wealth would become a changed social element; it would then consist of the accumulated products of human labor, instead of a hoggish monopoly of the products of God's labor; and the antagonism of capital and labor would forever cease. Capital could no longer grasp the largest share of the laborer's earnings, as a reward for not doing him all the injury the laws of the feudal aristocracy authorize, viz: the denial of all stock to work upon and all place to live in. To derive any profit from the laborer, it must first give him work; for it could no longer wax fat by levying a dead tax upon his existence. The hoary iniquities of Norman land pirates would cease to pass current as American law. Capital, with its power for good undiminished, would lose the power to oppress; and a new era would dawn upon the earth, and rejoice the souls of a thousand generations. Therefore forget not to vote yourself a farm.

JOHN HUMPHREY NOYES, 1811–1886

☆ Bible Communism and Complex Marriage

"I WAS BORN and brought up in a strange world," wrote Pierrepont Noyes, a son of John Humphrey Noyes, "a world bounded on four sides by walls of isolation; a world wherein the customs, laws, religions, and social formulas accumulated by civilization came to us only as the faint cries of philistine hordes outside our walls. Within that protected area, a prophet and his faithful followers, having separated themselves from the rest of mankind, were trying to live as lived those members of the Primitive Christian Church of whom it is written, 'No man called aught his own.' That little world was called the Oneida Community, and that prophet was my father."

For his little world, John Humphrey Noyes had proposed his

philosophy of "Bible Communism," not only as it related to property but also to the relationship of the sexes. "When the will of God is done on earth, as it is in heaven, there will be no marriage."

Mystic, visionary man of action, John Humphrey Noyes was born at Brattleboro, Vermont, the son of John and Polly (Hayes) Noyes. The elder Noyes was a successful businessman, active in state politics; Polly was the aunt of Rutherford B. Hayes, nineteenth President of the United States.

John Humphrey Noyes was graduated from Dartmouth College and studying law at the time of a great New England revival. The son of an agnostic, he turned to theology. With his first preaching assignment, he proclaimed the Perfectionist doctrine of a new freedom from the sense of sin. "I do not pretend to perfection in externals. I only claim purity of heart and the answer of a good conscience toward God."

Noyes founded what he called a "free church" in New Haven. In it, he preached that conversion brought a complete release from sin. His preachments were considered heresies in the community, and the Association of the Western District of New Haven County revoked his license to preach the gospel. However, the Association said, it was not "impeaching the Christian character of Mr. Noyes."

Noyes countered: "I have taken away their license to sin, and they keep on sinning. So, though they have taken away my license to preach, I shall keep on preaching."

His interpretation of what he called "perfectionism" and an unhappy love affair of his own led to his founding a colony in community living where complex marriage, male continence, and stirpiculture, the scientific breeding of humans, were to become the core of the social structure.

At Putney, the family home town, John Humphrey Noyes initially experimented with his theories. Among his first followers were his brother, two sisters, and their husbands.

Life at the little community was simple. Members built a small chapel and a store. Living expenses came from a common purse. Although communism of property emerged early in the community's establishment, complex marriage did not prevail until 1846. Before that time, Noyes did not feel that all the members were ready for this radical departure from conformity.

Putney neighbors accepted the community of Perfectionists until rumors began to circulate about the extension of communism into marriage. The village was horrified by "complex marriage." Clergymen preached sermons against these "free-lovers." Fathers sent their daughters to other parts of the country so they could not be lured into the trap.

The climax came on October 26, 1847, when John Humphrey Noyes was arrested and charged with violation of the ninety-ninth chapter of the Revised Statutes of the State of Vermont: adultery. Noyes was not daunted and declared, "We shall beat the devil at his game." Members of the colony prevailed on him, however, to leave Putney and avoid trouble with the town's citizens.

The Putney Perfectionists began to move. Noyes, who had gone to New York, was already working on bringing the dispersed community together again. The exiles from Putney joined with a new colony at Oneida, and by January 1849 there were eighty-seven members. Within the next twenty-six years, the membership rose to 298.

Farming and logging were the main industries at Oneida in the early years. Then, a steel trap invented by a new recruit to Oneida was put on the market and became an immediate financial success. Silk manufacture and fruit canning added to the community's income. Then the members began to produce silver flatware. Oneida became a thriving, industrial, profitable organization.

"The social principles of the Oneida Communists," said a handbook of the Oneida Community published in 1875, "naturally result from their religious principles. They affirm that the same spirit which on the day of Pentecost abolished exclusiveness in regard to money tends to obliterate all other property distinctions. Hence, in their society, where selfish ownership is unrecognized, the unit which in ordinary society is limited to one man and one woman is extended—complex marriage takes the place of simple—many small families are merged in one large family."

The handbook stressed that the communities "abhor rapes whether under the cover of marriage or elsewhere."

From the principle of Bible Communism grew two others which were part of the Oneida life: male continence and stirpiculture. Noyes explained his discovery of male continence: "Within six years my wife went through the agonies of five births. Four were premature. Only one child lived. After our last disappointment I pledged my word to my wife that I would never again expose her to such fruitless suffering. I made up my mind to live apart rather than break this promise. This was in the summer of 1844. At that time the solution came to me as an inspiration, that the social function could be separated from the procreative. I found that the self-control required was not difficult. This was a great deliverance. We had escaped the horrors and the fear of involuntary propagation, and our married life was happy as never before."

To the objection that male continence is "unnatural and unauthorized by the example of the lower animals," Noyes responded that cooking, wearing clothes, living in houses, are unnatural in the same sense. He pointed out that "the real meaning of this objection is that male continence is an interruption of a natural act. But every instance of self-denial is an interruption of some natural act. The man who contents himself with a look at a beautiful woman, the lover who stops at a kiss are conscious of such an interruption."

This led Noyes into stirpiculture: "Male continence not only relieves us of undesirable propagation but opens the way for scientific propagation. . . . The time will come when scientific combination will be freely and successfully applied to human generation."

This phase of the Oneida adventure was inaugurated in 1869 when fifty-three young women signed resolutions that "we do not belong to ourselves in any respect, but . . . we do belong first to

God, and second to Mr. Noyes as God's true representative." They offered to "cheerfully resign all desire to become mothers, if for any reason Mr. Noyes deem us unfit material for propagation." John Noyes himself directed the mating and in some instances "forbade" it. Noyes, who was in his sixties during the decade of the stirpiculture regime, fathered nine of the fifty-eight children born.

Though pressure against this self-contained community existed from its start, it was not until the early 1870's that an organized crusade was initiated against it. A federal obscenity law was passed in 1873 which considered information on contraception as lewd, lascivious, and obscene, and banned it in the United States mails. Correspondence on Noyes's doctrine of male continence was forbidden. The General Association of the Congregational Church of New York denounced the community as a "pernicious institution, which rests substantially on a system of organized fanaticism and lust." Critics called Oneida the "Utopia of Obscenity."

And now dissension rose within the community itself. There were demands that John Noyes leave and threats to lodge a complaint with the district attorney charging Noyes with some form of sexual delinquency.

When Noyes's followers "expressed fear that arrest . . . on a charge of sexual irregularities would result in an open scandal and wreck the community," Noyes left for Ontario. Two months later, in August 1879, in a letter to Oneida, he suggested certain modifications of the colony's structure. He urged the community to continue to hold the business and property in common, but to abandon complex marriage. He emphasized that he was not renunciating his philosophy; he had instead come to terms with the idea that the world was obviously not ready for such a step.

Almost two years later, Noyes proposed that community property, too, come to an end and that a stock company be formed. The members now became stockholders as well as employees of Oneida Community, Ltd.

Five years later, when John Noyes died, Oneida Community,

Ltd. had a working capital in excess of $500,000 and was paying a 6 per cent dividend annually. Oneida continues today as a thriving commercial enterprise.

★ BIBLE COMMUNISM

Showing that marriage is not an institution of the Kingdom of Heaven, and must give place to Communism.

Proposition 5. In the Kingdom of Heaven, the institution of marriage, which assigns the exclusive possession of one woman to one man, does not exist. Matt. 22: 23-30.

6. In the Kingdom of Heaven the intimate union of life and interest, which in the world is limited to pairs, extends through the whole body of believers; i.e. complex marriage takes the place of simple. John 17: 21. Christ prayed that all believers might be one, even as he and the Father are one. His unity with the Father is defined in the words, "All mine are thine, and all thine are mine." John 17:10. This perfect community of interests, then, will be the condition of all, when his prayer is answered. The universal unity of the members of Christ, is described in the same terms that are used to describe marriage unity. Compare 1 Cor. 12:12-27, with Gen. 2:24. See also 1 Cor. 6:15-17, and Eph. 5:30-32. . . .

8. Admitting that the community principle of the day of Pentecost, in its actual operation at that time, extended only to material goods, yet we affirm that there is no intrinsic difference between property in persons and property in things; and that the same spirit which abolished exclusiveness in regard to money would abolish, if circumstances allowed full scope to it, exclusiveness in regard to women and children. Paul expressly places property in women and property in goods in the same category, and speaks of them together, as ready to be abolished by the advent of the Kingdom of Heaven. "The time," says he, "is short; it remaineth that they that have wives be as though they had none; and they

---

From "Bible Communism," a pamphlet published by John Humphrey Noyes in February 1849.

that buy as though they possessed not; for the fashion of this world passeth away." 1 Cor. 7: 29–31.

9. The abolishment of appropriation is involved in the very nature of a true relation to Christ in the gospel. This we prove thus: The possessive feeling which expresses itself by the possessive pronoun *mine*, is the same in essence when it relates to persons, as when it relates to money or any other property. Amativeness and acquisitiveness are only different channels of one stream. They converge as we trace them to their source. Grammar will help us to ascertain their common center; for the possessive pronoun *mine* is derived from the personal pronoun *I*; and so the possessive feeling, whether amative or acquisitive, flows from the personal feeling, that is, it is a branch of egotism. Now egotism is abolished by the gospel relation to Christ. The grand mystery of the gospel is vital union with Christ; the merging of self in his life; the extinguishment of the pronoun *I* at the spiritual center. Thus Paul says, "I live, yet not I, but Christ liveth in me." The grand distinction between the Christian and the unbeliever, between heaven and the world is, that in one reigns the We-spirit, and in the other the I-spirit. From *I* comes *mine*, and from the I-spirit comes exclusive appropriation of money, women, etc. From *we* comes *ours*, and from the We-spirit comes universal community of interests.

10. The abolishment of exclusiveness is involved in the love-relation required between all believers by the express injunction of Christ and the apostles, and by the whole tenor of the New Testament. "The new commandment is, that we love one another," and that, not by pairs, as in the world, but en masse. We are required to love one another fervently. The fashion of the world forbids a man and woman who are otherwise appropriated, to love one another fervently. But if they obey Christ they must do this; and whoever would allow them to do this, and yet forbid them (on any other ground than that of present expediency), to express their unity, would "strain at a gnat and swallow a camel"; for unity of hearts is as much more important than any external expression of it, as a camel is larger than a gnat. . . .

12. The abolishment of the marriage system is involved in Paul's doctrine of the end of ordinances. Marriage is one of the "ordinances of the worldly sanctuary." This is proved by the fact that it has no place in the resurrection. Paul expressly limits it to life in the flesh. Rom. 7: 2, 3. The assumption, therefore, that believers are dead to the world by the death of Christ (which authorized the abolishment of Jewish ordinances), legitimately makes an end of marriage. Col. 2: 20.

13. The law of marriage is the same in kind with the Jewish law concerning meats and drinks and holy days, of which Paul said that they were "contrary to us, and were taken out of the way, being nailed to the cross." Col. 2: 14. The plea in favor of the worldly social system, that it is not arbitrary, but founded in nature, will not bear investigation. All experience testifies (the theory of the novels to the contrary notwithstanding), that sexual love is not naturally restricted to pairs. Second marriages are contrary to the one-love theory, and yet are often the happiest marriages. Men and women find universally (however the fact may be concealed), that their susceptibility to love is not burnt out by one honeymoon, or satisfied by one lover. On the contrary, the secret history of the human heart will bear out the assertion that it is capable of loving any number of times and any number of persons, and that the more it loves the more it can love. This is the law of nature, thrust out of sight and condemned by common consent, and yet secretly known to all.

14. The law of marriage "worketh wrath." 1. It provokes to secret adultery, actual or of the heart. 2. It ties together unmatched natures. 3. It sunders matched natures. 4. It gives to sexual appetite only a scanty and monotonous allowance, and so produces the natural vices of poverty, contraction of taste and stinginess or jealousy. 5. It makes no provision for the sexual appetite at the very time when that appetite is the strongest. By the custom of the world, marriage, in the average of cases, takes place at about the age of twenty-four; whereas puberty commences at the age of fourteen. For ten years, therefore, and that in the very flush of life, the sexual appetite is starved. This law of society bears

hardest on females, because they have less opportunity of choosing their time of marriage than men. This discrepancy between the marriage system and nature, is one of the principal sources of the peculiar diseases of women, of prostitution, masturbation, and licentiousness in general. . . .

17. The restoration of true relations between the sexes is a matter second in importance only to the reconciliation of man to God. The distinction of male and female is that which makes man the image of God, i.e. the image of the Father and the Son. Gen. 1: 27. The relation of male and female was the first social relation. Gen. 2: 22. It is therefore the root of all other social relations. The derangement of this relation was the first result of the original breach with God. Gen. 3: 7; comp. 2: 25. Adam and Eve were, at the beginning, in open, fearless, spiritual fellowship, first with God, and secondly, with each other. Their transgression produced two corresponding alienations, viz., first, an alienation from God, indicated by their fear of meeting Him and their hiding themselves among the trees of the garden; and secondly, an alienation from each other, indicated by their shame at their nakedness and their hiding themselves from each other by clothing. These were the two great manifestations of original sin—the only manifestations presented to notice in the record of the apostasy. The first thing then to be done, in an attempt to redeem man and reorganize society, is to bring about reconciliation with God; and the second thing is to bring about a true union of the sexes. In other words, religion is the first subject of interest, and sexual morality the second, in the great enterprise of establishing the Kingdom of Heaven on earth. . . .

19. From what precedes, it is evident that any attempt to revolutionize sexual morality before settlement with God, is out of order. Holiness must go before free love. Bible Communists are not responsible for the proceedings of those who meddle with the sexual question before they have laid the foundation of true faith and union with God.

20. Dividing the sexual relation into two branches, the amative and propagative, the amative or love-relation is first in im-

portance, as it is in the order of nature. God made woman because "he saw it was not good for man to be alone"; Gen. 2: 18; i.e., for social, not primarily for propagative, purposes. Eve was called Adam's "help-meet." In the whole of the specific account of the creation of woman, she is regarded as his companion, and her maternal office is not brought into view. Gen. 2: 18–25. Amativeness was necessarily the first social affection developed in the garden of Eden. The second commandment of the eternal law of love, "Thou shalt love thy neighbor as thyself," had amativeness for its first channel; for Eve was at first Adam's only neighbor. Propagation and the affections connected with it, did not commence their operation during the period of innocence. After the fall God said to the woman, "I will greatly multiply thy sorrow and thy conception"; from which it is to be inferred that in the original state, conception would have been comparatively infrequent.

21. The amative part of the sexual relation, separate from the propagative, is eminently favorable to life. It is not a source of life (as some would make it), but it is the first and best distributive of life. Adam and Eve, in their original state, derived their life from God. Gen. 2: 7. As God is a dual being, the Father and the Son, and man was made in his image, a dual life passed from God to Man. Adam was the channel specially of the life of the Father, and Eve of the life of the Son. Amativeness was the natural agency of the distribution and mutual action of these two forms of life. In this primitive position of the sexes (which is their normal position in Christ), each reflects upon the other the love of God; each excites and develops the divine action in the other.

22. The propagative part of the sexual relation is in its nature the expensive department. 1. While amativeness keeps the capital stock of life circulating between two, propagation introduces a third partner. 2. The propagative act is a drain on the life of man, and when habitual, produces disease. 3. The infirmities and vital expenses of woman during the long period of pregnancy, waste her constitution. 4. The awful agonies of child-

birth heavily tax the life of woman. 5. The cares of the nursing period bear heavily on woman. 6. The cares of both parents, through the period of the childhood of their offspring, are many and burdensome. 7. The labor of man is greatly increased by the necessity of providing for children. A portion of these expenses would undoubtedly have been curtailed, if human nature had remained in its original integrity, and will be, when it is restored. But it is still self-evident that the birth of children, viewed either as a vital or a mechanical operation, is in its nature expensive; and the fact that multiplied conception was imposed as a curse, indicates that it was so regarded by the Creator. . . .

25. The foregoing principles concerning the sexual relation, open the way for association. 1. They furnish motives. They apply to larger partnerships the same attractions that draw and bind together pairs in the worldly partnership of marriage. A community home in which each is married to all, and where love is honored and cultivated, will be as much more attractive than an ordinary home, as the community outnumbers a pair. 2. These principles remove the principal obstructions in the way of association. There is plenty of tendency to crossing love and adultery, even in the system of isolated households. Association increases this tendency. Amalgamation of interests, frequency of interview, and companionship in labor inevitably give activity and intensity to the social attractions in which amativeness is the strongest element. The tendency to extra-matrimonial love will be proportioned to the condensation of interests produced by any given form of association; that is, if the ordinary principles of exclusiveness are preserved, association will be a worse school of temptation to unlawful love than the world is, in proportion to its social advantages. Love, in the exclusive form, has jealousy for its complement; and jealousy brings on strife and division. Association, therefore, if it retains one-love exclusiveness, contains the seeds of dissolution; and those seeds will be hastened to their harvest by the warmth of associate life. An association of states with custom-house lines around each, is sure to be quarrelsome. The further states in that situation are apart, and the more their

interests are isolated, the better. The only way to prevent smuggling and strife in a confederation of contiguous states, is to abolish custom-house lines from the interior, and declare free trade and free transit, collecting revenues and fostering home products by one custom-house line around the whole. This is the policy of the heavenly system—"that they *all* [not two and two] may be one." . . .

27. In vital society labor will become attractive. Loving companionship in labor, and especially the mingling of the sexes, makes labor attractive. The present division of labor between the sexes separates them entirely. The woman keeps house, and the man labors abroad. Instead of this, in vital society men and women will mingle in both of their peculiar departments of work. It will be economically as well as spiritually profitable, to marry them in-doors and out, by day as well as by night. When the partition between the sexes is taken away, and man ceases to make woman a propagative drudge, when love takes the place of shame, and fashion follows nature in dress and business, men and women will be able to mingle in all their employments, as boys and girls mingle in their sports; and then labor will be attractive.

EDWARD KELLOGG, 1790–1858

☆ The Safety Fund: A New Monetary System

THE DREAM STARTED with Edward Kellogg; the agitation to bring it about came later from such forces as labor and the Greenbacks. The panacea offered: a new monetary system.

Kellogg, son of a farmer, was born in Norwalk, Connecticut. When he was only a youth, he was already traveling New Jersey, Pennsylvania, Maryland, and Virginia, successfully selling dry goods merchandise.

In 1830 he moved to New York, where he soon became the senior partner of the dry goods firm of Kellogg and Baldwin, and later chief of Edward Kellogg and Company.

At about the same time, he began to apply himself seriously to theology. "When matters of business were not immediately before him," wrote his daughter, Mary Kellogg Putnam, "he studied ardently in his own thoughts the relations of man to his Creator and to his fellow man; on his way from one engagement to another, he usually pondered the meaning of some text of Scripture."

Mrs. Putnam recalled that "during those years he did not speak of business matters at home, but he talked much with friends and neighbors about theological doctrines, principles of morality, about political questions and the management of the banks."

The Panic of 1837 had a sobering effect on Kellogg. Collections of accounts from people who owed him money were either slow or not forthcoming. Though his own assets were in excess of liabilities, he "was obliged to suspend payment and saw his affairs thrown into what seemed to be almost inextricable confusion."

Kellogg felt the cause of the panic was in the existing monetary system. After studying that system, he decided that the cause of the nation's ills was usury, which could be combated only by the establishment of a national bank.

Kellogg then suggested that a friend, Whitehook, write a pamphlet setting forth Kellogg's ideas. *Usury and Its Effects: A National Bank a Remedy*, by Whitehook, appeared in 1841. This pamphlet advanced Kellogg's theory that a national bank capitalized at $50 million be created with branches in every state. Dividends would be limited to 5 or 6 per cent. When surplus profit exceeded 5 per cent on the capital, the rate of interest on the loan would be reduced.

But Kellogg was not completely satisfied with his "remedy." The more he studied, the more he realized that he had not solved the basic problem of usurious rates of interest.

A friend remonstrated with him: "This is the most difficult part of political economy; no one has ever understood it. It has puzzled the wisest heads from the beginning until now, and you cannot solve it: you will only succeed in bewildering yourself. Besides, your own affairs are in a very perplexing condition and require all your attention; and it is *against your interest* to do anything about it."

Kellogg replied: "I have an interest in the human family, and I have discovered something that is for their benefit. I shall write it; I should if I knew that I could make a million dollars if I did not; and that if I did, I should live on a crust of bread and die in a garret."

Two years later, Kellogg had formulated his answer. In the summer of 1843, he published *Usury: the Evil and the Remedy* at his own expense. The *New York Tribune* called the pamphlet "a powerful essay. . . . The intent of the author is evidently to probe the evil to the bottom, and not to rest in mere grumbling at it, but devise and suggest adequate means for its removal."

In the meantime, Kellogg had acquired enough property so that he could retire and devote his time to the study of finance. Five years later, again at his own expense, he published a new book which was to become the basis of his monetary panacea.

Published in 1849, the book was titled *Labor and Other Capital: the Rights of Each Secured and the Wrongs of Both Eradicated; or, an Exposition of the Cause Why Few Are Wealthy and Many Poor, and the Delineation of a System Which, Without Infringing the Rights of Property, Will Give to Labor Its Just Reward.*

In the Appendix, Kellogg urged leaders of the French Revolution of 1848 to consider his proposal: "The Safety Fund is recommended to the French government; first, because it strikes at the root of the cause that produced the oppression, and will therefore prove a sure remedy for the complaints of the people; second, because it will render the republic stable, and to political, add social freedom; and third, because it will insure peace by the general diffusion of competency, intelligence, and happiness." Kellogg sent his book to Proudhon and members of the French assembly, as well as to statesmen in the United States and in other countries.

The book, however, attracted little attention. It was called "impractical" and "utopian." Kellogg insisted: "The millennium can never come until this system goes into operation; but then it can come!" Kellogg was working on a new edition of *Labor and Other Capital* when he died. His daughter published the revised edition including "numerous additions from his manuscripts" and a biographical sketch of her father. The new title was *Labor and Capital; A New Monetary System: the Only Means of Securing the Respective Rights of Labor and Property, and of Protecting the Public from Financial Revulsions.*

In the years following, Kelloggism attracted the interest of such labor bodies as the National Labor Union, and even the Knights of Labor flirted briefly with it in 1885. The National Labor Union, which had an interest in establishing producers' cooperatives, saw in Kellogg's idea a means of obtaining credit at a low interest rate for the founding of cooperatives. Kelloggism was also the intellectual basis of the Greenback movement.

In the decades after Kellogg first formulated his philosophy, "labor leaders turned with almost complete unanimity to a panacea offered . . . by an obscure writer [Kellogg] on political economy," according to Chester MacArthur Destler in his *American Radicalism, 1865–1901*.

★ A NEW MONETARY SYSTEM

In the plan here proposed for the formation of a national currency by the general government, all the money circulated in the United States will be issued by a national institution, and will be a representative of actual property; therefore it can never fail to be a good and safe tender in payment of debts. It will be loaned to individuals in every state, county, and town, at a uniform rate of interest, and therefore will be of invariable value throughout the union. All persons who offer good and permanent security will be at all times supplied with money, and for any term of years during which they will regularly pay the interest. Therefore, no town, county, or state need be dependent upon any other for money, because each has real property enough to secure many times the amount which it will require. If more than the necessary amount of money be issued, the surplus will be immediately funded, and go out of use without injury. It will be impossible for foreign nations, or any number of banks, or capitalists, to derange the monetary system, either by changing the rate of interest, or by inducing

From Edward Kellogg, *Labor and Other Capital* (New York, 1849).

a scarcity or a surplus of money. It will be the duty of the government to ascertain as nearly as possible what rate of interest will secure to labor and capital their respective rights, and to fix the interest at that rate.

The plan requires the general government to establish an institution, with one or more branches in each state. This institution may appropriately be called the National Safety Fund: first, because the money of this institution will always be safe; second, because it will secure property and labor from the tyranny now exercised over them by the capricious power of money.

To make this currency a true representative of property, the Safety Fund must issue its money only in exchange for mortgages secured by double the amount of productive-landed estate. The money, when put in circulation, will represent and be secured by the first half of productive property, and the interest upon the mortgages will be secured by a portion of the yearly products or income of the property. The Safety Fund will issue its money, bearing no interest, for the mortgages bearing interest. We have shown that money to maintain its value must not only represent property, but must always be capable of being loaned for an income. It is therefore necessary to provide not only for the issue, but also for the funding of the money.

The first of the following obligations will be the money of the institution; the second will be a note bearing interest for the funding of the money:

No.____ MONEY. *Dated*____

$500. $500.

The United States will pay to the bearer five hundred dollars in a Safety Fund note, on demand, at the Safety Fund Office in the city of ________

No.____ SAFETY FUND NOTE. *Dated*____

$500. $500.

One year from the first day of May next, or at any time there-

after, the United States will pay to A. B., or order, in the city of ________ five hundred dollars; and, until such payment is made, will pay interest thereon on the first day of May in each year, at the rate of one per cent per annum.

The "money" will bear no interest, but may always be exchanged for the Safety Fund notes, which will bear interest. Those who may not wish to purchase property or pay debts with their money, can always loan it to the institution for a Safety Fund note, bearing an interest of one per cent per annum. Therefore the money will always be good; for it will be the legal tender for debts and property, and can always be invested to produce an income.

Money being loaned at one and one-tenth per cent, and Safety Fund notes bearing but one per cent, the difference of ten per cent in the interest will induce owners of money to lend to individuals, and thus prevent continual issues and funding of money by the institution.

The Safety Fund notes are made payable a year after date, to prevent the unnecessary trouble of funding money for short periods. It is not probable that the institution will issue notes for a less amount than $500. People having small amounts will seldom wish to fund them. They will loan to individuals, or purchase property. If, however, it be deemed desirable to fund small amounts, they may be received, and credited in a small book, as in savings banks, and the interest paid upon these credits as upon Safety Fund notes. . . .

★ ADVANTAGES OF THE SAFETY FUND

The Safety Fund will loan money at a low rate of interest to all applicants furnishing the requisite landed security; hence every town, county, and state which has the power to perform the labor can make any internal improvement without pledging its property to large cities or to foreign nations to borrow money. . . .

The value of money being made uniform, all kinds of stocks will maintain a uniform value, according to the percentage interest which they will yield, and the time they have to run before the payment of the principal. If they bear a higher rate of interest than the legal one, of course they will be above par. All the state stocks which the states have reserved the right to pay before maturity, will be paid with money borrowed at one and one-tenth per cent. Even if the bonds of some states have a number of years to run, the states can much more easily pay five, six, or seven per cent interest per annum upon them during the period, than they can under the present monetary system, because the value of their labor and products will be increased. The same will be true of all private bonds and mortgages having a number of years to run. A few years will extinguish all these old loans, and then there will be a nearly uniform rate of interest on all obligations throughout the nation.

Although all useful trades and occupations are mutually beneficial and necessary, yet in most nations a jealousy exists between the agricultural and manufacturing interests. But in reality the natural tendency of the prosperity of one is to increase the prosperity of the other. The object of both is to supply themselves and each other with food, clothing, and the other comforts of life. When they have a just representative of their products, and can easily exchange them with one another, the prices of the products of both will naturally adjust themselves, so that both will receive the proper reward of their labor, while each will contribute to the benefit of the other. So long as the poverty of producers is supposed to be caused by overproduction, and the sale of too many products, the evil will be attributed to laws favoring one class of producers to the disadvantage of others. But when the real cause of the oppression, that is, the monopolizing power of money, is rectified, the various branches of productive industry will harmonize and promote one another's welfare.

Some may not understand how the rate of interest on money affects the compensation of labor. Suppose the owner of a small farm is obliged to work early and late for a mere subsistence. He has little or no means to spare for the education of his children, and in fact cannot give them time to attend school. If this man should be told that the high rate of interest at which money is loaned deprives him and his family of the comforts of life and the means of education, he would very naturally ask, "How can that be? I never borrow money and pay interest, nor do I lend money and receive interest. The payment of a high rate of interest by others does not affect me; it does not diminish my crops. I raise food for my family, and the produce that I can spare I sell, and buy such other articles as we need, and the storekeeper does not charge me any interest. I have enough to do to live, without troubling myself about the interest on money." He is indeed aware that many people live with far less labor than he does, and have many more comforts, and this he attributes to their good fortune. He does not grasp the subject sufficiently to perceive that the interest on money is a standard or governing power, which compels him to contribute his proportion of the products required to support all the non-producers in this country, and probably some of the capitalists of Europe. He does not see that a large per cent is taken from the price of his products by the purchaser, in order to enable the latter to pay his interest and live by the purchase and sale; and that, for the same reason, when he purchases, a large per cent is added to the price of every article produced by the labor of others. This difference in price must be sufficient to support all who live upon income without labor.

Let the Safety Fund be established, and interest be reduced to one and one-tenth per cent, and after a year or two let inquiry be made of the same farmer about his welfare. He would probably say, "I am doing very well; I am much better off than I was two or three years ago. I send my children to school, and have a good living." Should he be told that his prosperity was owing to a sound currency and low rate of interest, he might say, "I do not borrow any money from the Safety Fund, and I have no money to lend upon interest. I raise corn and potatoes as formerly, and sell them to the same merchants. I do not see how the reduction of the interest on money that other people borrow is any benefit to me." Although he do not perceive the causes of his past privations or of his present comforts, he will be as sensible as any one of the improvements in his condition. Should a man suffer intense pain, and be informed that it was caused by the disorder of a nerve, he might not understand this, nor think so small a cause could occasion such acute suffering. Should the proper remedy be applied, the nerve recover its tone, and the pain cease, he would be conscious of health, although he might not understand how the pain was removed. Whether a man understand the laws relating to his physical system or not, he will suffer if any organ do not perform its duty; and whether laborers understand the constitution of money or not, they must suffer all the consequences of its imperfect or deranged organization.

When the natural reward of labor is secured to the laborer, poverty cannot exist in any family whose members are able and willing to work. And those who can so easily provide for their own wants, will cheerfully contribute to the support of the sick and needy. They will be able to supply themselves amply with the comforts of life, and have an abundance of time for intellectual and moral culture. The incentives to vice will be comparatively few. Avarice first arises from the fear of want; to remove want will therefore in a great measure remove this vice, and the unnumbered evils which are its attendants. It is frequently said that the people must reform, and that not until then may we hope for good laws. Not so: we might as well expect families to grow up virtuous where the parents are cruel, profligate, and vicious, as to expect nations to be virtuous under oppressive laws. Make the laws a standard of right, and their benefits must secure an improvement in the morals of the people. . . .

So long as monetary laws continue a standard that will wrest products from producers, and place and protect them in the hands of non-producers, they will require for their support the aid of the sword and bayonet, because man's natural sense of right revolts against the usurpation and the injustice of such protection. But when monetary laws shall sustain a just standard of value, which will award and protect products in the hands of their producers, they will of course conform to the natural laws of production, which were ordained by a higher than human power. The distribution then being according to justice, strife will cease, because a man having his own rights respected and protected, will naturally respect and protect the rights of others. The time is not far distant when this truth will be known and appreciated by all civilized nations, and the mistaken power of legal *might*, which has such dominion over man, will wither before the higher power of *right*.

Part II

INDUSTRIALIZATION

[IMAGES: 1865–1893]

SURRENDER AT APPOMATTOX, *a defeated and bitter South. Cities and towns are burned; mills, haystacks, bridges, livestock, barns are destroyed; transportation breaks down; the economy is paralyzed, Confederate money worthless. In the North, a booming economy; production, prices, and profits soar; wages lag. President Lincoln pleads: "With malice toward none, with charity for all . . ."*

Assassination.

Reconstruction brings the carpetbaggers and scalawags, the birth of the Granger Union, the Greenback movement, the national labor unions, the Eight-Hour Day League, the Farmers' Alliance, the Knights of Labor, the Equal Rights party, the National Labor Reform party, Molly Maguires, Ku Klux Klan, the Tweed Ring.

Haymarket tragedy.

U. S. Grant is President. Horace Greeley, Grover Cleveland, Booker T. Washington, Homestead, Brigham Young, and the Chicago Fire make headlines.

George Westinghouse patents the air brake, and Alexander Graham Bell invents the telephone. William Dean Howells writes realistic novels, Edward Bellamy utopian fiction, Mark Twain pungent morality tales. Joel Chandler Harris, Henry James, Bret Harte, Louisa May Alcott, James Whitcomb Riley.

The cities are rising—the factory system, the transcontinental railroad; the "Crime of '73" and the Panic of 1873. Gold. Economic depression, unemployment, bank failures, an upsurge in crime, industrial unrest.

It is the age of corporate growth, of trusts and new folk heroes called "Coal Baron," "Steel King," "Railway Magnate," "Robber Baron." Mark Twain and Charles Dudley Warner call it the Gilded Age ("I wasn't worth a cent two years ago, and now I owe over a million dollars"). Jay Gould, James J. Hill, John D. Rockefeller, Andrew Carnegie, Philip Armour, Gustavus Swift, J. Pierpont Morgan.

Horatio Alger.

IRA STEWARD, 1831–1883

☆ The Eight-Hour Day: "Pleasure Economy"

IRA STEWARD was the "eight-hour monomaniac." For the eight-hour day he lived, worked, fought, and agitated with zest and with fanatical zeal. He espoused this cause from the stump, through journals, and in discussions for more than three decades.

Steward was born and educated in New London, Connecticut. When he was nineteen, he was apprenticed as a machinist in Providence, Rhode Island, under the twelve-hour-day system. Within a year, he was dismissed by his employer for his "peculiar views" in agitating for shorter hours.

The eight-hour day became Steward's cause.

As a delegate to the 1863 convention of the International Union of Machinists and Blacksmiths of North America, he introduced a resolution calling for the eight-hour day. The resolution read in part:

"*Resolved,* That from east to west, from north to south, the most important change to us as workingmen, to which all else is subordinate, is a permanent reduction to eight of the hours exacted for each day's work.

"*Resolved,* That since this cannot be accomplished until a public sentiment has been educated, both among the employers and the employés, we will use the machinery of agitation, whether it be among those of the religious, political, reformatory, or moneyed enterprises of the day, and to secure such reduction we pledge our money and our courage.

"*Resolved,* That such reduction will never be made until overwork, as a system, is prohibited, nor until it is universally recognized that an increase of hours is a reduction of wages. . . .

"*Resolved,* That a reduction of hours is an increase of wages. . . ."

The International Union of Machinists donated $400 for the eight-hour-day agitation; the Boston Trades Assembly contributed a similar amount.

For the next seven years Steward persistently appeared before legislative committees in Massachusetts pleading, arguing, urging the passage of an eight-hour law.

Because of Steward's agitation, a joint committee of the Massachusetts legislature, at the close of its May 1865 session, recommended to the governor that an unsalaried commission be named to study the question and report back at the next session. Steward and his followers were jubilant. Steward urged trade unionists to thank the committee for this action and concluded his appeal with a couplet:

"Let all now cheer, who never cheered before,
And those who always cheer now cheer the more."

After a period of study, the commission made its report to the legislature. Although the commission recommended a reduction of the current working day, which was normally eleven hours, it opposed the arbitrary limitations of an eight-hour work day for such reasons as that many industries would be unable to observe such a time limit and that different kinds of work required different measures of time for completion. The commission did, however, recommend that a salaried commission make a more intensive study of hours of labor and their effect. Such a commission was appointed, but its report opposed, two to one, any law restricting hours of work.

The agitation continued. At the convention of the New England Reform League in June 1869, to which Steward was a delegate, the president, Ezra A. Heywood, and others stressed that it was vital for the country to find a solution to the monetary problem. A series of resolutions was introduced to that effect. Steward and his friends objected to this emphasis. They offered a substitute resolution that "the whole power and strength of the labor-reform movement should be concentrated upon the single and simple idea of first reducing the hours of labor, that the masses may have more time to discuss for themselves all other questions in labor reform."

But the New England Reform League remained unconvinced, and in August 1869, two months after the convention, Steward and his friends founded the Boston Eight-Hour League. To Ira Steward, there continued to be only one solution to the labor problem: the eight-hour work day. It remained his single-purpose, all-encompassing philosophy. He insisted that a higher standard of living could be achieved only with fewer hours of labor. Otherwise, he felt, there could be no social progress.

The intensity of Steward's engrossment in the eight-hour day was described by a friend in the *American Workman:* "Meet him any day, as he steams along the street (like most enthusiasts he is always in a hurry) and although he will apologize and excuse himself if you talk to him of other affairs, and say that he is sorry, that he must rush back to his shop, if you only introduce the pet topic of 'hours of labor,' and show a little willingness to listen, he will stop and plead with you till nightfall."

Steward was in the midst of detailing his philosophy in a book when he died. Notes and manuscripts were willed to his friend George Gunton, who incorporated Steward's ideas into his own book, *Wealth and Progress: A Critical Examination of the Wage Question and Its Economic Relation to Social Reform.* In his book, Gunton gives credit to Steward: "The central thought [of this book] . . . and the first effort at its statement belongs to Ira Steward," he wrote in the "Introduction." "For more than twenty years he was the real leader and inspiration of the labor movement in that state; and to him, more than any other person, we are indebted for the Massachusetts Labor Bureau—the first, and today the best, institution of its kind in the world."

Ira Steward died in Plano, Illinois, many years before the eight-hour day became a reality. No words of prayer were said at his funeral, nor was there a ceremony of any kind. In accordance with his request, he was quietly buried with only his wife and nearest relatives present.

The philosophy of the life-long agitator for a "pleasure economy" can be summarized in the jingle reportedly written by his wife:

"Whether you work by the piece or work by the day,
Decreasing the hours increases the pay."

★ A REDUCTION OF HOURS, AN INCREASE OF WAGES

"Well," says a workingman, "I should certainly be very glad to work less hours, but I can scarcely earn enough by working ten to make myself and family comfortable."

Sir, as strange as it may seem to you at first blush, it is a fact that your wages will never be permanently increased until the hours of labor are reduced. Have you never observed that those who work the hardest and longest are paid the least, especially if the employment is very disagreeable, while those whose employment is more agreeable usually receive more, and many who do nothing receive more than either?

You are receiving your scanty pay precisely because you work so many hours in a day, and my point now is to show why this is true, and why reducing the hours for the masses will eventually increase their wages. . . .

Pamphlet by Ira Steward, published by the Boston Labor Reform Association, 1865.

The truth is, as a rule, that men who labor excessively are robbed of all ambition to ask for anything more than will satisfy their bodily necessities, while those who labor moderately have time to cultivate tastes and create wants in addition to mere physical comforts. How can men be stimulated to demand higher wages when they have little or no time or strength to use the advantages which higher wages can buy, or procure?

Take an extreme case for illustration of this—that of an average operative or mechanic employed by a corporation fourteen hours a day. His labor commences at half past four in the morning, and does not cease until half past seven P.M. How many newspapers or books can he read? What time has he to visit or receive visits? To take baths? To write letters? To cultivate flowers? To walk with his family? Will he not be quite as likely to vote in opposition to his real interests as in favor? What is his opinion good for? Will any one ask his advice? Which will he most enjoy, works of art, or rum? Will he go to meeting on Sunday? Does society care whether he is happy or miserable? Sick or well? Dead or alive? How often are his eyes tempted by the works of art? His home means to him his food and his bed. His life is work, with the apparition, however, of some time being without, for his work means bread! "Only that and nothing more." He is debased by excessive toil! He is almost without hope! . . .

From the fourteen-hour system let us turn to that of eight hours for a day's work, and see if the real secret of low and high wages does not lie in the vast difference which the two systems make in the daily habits and ways of living of the masses. In the eight-hour system, labor commences at seven o'clock A.M., and, as an hour and a half is allowed for dinner, the labor of the day ends at half past four in the afternoon, instead of half past seven in the evening. Think carefully of the difference between the operative and mechanic leaving his work at half past seven (after dark, the most of the year), and that of the more leisurely walk home at half past four P.M., or three hours earlier. Remember also that there is a vast difference in the strength and feelings of those who commence two hours and a half later, or at seven o'clock. It is the hard practical necessary differences between the two systems which control the daily habits and thoughts of all who are living under them.

You can hardly dwell too long upon this point, for upon it turns this whole question of social science—poverty and wealth—vice and virtue—ignorance and knowledge. The follies, burdens, and crimes of our later civilization are hanging upon this question, and the temptation to leave the simple, and comparatively unimportant fact that reducing the hours will increase the wages, and launch out upon broader and more sublime results, is almost irresistible. The simple increase of wages is the first step on that long road which ends at last in a more equal distribution of the fruits of toil. For wages will continue to increase until the capitalist and laborer are one. But we must confine ourselves to the first simple fact that a reduction of hours is an increase of wages; and when we are perfectly satisfied of its soundness we can build upon it until the consequences grow to the extent of our comprehension or imagination.

Think then of the difference which will soon be observed in a man or woman emancipated by the eight-hour system from excessive toil! Not the first day nor the first week, perhaps, but in a very little while. The first feeling may be one merely of simple relief; and the time for a while may be spent, as are many of the Sabbaths, by the overworked, in sleeping and eating, and frequently in the most debasing amusements. The use which a man makes of his leisure depends largely upon the use which has been made of him. If he has been abused, he will be pretty sure to abuse his first opportunities. An hour in the hands of John Quincy Adams meant a golden opportunity—in the hands of a Newcastle collier it means debauchery—and in the hands of a New England operative, an hour extra will mean the difference balanced, or divided between the two.

Many make the mistake of supposing that leisure will be abused by workingmen, as if leisure of itself were necessarily corrupting. Leisure, however, is neither positively good, or bad. Leisure, or time is a bland—a negative—a piece of white paper upon which we stamp, picture, or write, our past characters. If we have been soured and disappointed by a life of poverty and drudgery, if opportunities have been few and far between, if education has been neglected and habits of thought and observation have not been cultivated—if we have inherited qualities which are ever leading us into temptation, we shall be sure to stamp this humiliating record upon the first leisure hour in the eight-hour system. The most of men will make a clumsy use of any thing which they have not become familiar with. Progress in the arts and sciences is marked by a line of accidents, burnings, explosions, losses, and deaths, to which we may liken the abuse of the laborer's first opportunities. But the remedy is not in depriving him of his chance to experiment. . . .

Mankind will be virtuous and happy when they have full power to choose between good and evil, with plenty of motives for deciding right. Men will not abuse power when they are made responsible for its abuse. While therefore giving the masses more time will give them increased power to do wrong, the motives to do right will increase very much faster.

Assuming that the leisure we propose is not so positively debasing, let us return to the main question. My theory is,

1st. That more leisure, will create motives and temptations for the common people to ask for more wages.

2d. That where all ask for more wages, there will be no motive for refusing, since employers will all fare alike.

3d. That where all demand more wages, the demand cannot be resisted.

4th. That resistance would amount to the folly of a "strike" by employers themselves, against the strongest power in the world, viz., the habits, customs, and opinions, of the masses.

5th. That the change in the habits and opinions of the people through more leisure will be too gradual to disturb or jar the commerce and enterprise of capital.

6th. That the increase in wages will fall upon the wastes of society, in its crimes, idleness, fashions, and monopolies, as well as the more legitimate and honorable profits of capital, in the production and distribution of wealth, and

7th. In the mechanical fact, that the cost of making an article depends almost entirely upon the number manufactured is a practical increase of wages, by tempting the workers through their new leisure to unite in buying luxuries now confined to the wealthy, and which are costly because bought only by the wealthy.

The first point in this theory is the vital one "that more leisure will create motives and temptations for the most ordinary laborer to insist upon higher wages." A few, comparatively, insist upon more pay now, but they are in competition with the great body of laborers who do not, and who never will, until, in the language of John Stuart Mill, "a change has been wrought in their ideas and requirements."

There is a law or two in this case which proves, on examination, to be a blessing in disguise. The law is first, that if one employer pays for the same quality and quantity of labor enough more than another that his business will be ruined, and his workmen finally thrown out of employment; and second, that if a workman of superior tendencies to the majority of his fellows, is not paid more than they for performing the same kind of labor his general influence and his opportunities for usefulness will be cramped and limited accordingly. The blessing in disguise is this—the necessity created by these two laws, of elevating all who labor! Every laborer in rags is a walking admonition to those who are not: for he says, unconsciously of course, "I must continue to labor for what my rags cost, until I am placed in a position where I am ashamed to wear them; and as long as I am paid only enough to buy rags, you cannot be paid much more; so please help me up!" Every laborer who saves rent by living in crowded tenement houses, narrow alleys, and unhealthy localities, can underbid the few who will not live in them. Parents who do not educate their children, but send them into factories and shops, can underbid those who do. Men who do not marry can underbid those who do. The charm of the eight-hour system is, that it gives time and opportunity for the ragged—the unwashed—the ignorant and ill-mannered, to become ashamed of themselves and their standing in society.

When an intelligent workingman applies for employment, he don't want to meet a fellow laborer offering to do about the same thing for fifty or seventy-five cents less per day; yet he will be there "every time" until allowed the leisure necessary to be reached through his low pride or envy, if nothing higher, by wife, children, neighbors, and society generally. Give the masses time to come together and they cannot be kept apart; for man is a social being; and when they come together expenses multiply, because the inferior will struggle to imitate the superior in many things which cost. To see is to desire, from babyhood to old age; to desire is to struggle, and to struggle is to succeed, sooner or later.

Imagine operatives or laborers of average capacity leaving work at half past four; they are liable to meet those whose good opinion is worth everything to them, and they think that a neat personal appearance is positively necessary; and it must be confessed that, while fine clothes do not make a man, we all look at them as a certain sort of index to his character.

Men who are governed only by their pride are low indeed; but those who have no pride at all are very much lower. We must take human nature as we find it; hoping and believing that the era of personal display will be succeeded by one of mental and moral accomplishment. A valuable point has been gained in pushing the man into a position where he is made to feel the imperative necessity of dress, and for this he will struggle. An operative running from the shop in the evening tired, hungry, and unwashed, has not time to be ashamed of his personal appearance; and our modern laborer passing through the streets at six, has not time and strength enough: but the improvement which has been made in the personal appearance of ten-hour laborers, over those of the twelve- and fourteen-hour system, is suggestive of what two hours more of leisure may soon accomplish.

Many things can be done for self, family, and domicile which cost nothing but time and labor; but when done are sure to suggest one or two things more costing money. There is time after eight hours' labor to attend an evening concert, which adds a little to the expense, but much to the enjoyment of the family. . . .

Without attempting to settle, definitely, how much common labor is worth—for it is a broad question—I will make the claim that no man's compensation should be so low, that it will not secure for himself and family a comfortable home—education for his children, and all of the influence to which he is entitled by his capacity, virtue, and industry. . . .

In the eight-hour system a dollar will be worth more than a dollar in the long-hour system—not immediately, of course—but in a comparatively short time. The reason of this lies in the fact which every good mechanic understands, that the cost of making an article depends almost entirely on the number manufactured. It pays to build elaborate machinery, to manufacture something which every one will buy; while [those] who make the manufacture a study will improve upon their machinery and reduce the cost continually, especially if in competition with others equally anxious to produce something which everybody wants. One of the reasons why a calendar clock, for instance, or an oval picture frame, or a law book, costs so much is because so few buy. While a common clock, excursion tickets, water pails and Bibles are wanted by everybody, and are cheapened accordingly; and when everybody can be made to feel that they must have certain luxuries now confined to the wealthy, they will be cheapened accordingly. How much do you imagine a single copy of the *Atlantic Monthly* or of *Our Young Folks* would cost if bought by ten times their present number of subscribers? One could spend hours in describing the saving which this patronage would make in the manufacture of those publications alone. Meantime you who will buy the *Atlantic* or *Our Young Folks* are paying the present prices because there are so many who will not buy at all. Your loss is doubled; they keep your wages down because they do without these publications, and keep the prices of these publications up, because they do without them.

Here then is an increase of wages, practically, at the expense of no one; and the general fact that much of the increase is to fall upon the wastes of society, caused by its idleness, crimes, fashions, and accidents at last, and that the increase will be very gradual, ought to disarm all opposition. . . .

Because fathers are paid low wages they send their children—who ought to be at school—into factories and shops to do cheaply what women ought to be fairly paid for doing. Because husbands are underpaid, they consent that their wives may crowd the labor market in competition with maidens who have no husbands to make up for their low wages. And because single men are not paid enough for their daily labor, they do not marry; and thus the maidens who ought to be married, and the wives who ought to be out of the labor market and attending to themselves and families, and the children who ought to be at school, are bringing down woman's wages until her cry of want and despair is splitting the ears of the nation! It is fashionable to sympathize with the "poor sewing girl," but when will men dare to go to the root of the difficulty? . . .

The eight-hour system will put the man who made the shoes and the man who bought them together; and they will compare the prices paid for labor and the sale of the shoes; and observing the great difference, will begin to think! This thought and its consequences melt back into the hands which produced it, the wealth of the world. It means anti-pauperism, anti-aristocracy, anti-monopoly, anti-slavery, anti-prostitution, anti-crime, want, waste, and idleness; and the vast moral and material consequences flowing from such a conference justify the legislation necessary to secure the time.

SUSAN B. ANTHONY, 1820–1906

☆ Suffrage for Women

WHEN SUSAN B. ANTHONY BEGAN her agitation, the unmarried woman had virtually no rights, the married woman even fewer. Women could not own property, make contracts, bring suits, or give testimony in court. The right of women to speak in public was forbidden "by a sentiment stronger than law." The dream of higher education for women was only a gleam in the eyes of a few, a very few.

For almost sixty years Miss Anthony agitated, argued, lectured, and wrote, always in the interest of reform. But early in her career as a reformer, she was led to one purpose: the enfranchisement of women.

Susan B. Anthony was the second of eight children of Daniel and Lucy Read Anthony. She was born in Adams, Massachusetts, and educated in a private school established by her Quaker father, who believed in the education and economic independence of women. At fifteen she was teaching there during the summers.

Susan continued her own education at a Friends' boarding school in Philadelphia. In 1846 she became "headmistress" of the "Female Department" at the Canajoharie (New York) Academy, a position she held for three years, until she left to devote her full time to temperance agitation.

It was eight years before Susan Anthony made her first public speech. At a supper given by the Daughters Union of Canajoharie, Miss Anthony spoke on behalf of temperance. "In my humble opinion," she told an audience of more than two hundred women, "all that is needed to produce a complete temperance and social reform in this age of moral suasion, is for our sex to cast their united influence into the balance."

In May 1851, Susan Anthony attended the Anti-Slavery Anniversary Convention in Syracuse. At about the same time, she fulfilled a long-cherished desire to meet the suffragist and reformer, Elizabeth Cady Stanton. Her introduction to this remarkable woman was the beginning of Susan's lifelong career as a woman suffragist.

Sometime later Susan Anthony met with Mrs. Stanton, Lucy Stone, Horace Greeley, and several others to discuss the founding of the People's College. The women were determined that the school be coeducational. Greeley pleaded with them not to agitate the question. He promised he would see to it that the constitution and bylaws would admit both sexes. Greeley kept his promise. However, before the college opened, it merged with Cornell University.

The Sons of Temperance held a mass meeting in Albany, New York, and invited the Daughters to send representatives. Susan Anthony was one of the delegates to this 1852 convention. During the discussion of a certain motion, Miss Anthony asked permission from the chairman to speak. The chairman told her that while women were welcome to learn at these meetings, their opinions were not invited. Miss Anthony, with three or four other women, walked out of the hall. Most of the women there, however, remained and decried these rebels as "bold, meddlesome disturbers."

After working for many years for female suffrage, Susan Anthony decided to test women's right to vote. She and several other ladies registered for the November 1872 election. They received their ballots, marked them, and dropped them into the ballot box with the approval of two of the three male inspectors.

Within a short time, Miss Anthony and the other women were indicted for having "knowingly voted without having a lawful right to vote" because of being "a person of the female sex." At the same time, all three inspectors were indicted for having "knowingly and wilfully received the votes of persons not entitled to vote."

Of the women voters, only Miss Anthony was brought to trial. A *nolle prosequi* was entered upon the other indictments.

The trial was brief. It was readily admitted that Susan B. Anthony had registered and had voted. The court ordered the jury to find the defendant guilty. The judge refused to have the jury polled. The defense's move for a new trial was denied.

The judge ordered the defendant to stand up.

Judge: Has the prisoner anything to say why sentence shall not be pronounced?

Miss Anthony: Yes, your honor, I have many things to say; for in your ordered verdict of guilty, you have trampled under foot every vital principle of our government. My natural rights, my civil rights, my political rights, my judicial rights, are all alike ignored. Robbed of the fundamental privilege of citizenship, I am degraded from the status of a citizen to that of a subject; and not only myself individually, but all of my sex, are, by your honor's verdict, doomed to political subjection under this, so-called, form of government.

Judge: The Court cannot listen to a rehearsal of arguments the prisoner's counsel has already consumed three hours in presenting.

Miss A.: May it please your honor . . . Your denial of my

citizen's right to vote, is the denial of my right of consent as one of the governed, the denial of my right of representation as one of the taxed, the denial of my right to a trial by a jury of my peers as an offender against law, therefore, the denial of my sacred rights to life, liberty, property and—

Judge: The Court cannot allow the prisoner to go on.

Miss A.: But your honor will not deny me this one and only poor privilege of protest against this high-handed outrage upon my citizen's rights. May it please the Court to remember that since the day of my arrest last November, this is the first time that either myself or any person of my disfranchised class has been allowed a word of defense before judge or jury—

Judge: The prisoner must sit down—the Court cannot allow it.

Miss A.: All of my prosecutors, from the Eighth Ward corner grocery politician, who entered the complaint, to the United States marshal, commissioner, district attorney, district judge, your honor on the bench, not one is my peer, but each and all are my political sovereigns; and had your honor submitted my case to the jury, as was clearly your duty, even then I should have had just cause of protest, for not one of those men was my peer. . . .

Judge: The Court must insist—the prisoner has been tried according to the established forms of law.

Miss A.: Yes, your honor, but by forms of law all made by men, interpreted by men, administered by men, in favor of men, and against women; and hence, your honor's ordered verdict of guilty, against a United States citizen for the exercise of '*that citizen's right to vote,*' simply because that citizen was a woman and not a man. . . .

Judge: The Court orders the prisoner to sit down. It will not allow another word.

Miss A.: When I was brought before your honor for trial, I hoped for a broad and liberal interpretation of the Constitution. . . . But failing to get this justice—failing, even, to get a trial by a jury *not* of my peers—I ask not leniency at your hands—but rather the full rigors of the law.

Judge: The Court must insist—

The prisoner sat down.

The judge ordered the prisoner to stand up. Miss Anthony rose.

Judge: The sentence of the Court is that you pay a fine of one hundred dollars and the costs of the prosecution.

Miss A.: May it please your honor, I shall never pay a dollar of your unjust penalty. All the stock in trade I possess is a $10,000 debt, incurred by publishing my paper—*The Revolution*—four years ago, the sole object of which was to educate all women to do precisely as I have done, rebel against your man-made, unjust, unconstitutional forms of law, that tax, fine, imprison and hang women, while they deny them the right of representation in the government; and I shall work on with might and main to pay every dollar of that honest debt, but not a penny shall go to this unjust claim. And I shall earnestly and persistently continue to urge all women to the practical recognition of the old revolutionary maxim, that "Resistance to tyranny is obedience to God."

Judge: Madam, the Court will not order you committed until the fine is paid.

She never paid the fine, and she continued to agitate and lecture on the enfranchisement of women.

Shortly before she died at the age of eighty-six, on her return from the National Suffrage convention in Baltimore, Miss Anthony told a friend, "I have been striving for over sixty years for a little bit of justice no bigger than that," measuring a little space on one finger, "and yet I must die without obtaining it. Oh, it seems so cruel."

She died leaving "every dollar" she had to the "cause."

In 1920, the centennial year of Susan B. Anthony's birth, the last of the thirty-six states required by the constitution of the United States to make the suffrage amendment a law voted for ratification. The words of the amendment are almost identical to those written by Miss Anthony in 1875. The constitutional amendment reads: "The right of citizens of the United States to vote shall not be denied or abridged by the United States or by any state on account of sex."

★ WOMEN'S SUFFRAGE

The reward of virtue for the homeless, friendless, penniless woman is ever a scanty larder, a pinched, patched, faded wardrobe, a dank basement or rickety garret, with the colder, shabbier scorn and neglect of the more fortunate of her sex. Nightly, as weary and worn from her day's toil she wends her way through the dark alleys toward her still darker abode, where only cold and hunger await her, she sees on every side and at every turn the gilded hand of vice and crime outstretched, beckoning her to food and clothes and shelter; hears the whisper in softest accents, "Come with me and I will give you all the comforts, pleasures, and luxuries that love and wealth can bestow." Since the vast multitudes of human beings, women like men, are not born to the courage or conscience of the martyr, can we wonder that so many poor girls fall, that so many accept material ease and comfort at the expense of spiritual purity and peace? Should we not wonder, rather, that so many escape the sad fate?

Clearly, then, the first step toward solving this problem is to lift this vast army of poverty-stricken women who now crowd our cities, above the temptation, the necessity, to sell themselves, in marriage or out, for bread and shelter. To do that, girls, like boys, must be educated to some lucrative employment; women, like men, must have equal chances to earn a living. If the plea that poverty is the cause of women's prostitution be not true, perfect equality of chances to earn honest bread will demonstrate the

---

From "Social Purity," a lecture delivered in Chicago, 1875.

falsehood by removing that pretext and placing her on the same plane with man. Then, if she is found in the ranks of vice and crime, she will be there for the same reason that man is and, from an object of pity she, like him, will become a fit subject of contempt. From being the party sinned against, she will become an equal sinner, if not the greater of the two. Women, like men, must not only have "fair play" in the world of work and self-support, but, like men, must be eligible to all the honors and emoluments of society and government. Marriage, to women as to men, must be a luxury, not a necessity; an incident of life, not all of it. And the only possible way to accomplish this great change is to accord to women equal power in the making, shaping, and controlling of the circumstances of life. That equality of rights and privileges is vested in the ballot, the symbol of power in a republic. Hence, our first and most urgent demand—that women shall be protected in the exercise of their inherent, personal, citizen's right to a voice in the government, municipal, state, national.

Alexander Hamilton said one hundred years ago, "Give to a man the right over my subsistence, and he has power over my whole moral being." No one doubts the truth of this assertion as between man and man; while, as between man and woman, not only does almost no one believe it, but the masses of people deny it. And yet it is the fact of man's possession of this right over woman's subsistence which gives to him the power to dictate to her a moral code vastly higher and purer than the one he chooses for himself. Not less true is it, that the fact of woman's dependence on man for her subsistence renders her utterly powerless to exact from him the same high moral code she chooses for herself.

Of the eight million women over twenty-one years of age in the United States, 800,000, one out of every ten, are unmarried, and fully one-half of the entire number, four million, support themselves wholly or in part by the industry of their own hands and brains. All of these, married or single, have to ask man, as an individual, a corporation, or a government, to grant to them even the privilege of hard work and small pay. The tens of thousands of poor but respectable young girls soliciting copying, clerkships, shop work, teaching, must ask of men, and not seldom receive in response, "Why work for a living? There are other ways!"

Whoever controls work and wages, controls morals. Therefore, we must have women employers, superintendents, committees, legislators; wherever girls go to seek the means of subsistence, there must be some woman. Nay, more; we must have women preachers, lawyers, doctors—that wherever women go to seek counsel—spiritual, legal, physical—there, too, they will be sure to find the best and noblest of their own sex to minister to them.

Independence is happiness. "No man should depend upon another; not even upon his own father. By depend I mean, obey without examination—yield to the will of any one whomsoever." This is the conclusion to which Pierre, the hero of Madame Sand's *Monsieur Sylvestre,* arrives, after running away from the uncle who had determined to marry him to a woman he did not choose to wed. In freedom he discovers that, though deprived of all the luxuries to which he had been accustomed, he is happy, and writes his friend that "without having realized it, he had been unhappy all his life; had suffered from his dependent condition; that nothing in his life, his pleasures, his occupations, had been of his own choice." And is not this the precise condition of what men call the "better half" of the human family?

In one of our western cities I once met a beautiful young woman, a successful teacher in its public schools, an only daughter who had left her New England home and all its comforts and luxuries and culture. Her father was a member of Congress and could bring to her all the attractions of Washington society. That young girl said to me, "The happiest moment of my life was when I received into my hand my first month's salary for teaching." Not long after, I met her father in Washington, spoke to him of his noble daughter, and he said: "Yes, you woman's rights people have robbed me of my only child and left the home of my old age sad and desolate. Would to God that the notion of supporting herself had never entered her head!" Had that same lovely, cultured, energetic young girl left the love, the luxury, the protection of that New England home for marriage instead of self-support, had she gone out to be the light and joy of a husband's life, instead of her own; had she but chosen another man, instead of her father, to decide for her all her pleasures and occupations; had she but taken another position of dependence, instead of one of independence, neither her father nor the world would have felt the change one to be condemned. . . .

Fathers should be most particular about the men who visit their daughters, and, to further this reform, pure women not only must refuse to meet intimately and to marry impure men, but, finding themselves deceived in their husbands, they must refuse to continue in the marriage relation with them. We have had quite enough of the sickly sentimentalism which counts the woman a heroine and a saint for remaining the wife of a drunken, immoral husband, incurring the risk of her own health and poisoning the lifeblood of the young beings that result from this unholy alliance. Such company as ye keep, such ye are! must be the maxim of married, as well as unmarried, women. . . .

So long as the wife is held innocent in continuing to live with a libertine, and every girl whom he inveigles and betrays becomes an outcast whom no other wife will tolerate in her house, there is, there can be, no hope of solving the problem of prostitution. As long experience has shown, these poor, homeless girls of the world can not be relied on, as a police force, to hold all husbands true to their marriage vows. Here and there, they will fail, and where they do, wives must make not the girls alone, but their husbands also suffer for their infidelity, as husbands never fail to do when their wives weakly or wickedly yield to the blandishments of other men. . . .

In a western city the wives conspired to burn down a house of ill-fame in which their husbands had placed a half-dozen of the demimonde. Would it not have shown much more womanly wisdom and virtue for those legal wives to have refused to recognize their husbands, instead of wreaking their vengeance on the heads of those wretched women? But how could they without finding themselves, as a result, penniless and homeless? The person, the services, the children, the subsistence, of each and every one of those women belonged by law, not to herself, but to her unfaithful husband.

Now, why is it that man can hold woman to this high code of morals, like Caesar's wife—not only pure but above suspicion—and so surely and severely punish her for every departure, while she is so helpless, so powerless to check him in his license, or to extricate herself from his presence and control? His power grows out of his right over her subsistence. Her lack of power grows out of her dependence on him for her food, her clothes, her shelter.

Marriage never will cease to be a wholly unequal partnership until the law recognizes the equal ownership in the joint earnings and possessions. The true relation of the sexes never can be attained until woman is free and equal with man. Neither in the making nor executing of the laws regulating these relations has woman ever had the slightest voice. The statutes for marriage and divorce, for adultery, breach of promise, seduction, rape, bigamy, abortion, violating these laws and what shall be their punishment, with judge, jury, and advocate all men, with no woman's voice heard in our courts, save as accused or witness, and in many cases the married woman is denied the poor privilege of testifying as to her own guilt or innocence of the crime charged against her.

Since the days of Moses and the prophets, men and ministers have preached the law of "visiting the iniquity of the fathers upon the children and the children's children, to the third and fourth generations." But with absolute power over woman and all the conditions of life for the whole six thousand years, man has proved his utter inability either to put away his own iniquities or to cease to hand them down from generation to generation; hence, the only hope of reform is in sharing this absolute power with some other than himself, and that other must be woman. When no longer a subject, but an equal—a free and independent sovereign, believing herself created primarily for her own individual happiness and development and secondarily for man's, precisely as man believes himself created first for his own enjoyment and second for that of woman—she will constitute herself sole umpire in the sacred domain of motherhood. Then, instead of feeling it her Christian duty to live with a drunken, profligate husband, handing down to her children his depraved appetites and passions, she will *know* that God's curse will be upon her and her children if she flee not from him as from a pestilence.

It is worse than folly, it is madness, for women to delude themselves with the idea that their children will escape the terrible penalty of the law. The taint of their birth will surely follow them. For pure women to continue to devote themselves to their man-appointed mission of visiting the dark purlieus of society and struggling to reclaim the myriads of badly-born human beings swarming there, is as hopeless as would be an attempt to ladle the ocean with a teaspoon; as unphilosophical as was the undertaking of the old American Colonization Society, which, with great labor and pains and money, redeemed from slavery and transported to Liberia annually four hundred Negroes; or the fugitive slave societies, which succeeded in running off to Canada, on their "underground railroads," some forty thousand in a whole quarter of a century. While those good men were thus toiling to rescue the four hundred or the forty thousand individual victims of slavery, each day saw hundreds and each year thousands of human beings born into the terrible condition of chattelism. All see and admit now what none but the abolitionists saw then, that the only effectual work was the entire overthrow of the system of slavery; the abrogation of the law which sanctioned the right of property in man.

In answer to my proposal to speak in one of the cities of Iowa, an earnest woman replied, "It is impossible to get you an audience; all of our best women are at present engaged in an effort to establish a 'Home for the Friendless.' All the churches are calling for the entire time of their members to get up fairs, dinners, concerts, etc., to raise money. In fact, even our women suffragists are losing themselves in devotion to some institution."

Thus, wherever you go, you find the best women, in and out of the churches, all absorbed in establishing or maintaining benevolent or reform institutions: charitable societies, souphouses, ragged schools, industrial schools, mite societies, mission schools—at home and abroad—homes and hospitals for the sick, the aged, the friendless, the foundling, the fallen; asylums for the orphans, the blind, the deaf and dumb, the insane, the inebriate, the idiot. The women of this century are neither idle nor indifferent. They are working with might and main to mitigate the evils which stare them in the face on every side, but much of their work is without knowledge. It is aimed at the effects, not the cause; it is plucking the spoiled fruit; it is lopping off the poisonous branches of the deadly upas tree, which but makes the root more vigorous in sending out new shoots in every direction. A right understanding of physiological law teaches us that the cause must be removed; the tree must be girdled; the taproot must be severed.

The taproot of our social upas lies deep down at the very foundations of society. It is woman's dependence. It is woman's subjection. Hence, the first and only efficient work must be to emancipate woman from her enslavement. The wife must no longer echo the poet Milton's ideal Eve, when she adoringly said to Adam, "God, thy law; thou, mine!" She must feel herself accountable to God alone for every act, fearing and obeying no man, save where his will is in line with her own highest idea of divine law. . . .

If the divine law visits the sins of the fathers upon the children, equally so does it transmit to them their virtues. Therefore, if it is through woman's ignorant subjection to the tyranny of man's appetites and passions that the life current of the race is corrupted, then must it be through her intelligent emancipation that the race shall be redeemed from the curse, and her children and children's children rise up to call her blessed. When the mother of Christ shall be made the true model of womanhood and motherhood, when the office of maternity shall be held sacred and the mother shall consecrate herself, as did Mary, to the one idea of bringing forth the Christ-child, then, and not till then, will this earth see a new order of men and women, prone to good rather than evil.

I am a full and firm believer in the revelation that it is through woman that the race is to be redeemed. And it is because of this faith that I ask for her immediate and unconditional emancipation from all political, industrial, social, and religious subjection.

HENRY GEORGE, 1839–1897
☆ The Single Tax

IT TOOK EIGHT YEARS after *Progress and Poverty* was published for "Single Tax" to become the descriptive phrase for the Henry George movement. The term had initially appeared in George's book when he referred to "the effect of substituting for the manifold taxes now imposed a single tax on the value of land." It was a George disciple, however, who first used the term "single tax" to describe the Henry George philosophy. The name was accepted with remarkable rapidity. Yet George, who also used it, did not feel it really expressed "all that a perfect name would convey."

Henry George, the second of ten children, was born in Philadelphia. His father, a vestryman in St. Paul's Episcopal Church, was a publisher of religious books. The young George attended church regularly and was brought up with morning and evening prayers.

His formal education ended at fourteen when he went to work as an office boy. But the sea excited him, and two years later he signed up as a foremast boy on a ship bound for Australia and India. On his return home, he subbed as a typesetter and wrote as an avocation. He took to the sea again, and when he returned, he worked as a typesetter once more.

George spent the next years at a succession of typesetting jobs. Occasionally, one would last long enough to provide some financial security, but for the most part, he found it difficult to support a wife and growing family.

During this time, he was also writing on social issues, although his first article was not published until 1865.

In 1866, George joined the newly established *San Francisco Times*, first as a reporter, then as an editorial writer, and finally as managing editor. Although his own economic situation had now improved considerably, George remembered vividly his days of poverty and continued to seek a solution to the causes of poverty in a land of plenty.

The completion of the first transcontinental railroad and the resultant increase in land values gave George his initial impetus to set down on paper his thoughts on land and wealth. He had gone for a horseback ride, he recalled. "Absorbed in my own thoughts, I had driven the horse into the hills until he panted. Stopping for breath, I asked a passing teamster, for want of something better to say, what land was worth there. He pointed to some cows grazing off so far that they looked like mice and said: 'I don't know exactly, but there is a man over there who will sell some land for a thousand dollars an acre.' Like a flash it came upon me that there was the reason of advancing poverty with advancing wealth. With the growth of population, land grows in value, and the men who work it must pay more for the privilege. I turned back, amidst quiet thought, to the perception that then came to me and has been with me ever since."

When George started to write *Progress and Poverty*, the country was in the midst of an industrial depression; strikes and riots were taking place in the east; the draught in California aggravated the economy there.

The book was completed in 1879 and sent to a New York publisher, Appleton & Co., who returned the manuscript with the comment, "It has the merit of being written with great clearness and force, but is very aggressive. There is very little to encourage the publication of any such work at this time." Two other New York publishers also rejected the work which was destined to excite the imagination of millions.

A friend of George's printed several hundred copies. Appleton then agreed to publish the book if the author would supply the plates. This George did.

Sales at first were sluggish. Henry George went to New York in the hope of stimulating the sale of the book and to find work on one of the newspapers there.

But jobs were scarce. George began to lecture. His interest in the land problem found sympathetic ears, particularly among the Irish in New York who were at that moment interested in the agitation going on in Ireland against landlordism. George wrote a pamphlet, *The Irish Land Question,* later retitled *The Land Question.* The booklet's wide circulation acted as a stimulant to sales of *Progress and Poverty*; more newspapers and magazines began to review the book. George was catapulted into fame in the United States as well as in England and Ireland. *Progress and Poverty* had initiated a social movement, with Henry George as its prophet.

In 1886, George was asked by a united labor movement in New York to be its candidate for mayor of that city. He accepted because "the campaign will bring the land question into practical politics and do more to popularize its discussion than years of writing would do."

So worried was the Tammany machine about George's candidacy that it went outside its ranks for its own candidate. The Republican party nominated Theodore Roosevelt. When the vote was counted, the Democratic candidate, Abram S. Hewitt, won with 90,552 votes; George came in second with 68,110 votes, and Roosevelt third with 60,435.

There followed feverish activity in organizing Land and Labor clubs and Single Tax clubs to further Henry George's principles. George also ran unsuccessfully for secretary of the state of New York.

In 1897, he was nominated for mayor of New York on the ticket of the newly formed "Party of Thomas Jefferson." In the midst of the campaign, Henry George, mayoral candidate, writer, and philosopher, died suddenly of apoplexy.

Today, scattered groups throughout the country still actively support the single-tax movement.

★ HOW EQUAL RIGHTS TO THE LAND MAY BE ASSERTED AND SECURED

We have traced the want and suffering that everywhere prevail among the working classes, the recurring paroxysms of industrial depression, the scarcity of employment, the stagnation of capital, the tendency of wages to the starvation point, that exhibit themselves more and more strongly as material progress goes on, to the fact that the land on which and from which all must live is made the exclusive property of some.

We have seen that there is no possible remedy for these evils but the abolition of their cause, we have seen that private property in land has no warrant in justice, but stands condemned as the denial of natural right—a subversion of the law of nature that as social development goes on must condemn the masses of men to a slavery the hardest and most degrading.

We have weighed every objection, and seen that neither on the ground of equity or expediency is there anything to deter us from making land common property by confiscating rent.

But a question of method remains. How shall we do it?

We should satisfy the law of justice, we should meet all eco-

---

From Henry George, *Progress and Poverty* (New York, 1879).

nomic requirements, by at one stroke abolishing all private titles, declaring all land public property, and letting it out to the highest bidders in lots to suit, under such conditions as would sacredly guard the private right to improvements.

Thus we should secure, in a more complex state of society, the same equality of rights that in a ruder state were secured by equal partitions of the soil, and by giving the use of the land to whoever could procure the most from it, we should secure the greatest production.

Such a plan, instead of being a wild, impracticable vagary, has (with the exception that he suggests compensation to the present holders of land—undoubtedly a careless concession which he upon reflection would reconsider) been indorsed by no less eminent a thinker than Herbert Spencer, who . . . says of it:

> Such a doctrine is consistent with the highest state of civilization; may be carried out without involving a community of goods, and need cause no very serious revolution in existing arrangements. The change required would simply be a change of landlords. Separate ownership would merge into the joint-stock ownership of the public. Instead of being in the possession of individuals, the country would be held by the great corporate body—society. Instead of leasing his acres from an isolated proprietor, the farmer would lease them from the nation. Instead of paying his rent to the agent of Sir John or his Grace, he would pay it to an agent or deputy agent of the community. Stewards would be public officials instead of private ones, and tenancy the only land tenure. A state of things so ordered would be in perfect harmony with the moral law. Under it all men would be equally landlords, all men would be alike free to become tenants. . . . Clearly, therefore, on such a system, the earth might be enclosed, occupied and cultivated, in entire subordination to the law of equal freedom.

But such a plan, though perfectly feasible, does not seem to me the best. Or rather I propose to accomplish the same thing in a simpler, easier, and quieter way than that of formally confiscating all the land and formally letting it out to the highest bidders.

To do that would involve a needless shock to present customs and habits of thought—which is to be avoided.

To do that would involve a needless extension of governmental machinery—which is to be avoided.

It is an axiom of statesmanship, which the successful founders of tyranny have understood and acted upon—that great changes can best be brought about under old forms. We who would be free men should heed the same truth. It is the natural method. When nature would make a higher type, she takes a lower one and develops it. This also is the law of social growth. Let us work by it. With the current we may glide fast and far. Against it, it is hard pulling and slow progress.

I do not propose either to purchase or to confiscate private property in land. The first would be unjust; the second, needless. Let the individuals who now hold it still retain, if they want to, possession of what they are pleased to call *their* land. Let them continue to call it *their* land. Let them buy and sell, and bequeath and devise it. We may safely leave them the shell, if we take the kernel. *It is not necessary to confiscate land; it is only necessary to confiscate rent.*

Nor to take rent for public uses is it necessary that the State should bother with the letting of lands, and assume the chances of the favoritism, collusion, and corruption this might involve. It is not necessary that any new machinery should be created. The machinery already exists. Instead of extending it, all we have to do is to simplify and reduce it. By leaving to land owners a percentage of rent which would probably be much less than the cost and loss involved in attempting to rent lands through state agency, and by making use of this existing machinery, we may, without jar or shock, assert the common right to land by taking rent for public uses.

We already take some rent in taxation. We have only to make some changes in our modes of taxation to take it all.

What I, therefore, propose, as the simple yet sovereign remedy, which will raise wages, increase the earnings of capital, extirpate pauperism, abolish poverty, give remunerative employment to whoever wishes it, afford free scope to human powers, lessen crime, elevate morals, and taste, and intelligence, purify government and carry civilization to yet nobler heights, is—*to appropriate rent by taxation.*

In this way the state may become the universal landlord without calling herself so, and without assuming a single new function. In form, the ownership of land would remain just as now. No owner of land need be dispossessed, and no restriction need be placed upon the amount of land any one could hold. For, rent being taken by the state in taxes, land, no matter in whose name it stood, or in what parcels it was held, would be really common property, and every member of the community would participate in the advantages of its ownership.

Now, insomuch as the taxation of rent, or land values, must necessarily be increased just as we abolish other taxes, we may put the proposition into practical form by proposing—

To abolish all taxation save that upon land values. . . . The value of land is at the beginning of society nothing, but as society develops by the increase of population and the advance of the arts, it becomes greater and greater. In every civilized country, even the newest, the value of the land taken as a whole is sufficient to bear the entire expenses of government. In the better developed countries it is much more than sufficient. Hence it will not be enough merely to place all taxes upon the value of the land. It will be necessary, where rent exceeds the present governmental revenues, commensurately to increase the amount demanded in taxation, and to continue this increase as society progresses and rent advances. But this is so natural and easy a matter, that it may be considered as involved, or at least understood, in the proposition to put all taxes on the value of land. That is the first step, upon which the practical struggle must be made. When the hare is once caught and killed, cooking him will follow as a matter of course. When the common right to land is so far appreciated that all taxes are abolished save those which fall upon rent, there is no danger of much more than is necessary to induce them to collect the public revenues being left to individual land holders.

Experience has taught me (for I have been for some years endeavoring to popularize this proposition) that wherever the idea of concentrating all taxation upon land values finds lodgment sufficient to induce consideration, it invariably makes way, but there are few of the classes most to be benefited by it, who at first, or even for a long time afterward, see its full significance and power. It is difficult for workingmen to get over the idea that there is a real antagonism between capital and labor. It is difficult for small farmers and homestead owners to get over the idea that to put all taxes on the value of land would be unduly to tax them. It is difficult for both classes to get over the idea that to exempt capital from taxation would be to make the rich richer, and the poor poorer. These ideas spring from confused thought. But behind ignorance and prejudice there is a powerful interest, which has hitherto dominated literature, education, and opinion. A great wrong always dies hard, and the great wrong which in every civilized country condemns the masses of men to poverty and want, will not die without a bitter struggle.

EDWARD BELLAMY, 1850–1898

☆ Nationalism

"IN UNDERTAKING TO WRITE *Looking Backward*," explained Edward Bellamy in the initial issue of the *Nationalist*, "I had, at the outset, no idea of attempting a serious contribution to the movement of social reform. The idea was of a mere literary fantasy, a fairy tale of social felicity. There was no thought of contriving a house which practical men might live in."

Yet, four years later, he wrote in an article: "According to my best recollection it was in the fall or winter of 1886 that I sat down to my desk with the definite purpose of trying to reason out a method of economic organization by which the republic might guarantee the livelihood and material welfare of its citizens on a basis of equality corresponding to and supplementing their political equality."

Whether Edward Bellamy purposefully and deliberately set

out to create a utopia or whether his original idea was only meant to be "a mere literary fantasy," the author soon after publication of his book found himself the social prophet of a movement which proclaimed in its Declaration of Principles: "So long as competition continues to be the ruling factor in our industrial system, the highest development of the individual cannot be reached, the loftiest aims of humanity cannot be realized."

Edward Bellamy was born in Chicopee Falls, Massachusetts. As a youth he wanted to be a soldier, but his failure to pass the physical examination at West Point turned his attention first to law, then to journalism, and finally to literature.

During a trip to Europe, prior to his "reading law," as he traveled in the "great cities" and "among the hovels of the peasantry" Bellamy became aware of the "extent and consequences of man's inhumanity to man."

Though he was admitted to the bar, he never practiced law. He went into journalism instead, working on the *New York Post* and later on the *Springfield Union*. In 1878 his first novel, *Six to One*, was published. After *Dr. Heidenhoff's Process*, which first appeared serially in a newspaper, he was proclaimed by some literary critics as a lineal descendant of Nathaniel Hawthorne.

When Bellamy started to write *Looking Backward*, the country was in the midst of industrial unrest. The year 1886 saw labor's push for the eight-hour day and the explosion of the Haymarket bomb in Chicago.

Bellamy, reticent and retiring, was suddenly pushed into the national limelight with the publication of *Looking Backward*. He found himself the leader of a reform movement which promised to be a social, political, and economic panacea.

The book tells the story of Julian West, a young Bostonian who awakens in the year 2000 A.D. after more than a hundred-year sleep induced by hypnosis. He is introduced to this new world by a Dr. Leete and his daughter Edith, who provides the romance in the story. By 2000 A.D. the world has substituted cooperation for competition. It is based on the universal service of its people in an "army of production."

Soon after the publication of *Looking Backward* in January 1888, a Boston newspaperman, Cyrus Field Willard, wrote to Bellamy suggesting ways to promote the ideas Bellamy had expressed in the book. After several exchanges of letters, Bellamy told Willard to "go ahead" in forming an association "if you can find anybody to associate with . . . to support and propagate the Nationalist ideas of the book as offering the best solutions of the problems of the day. . . . No doubt eventually the formation of such Nationalist Clubs or associations among our sympathizers all over the country will be a proper measure." Bellamy also wrote Willard that he "thoroughly" approved Willard's idea of directing his "efforts more particularly to the conversion of the cultured and conservative class. That was precisely the special end for which *Looking Backward* was written."

The membership of the movement was generally middle class —ex-Civil War army officers, writers, theosophists, ministers, some Socialists and Populists.

Bellamy rejected the class-conscious philosophy of the Socialists; he also rejected the use of the name Socialism to describe his movement because he felt that to the average American Socialism was alien and immoral.

Within two years after *Looking Backward* appeared, there were more than 150 Nationalist clubs throughout the United States propagating the new social order through forums and periodicals. Bellamy and the Nationalists were at high tide. In some sections of the country they nominated their own political candidates; in other parts they united with Socialists and with the Populist Party to support a candidate.

But by 1892, the Nationalist movement had begun to disintegrate. Because the Nationalist program was general, it had attracted members easily. When it came to specific action, however, there was no unity of opinion. Bellamy was too frail to give the strong leadership such a movement required. The very rapidity of its growth was a weakness.

Many of the Nationalist members joined the Populists, and by 1895 Bellamy's movement had faded from the scene, although he attempted to revive it with a new novel, *Equality*, published in 1897, which was an extension of the ideas he expressed in *Looking Backward*.

While writing *Equality*, Bellamy contracted tuberculosis. He died in the spring of 1898 at the age of forty-eight.

The Nationalist movement was never revived. Considered by some as a Boston "fad," as "the sentimental nostrum of people who are out of all vital touch with workingmen," it did not bring about any specific reforms. But Bellamy's Nationalism did create a climate which made the public willing to accept social and economic change. Many men and women who would play an important role on the national scene in the years to come were influenced by it.

★ PRINCIPLES AND PURPOSES OF NATIONALISM

The time has now come in America as it has come sooner or later in the history of all republics, when by the increase of wealth and by gross disparity in its distribution, this equality in its three aspects—political, social, industrial—is threatened with complete subversion. In order, under the changed conditions, to make good the original pledge of the republic to its citizens, it has become necessary to re-establish and maintain by some deliberate plan that economic equality, the basis of all other sorts of equality which, when the republic was established, existed in a substantial degree by nature. The question is not of assuming a new obligation, but whether the original ends and purposes of the republican compact shall be repudiated. We demand that the republic keep faith with the people, and propose a plan of industrial reorganization which seems to us the only possible means by which that faith can be kept. We are the true conservative party, because we are devoted to the maintenance of republican institutions against the revolution now being effected by the money power. We pro-

---

Address by Edward Bellamy at Tremont Temple, Boston, on the Nationalist Club's first anniversary, December 19, 1889.

pose no revolution, but that the people shall resist a revolution. We oppose those who are overthrowing the republic. Let no mistake be made here. We are not revolutionists, but counter-revolutionists.

But while the guarantee of equality of citizens is thus a measure amply justified and necessitated by merely patriotic and national considerations, without looking further for arguments, we do, in proposing this action, look both further and higher, to the ends of the earth indeed, and the ultimate destiny of the race.

While historic, political, and economic conditions require that this movement should be conducted on national lines by each people for itself, we hold the economic equality of all men a principle of universal application, having for its goal the eventual establishment of a brotherhood of humanity as wide as the world and as numerous as mankind. Those who believe that all men are brothers and should so regard one another must believe in the equality of men, for equals only can be brothers. Even brothers by blood do but hate each other the more bitterly for the tie when the inheritance is unequally parted between them, while strangers are presently made to feel like brothers by equality of interest and community of loss and gain. Therefore we look to the establishment of equality among men as the physical basis necessary to realize that brotherhood of humanity regarded by the good and wise of all ages as the ideal state of society. We believe that a wonderful confluence, at the present epoch, of material and moral tendencies throughout the world, but especially in America, has made a great step in the evolution of humanity not only possible but necessary for the salvation of the race. We are surrounded by perils from which the only way of escape is the way upward.

The plan of industrial reorganization which Nationalism proposes is the very simple and obvious one of placing the industrial duty of citizens on the ground on which their military duty already rests. All able-bodied citizens are held bound to fight for the nation, and, on the other hand, the nation is bound to protect all citizens, whether they are able to fight or not. Why not extend this accepted principle to industry, and hold every able-bodied citizen bound to work for the nation, whether with mind or muscle, and, on the other hand, hold the nation bound to guarantee the livelihood of every citizen, whether able to work or not. As in military matters the duty to fight is conditioned upon physical ability, while the right of protection is conditioned only upon citizenship, so would we condition the obligation to work upon the strength to work, but the right to support upon citizenship only.

The result would be to substitute for the present ceaseless industrial civil war, of which it would be hard to say whether it is more brutal or more wasteful, a partnership of all the people, a great joint stock company to carry on the business of the country for the benefit of all equally, women with men, sick with well, strong with weak. This plan of a national business partnership of equals we hold not only to be demonstrably practicable, but to constitute as truly the only scientific plan for utilizing the energy of the people in wealth production, as it is the only basis for society consistent with justice, with the sentiment of brotherhood, with the teachings of the founder of Christianity, and, indeed, of the founders of all the great religions.

The realization of the proposed plan of industry requires as the preliminary step the acquisition by the nation through its government, national and municipal, of the present industrial machinery of the country. It follows, therefore, that the Nationalists' program must begin with the progressive nationalization of the industries of the United States. In proposing this course we are animated by no sentiment of bitterness toward individuals or classes. In antagonizing the money power we antagonize not men but a system. We advocate no rash or violent measures, or such as will produce derangement of business or undue hardship to individuals. We aim to change the law by the law, and the Constitution, if necessary, by constitutional methods. As to the order in which industries should be nationalized, priority should naturally be given to those the great wealth of which renders them perilous to legislative independence, to those which deal extortionately with the public or oppressively with employees, to those which are highly systematized and centralized and to those which can be readily assimilated by existing departments of government.

The following are some of the measures in the line of this policy for which the country appears to be quite ready:

First—The nationalization of the railroads whether by constituting the United States perpetual receiver of all lines, to manage the same for the public interest, paying over to the present security-holders, pending the complete establishment of nationalism, such reasonable dividends on a just valuation of the property as may be earned, or by some other practicable method not involving hardship to individuals.

The nationalization of the railroads is advisable for reasons apart from the Nationalist program proper. Firstly, the railroad corporations, by the corrupt use of their vast wealth to procure and prevent legislation, are among the most formidable of the influences which are debauching our government. Secondly, the power they wield irresponsibly over the prosperity of cities, states, and entire sections of the country, ought to be in the hands only of the general government. Thirdly, the desperate rivalry of the railroads, with its incidents of reckless extension, duplication, and rate wars, has long been a chief waste of the national resources and a cause of periodical business crises. Fourthly, the financial management of a large portion of the railroad system, together with its use for speculative purposes, has rendered railroad financiering the most gigantic gambling and general swindling business ever carried on in any country. Fifthly, the convenience and safety of the traveling public demand a uniform and harmonious railroad system throughout the country, nor is it likely that anything less will bring to an end the cruel slaughter of railroad employees now carried on by the corporations.

A second measure for which the people are certainly quite ready is the nationalization of the telegraphic and telephone services, and their addition to the Post Office, with which, as departments of transmission of intelligence, they should properly always have been connected.

Third—We propose that the express business of the country be assumed by the post offices, according to the successful practices of other countries.

Fourth—We propose that the coal-mining business which at present is most rapaciously conducted as respects the public, and most oppressively as regards a great body of laborers, be nationalized, to the end that the mines may be continuously worked to their full capacity, coal furnished consumers at cost and the miners humanely dealt with. It is suggested that all mines hereafter discovered or opened shall be regarded as public property subject to just compensation for land.

Fifth—We propose that municipalities generally shall undertake lighting, heating, running of streetcars and such other municipal services as are now discharged by corporations, to the end that such services may be more cheaply and effectually rendered; that a fruitful source of political corruption be cut off and a large body of laborers be brought under humaner conditions of toil.

Pending the municipalization of all such services as have been referred to, Nationalists enter a general protest against the grant to corporations of any further franchises whether relating to transit, light, heat, water, or other public services.

It is to be understood that all nationalized and municipalized business should be conducted at cost for use and not for profit, the amount at present paid in taxes by such businesses, being, however, charged upon them.

It is an essential feature of the method of Nationalism that as fast as industries are nationalized or municipalized, the conditions of the workers in them shall be placed upon a wholly humane basis. The hours of labor will be made reasonable, the compensation adequate, the conditions safe and healthful. Support in sickness, with pensions for disabled and superannuated workers, will be guaranteed.

The question will be asked, "How is this great force of public employees to be placed beyond the power of politicians and administrations to use for partisan purposes?" Nationalists respond by proposing a plan for organizing and maintaining all public departments of business that shall absolutely deprive parties or politicians of any direct or arbitrary power over their membership, either as to appointment, promotion, or removal.

In the first place, it is understood that upon the nationalization of any business the existing force of employees and functionaries would be as a body retained. It is proposed that the service should be forthwith strictly graded and subsequently recruited exclusively by admissions to the lowest grade. All persons desiring to enter the service should be free to file applications at the proper bureau upon passing certain simple mental or physical tests, not competitive in character and adapted only to minimum grade of qualifications. Upon vacancies occurring in the force or a need of increase, the desired additions should be taken from the list of applicants on file, either in order of filed applications or, more perfectly to prevent fraud, by the drawing of the requisite number of names from a wheel containing the entire list of eligibles.

The chief of the department should be appointed at the discretion of the political executive, whether of city, state or nation, in order that responsibility for the general management of the business might be brought home to an elective officer. With this exception, and perhaps the further exceptions in some cases of the chiefs of a few important subordinate branches of the service, all positions should be filled by promotion in order of grades, such promotions to be determined by superiority of record and with certain requirements of length of service. While the chief should have power of suspension, no discharge from the service should take place save by verdict of a tribunal expressly erected for that purpose, before which all charges of fault or incompetence, whether by superior against subordinate, by subordinate against superior or by the outside public against members of the force, should be laid.

It is believed that such a plan of organization would absolutely prevent administrative coercion of members of the public service for partisan ends, and it is urgently recommended by Nationalists that it be immediately applied to the Post Office and all other business departments of the general government, to the employees and to the public works departments of all municipalities.

The nationalization of the several great branches of public service and productions which have been enumerated would directly affect, greatly for the better, the condition of a million and a half of workers.

Here truly would be a bulwark against capitalism, against corporate usurpation, against industrial oppression. Here would be a mighty nucleus for the coming industrial army. Here, too, would be a great body of consumers whose needs would suggest and whose demands would sustain the beginning of the coming National distributive and productive system.

Even a single industry organized on such a basis as described and guaranteeing to its toilers security, health, safety, dignity and justice would be an object lesson of the advantage of Nationalism, even in its beginnings, which would greatly hasten the general adoption of the system. As a measure which cannot wait, seeing that at best, the consequences of its postponement must continue to be felt long after it is effected, we urge that such partisan support as may be needful to enable them to attend school to the age of seventeen at least, be provided under proper guards by the state for the children of parents unable to maintain them without aid from their labor, and that with this provision the employment of children should be unconditionally forbidden and their education made rigidly compulsory, to the end that equality of educational opportunities for all be established.

Seeing that it would be manifestly inconsistent to make the education of our children compulsory while permitting the unlimited importation of adult ignorance and vice, a necessary complement to any system of education would be such regulation of foreign immigration as, without prejudice to honest, intelligent poverty, should prevent the importation of persons grossly illiterate in their own language, of the defective and of criminals, merely political offenses not being considered crimes.

In reviewing the measures which have been mentioned as substantially representing, according to my belief, the present demands of Nationalists, it is observable that there is not one of them which is not demanded by considerations of humanity and public expediency quite without reference to Nationalism. A man has no need to be a Nationalist at all to advocate them. They have been freely and often favorably discussed by the press for years, and the leading political economists of this country and Europe are on record in favor of most if not all of them. As to some of the most important of these propositions, it is altogether probable that a majority of the American people, if they could be polled today would favor them. Nationalists may be, as some say, a very extravagant and fantastical set of people, but there is certainly nothing fantastical about the plan of action which they propose. There is not even anything which can be said to be greatly in advance of public opinion. This moderation is not accidental, nor yet a result of policy, but a necessary consequence of the method of Nationalism, which is essentially gradual and progressive rather than abrupt or violent, the method of evolution as opposed to that of revolution. . . .

While the nationalizing of land in such time and by such methods as shall involve least hardships to any is a part of the National plan, and while the Nationalists meanwhile favor all practicable measures to prevent land monopoly and protect tenants and farmers, they are not persuaded that any measure applying to land alone would furnish a sufficient remedy for existing industrial and social troubles.

While sympathizing with all efforts of workers to obtain small immediate improvements in their condition, Nationalists would have them reflect that no great improvements can be gained, and if gained, can be secure, under the present industrial system, and that the only effectual and peaceable way of replacing that system by a better one is offered by Nationalism. It is also pointed out that the plan of Nationalism, by the humane and just conditions which will be secured to the employees of every industry, as it comes under the public control, offers not only the greatest ultimate results, but the speediest and surest way for immediately benefiting great bodies of workers absolutely without a risk of derangement to business.

THE END OF INNOCENCE

[IMAGES: 1894–1919]

PULLMAN. *American Railway Union. Eugene Victor Debs: "While there is a lower class, I am in it." Clarence Darrow. John Peter Altgeld of Illinois. Coxey's Army. William Jennings Bryan: "You shall not crucify mankind upon a cross of gold." "Bully!" The Gibson Girl. Mr. Dooley. President Theodore Roosevelt invites Negro educator Booker T. Washington to White House luncheon.*

"The rights and interests of the laboring man will be protected and cared for—not by the labor agitators but by the Christian men to whom God in His infinite wisdom has given the control of the property interests of this country."— George F. Baer, president, Philadelphia and Reading Coal and Iron Company. "The working class and the employing class have nothing in common."— I.W.W. Preamble.

San Francisco earthquake. John Dewey. She Was Only a Bird in a Gilded Cage.

Muckrakers: Lincoln Steffens, Ida Tarbell, David Graham

Phillips. Ray Stannard Baker. Upton Sinclair and The Jungle. *Pure Food and Drug Act. Meat inspection. Republican insurgency. Gallinger-Pinchot controversy. Anti-trust. Joe Hill's* Long-Haired Preachers Come Out Every Night. *Jane Addams and the clothing strike, and Hull House. The Great Steel strike.*

Orville and Wilbur Wright at Kittyhawk. The diesel engine. Lee DeForest and radio. George Eastman and the Kodak camera. Waterman's fountain pen. X-ray. Thompson's sub-machine gun. Brandeis-Holmes dissents. Suffragettes march on Washington.

Preparedness. Woodrow Wilson: "The world must be made safe for democracy."

War.

Liberty Loan. Mooney and Billings. Henry Ford's "flivver," and the "peace ship." Emma Goldman and Alexander Berkman. Influenza epidemic.

Armistice.

JACOB S. COXEY, 1854–1951

☆ Coxey's Army

ON MAY 1, 1894, A STRAGGLY LINE of men trudged down Pennsylvania Avenue in Washington, D.C., toward the Capitol. Headed by "General" Jacob S. Coxey, this "army" of unemployed had walked from Massillon, Ohio, to the nation's capital to demand that Congress pass a "good roads" and "non-interest-bearing bonds" bill as a means of alleviating the Panic of 1893.

The march ended when Coxey and two of his aides were arrested as Coxey began a speech from the Capitol steps. The three were found guilty of carrying banners and walking on the grass of the Capitol grounds; each man was given a twenty-day jail sentence and a $5 fine.

Jacob S. Coxey was born in Selinsgrove, Pennsylvania. At the age of fifteen, he quit school and went to work in the rolling mills in Danville, Ohio, where his family had moved. In 1881 he moved to Massillon, where he purchased and operated a thriving sandstone quarry. He also acquired farming interests, and he bred horses, raced them, and sold them.

At the time of the march of the unemployed, Coxey's own wealth was estimated at $200,000. His standing in the community was that of "a worthy and honest man." He had already shown an interest in politics by his candidacy for the state senate in 1885, when he based his campaign on the "money inflation" issue.

The idea for a roads program came to him as he was driving home one evening. When he found himself running into ruts and mudholes, he came to the conclusion that the only way to have good roads was to have the federal government build them. He organized the J. S. Coxey Good Roads Association to promote the idea. To implement the road bill, he promoted non-interest-bearing bonds for public improvements.

Coxey, the successful businessman, met Carl Browne at the Silver Convention in Chicago in 1893. They became friends. Browne had been a printer, painter, cartoonist, editor, rancher, politician, and labor agitator; now he began to campaign for the good-roads bill. It was Browne who told Coxey about the marches which the California unemployed had been making to demand relief. It was Browne, too, who came up with the idea of a "petition in boots."

The march and the demands were to be Coxey's remedy for the Panic of 1893, which had been precipitated by a year of business failures, unemployment, discontent, strikes, and mortgaged farms. By the end of the year, two million Americans were unemployed. The resources of charitable organizations were "strained to the breaking point." To aid the needy, soup kitchens were opened; the *New York World* distributed more than a million loaves of bread and the *New York Herald* gave away thousands of dollars' worth of clothing.

Coxey and Browne formulated plans for a march which was designed to make the government aware of the plight of the people by demanding help from Congress in the form of legislation to give every man a job at a good wage. The march was called the "Commonweal of Christ." On one of its banners was painted the head of Christ, Who here bore a resemblance to Browne. The banner proclaimed: "Peace on Earth Good Will to Men. He Hath Risen, but Death to Interest on Bonds."

W. T. Snead, writing in the *Review of Reviews* in July 1894, described the scene: "First marched a Negro carrying the American banner. Then riding on a big gray horse came Browne in his buckskin coat, fringed down the sleeves and plastered with decorations. A broad-brimmed white sombrero covered his head, and round his neck he wore an amber necklace given him by his wife. . . . Coxey himself followed the band in a buggy drawn by two bay mares and driven by a Negro." The "army" was next, followed by about forty newspapermen.

As they marched through Pennsylvania, the Coxey bill for good roads and non-interest-bearing bonds for public improvements was being reported on unfavorably in the Senate by the Committee on Education and Labor.

When the "army" reached Washington, Coxey began his talk from the Capitol steps. As he was being arrested, he handed the manuscript of his speech to a bystander and asked that it be turned over to the press. In this prepared speech, Coxey had cited the constitutional right "to peacefully assemble and petition for the redress of grievances." He asserted: "We stand here today in behalf of millions of toilers whose petitions have been buried in committee rooms, whose prayers have been unresponded to, and whose opportunities for honest, remunerative, and productive labor have been taken from them by unjust legislation which protects idlers, speculators, and gamblers. We come to remind Congress, here assembled, of the declaration of a United States senator, that 'for a quarter of a century the rich have been growing richer and the poor poorer.' "

By the time the three men had served their twenty-day sentence, only remnants of their army remained in Washington.

Coxey remained active politically. He made many attempts to reach public office: in 1897 he was a candidate for Governor of Ohio; in 1916 he tried for the nomination as U. S. Senator; in

1924 and 1926 he ran for Congress as an "Independent Progressive"; he tried again for the Senate in 1928.

In 1931 Jacob S. Coxey was elected to his only term of public office: mayor of Massillon on the Republican ticket. Three years later he was defeated in the city's primary when he sought re-election. In 1936 he was nominated for President by the Farmer-Labor Party, but withdrew to support William Lemke of the Union Party, who was also pledged to fight against the "money changers and their servants, Landon and Roosevelt." In 1943 Coxey was defeated for mayor on the Democratic ticket.

At the age of ninety, seven years before he died, Coxey traveled to Washington and completed the speech he started to deliver in 1894 when he led Coxey's Army into that city.

★ COXEY'S ARMY

The aim and object of this march to Washington has been to awaken the attention of the whole people to a sense of their duty in impressing upon Congress the necessity for giving immediate relief to the four million of unemployed people, and their immediate families, consisting of twelve million to fifteen million more. The idea of the march is to attract the attention of the whole people of this country to the greatest question that has ever been presented to them—the money question. Believing that the people can only digest one idea at a time, it was necessary to get up some attraction that would overshadow other matters and have their minds centered upon this one idea and to understand it intelligently.

Knowing that this march would consume thirty-five days from Massillon to Washington, that it would attract their attention and we could present this money feature to them in an impressive sense and a business manner and thus be able to educate them more in six weeks' time than through any one political party in ten years.

From a speech made by Jacob Selcher Coxey at Camp California, Williamsport, Maryland, April 18, 1894.

Our plan is to arrive at Washington by May 1, next, and camp there until Congress takes some action upon the two bills that have been presented to them by Senator Peffer, viz.: "The Good Roads Bill" and "The Non-Interest-Bearing Bond Bill." Believing that the unemployed people and the business men of this country whose interests are identical will try and get to Washington the first week in May, from 300,000 to 500,000 strong. In this manner they will bring the strongest impression to bear upon Congress coming through the common people that has ever been made in the history of this country.

So long as Congress can keep the people isolated from each other all over the land, they will never grant them any relief, but when they come in a body like this, peaceably to discuss their grievances and demanding immediate relief, Congress can no longer turn a deaf ear, but will heed them and do it quickly.

The full text of the bill before Congress by which to build good roads, according to my plan, is as follows:

"Section 1. Be it enacted by the Senate and House of Representatives in Congress assembled: that the Secretary of the Treasury of the United States is hereby authorized and instructed to have engraved and printed, immediately after the passage of this bill, $500 million of treasury notes, a legal tender for all debts, public and private, said notes to be in denominations of one, two, five, and ten dollars, and to be placed in a fund to be known as the 'general county road fund system of the United States,' and to be expended solely for said purpose.

"Sec. 2. And be it further enacted, that it shall be the duty of the Secretary of War to take charge of the construction of the said General County Road system in the United States, and said construction to commence as soon as the Secretary of the Treasury shall inform the Secretary of War that the said fund is available, which shall not be later than ———; when it shall be the duty of the Secretary of War to inaugurate the work and expend the sum of $20 million per month, pro rata, with the number of miles of roads in each state and territory in the United States.

"Sec. 3. Be it further enacted, that all labor other than that of the Secretary of War, 'whose compensations are already fixed by law,' shall be paid by the day, and that the rate be not less than $1.50 per day for common labor, and $3.50 per day for team and labor, and that eight hours per day shall constitute a day's labor under the provisions of this bill."

For the propositions are, that Congress shall issue and appropriate $500 million of full legal tender treasury notes to the states and territories, pro rata, with the number of miles of roads in each state and territory at the rate of $20 million per month, for the improvements of the public roads of this country, and to give employment to the unemployed in making these improvements. Another provision of this bill says that all labor shall be generally by the day—no contract labor—and the rate shall be not less than $1.50 per day of eight hours.

This will settle the eight-hour question, because it brings into competition the government, which stands ready at all times to employ the idle labor in making public roads at $1.50 per day for a day of eight hours, and no employer of labor outside of government will be able to employ a single man for less than $1.50 per day of eight hours, so this will practically settle the eight-hour question.

The other matter under consideration is the Non-Interest-Bearing Bond Bill, now before Congress, as follows:

"Be it enacted by the Senate and House of Representatives, in Congress assembled, that whenever any state, territory, county, township, municipality, or incorporated town or village deem it necessary to make any public improvements, they shall deposit with the Secretary of the Treasury of the United States a non-interest-bearing, twenty-five-year bond, not to exceed one-half the assessed valuation of the property in said state, territory, county, township, municipality, or incorporated town or village, and said bond to be retired at the rate of 4 per cent per annum.

"Whenever the foregoing section of this act has been complied with, it shall be mandatory upon the Secretary of the Treasury of the United States to have engraved and printed treasury notes in the denominations of one, two, five, ten, and twenty dollars each, which shall be a full legal tender for all debts, public and private, to the face value of said bond, and deliver to said state, territory, county, township, municipality, or incorporated town or village 99 per cent of said notes, and retain 1 per cent for expense of engraving and printing same."

This non-interest, twenty-five-year bond bill grants to all states, counties, townships, municipalities, towns, or villages the right to draw their non-interest, twenty-five-year bond, not to exceed one-half the assessed valuation of their entire property, and to deposit the same with the Secretary of the Treasury at Washington. It will then be mandatory upon him to issue the face value of these bonds in full legal tender treasury notes of the denominations of one, two, five, ten, and twenty dollars each, returning 99 per cent of those notes to the states, counties, townships, municipalities, towns, or villages depositing these bonds, and the government retaining 1 per cent for the expense of engraving the treasury notes. The parties so receiving the money agree to repay it back at the rate of 4 per cent per annum, or in twenty-five annual installments without interest.

This will enable the states, counties, townships, municipalities, towns, or villages to make all the public improvements that they will need for all time to come without paying one cent of tribute to any one in the share of usury. They will be enabled to build their statehouses, their insane asylums, courthouses, infirmaries, and schoolhouses. All municipalities can build their own market-houses, public libraries, museums, engine-houses, schoolhouses, and public halls where people can come and discuss all questions that interest them; pave their own streets; own and build their own electric light plants, water works, street railroads, and other public improvements that are a convenience and comfort, and promote the advancement of the whole people.

After this system of public improvements is inaugurated, it will settle the money question, as it will supply all the money needed for the public convenience, and to develop the resources of the country, and not one dollar can go into circulation without a service being rendered and the value credited to the government direct in the shape of public improvements, which will be beneficial to all.

This will supply actual money in place of confidence money. This will substitute a cash system for a credit or script system. The business of this country has been done on confidence money. Now that the confidence has vanished, business has also vanished.

One year ago we had in circulation $1.5 billion in actual money, $1 billion of which was in the hands of the people making the small exchanges, $500 million was in the banks and bank reserves, and upon these reserves the banks of this country had created $4 billion of confidence money, and by the conspiracy of the money lenders of Europe in throwing their securities upon our markets and converting them into gold and withdrawing the gold from the country. Thus through the continued agitation of the daily press claiming that if the government did not stop the further purchase of silver through the Sherman bill, it would drive gold out of this country and create a panic.

They did, through these means scare the small depositors and employees of the country into withdrawing their savings and deposits from the banks, and when employers went to the banks to get accommodations in the shape of discounts, the banker said, "Self-preservation being the first law of nature, I must protect my depositors, and cannot therefore, discount your paper."

The manufacturer, expecting that there would be no trouble in using the paper that he had taken in payment for his goods, was nonplused and compelled to close down his works on account of not being able to realize upon this paper. This then became general throughout the country, business men were compelled to suspend, and thousands of millions of credit was affected. The paper confidence money which had been transacting the business of the country just the same as the actual money did, commenced to vanish, and as it vanished business vanished with it; workshops became idle and are now rusting away; men were thrown out of employment, and now devastation and ruin have spread over our land.

To cap the climax, when the money famine was at its height,

President Cleveland called an extra session of Congress to repeal the Sherman Act, which act did increase the volume of money at the rate of $4 million per month. Had it been left on the statute books, it would have made money a little easier, and by repealing that act business has become worse. There is little hope for the future in a business sense unless the two measures mentioned are passed. These would give immediate relief to the unemployed, in making public improvements and substitute actual money in place of confidence money that has already vanished, thus taking away all possibility of panics and hard times in the future and making it an impossibility for a man to seek work without finding it.

WILLIAM HOPE HARVEY, 1851–1936

☆ Coin's Financial School

FREE SILVER was offered as the all-encompassing solution to the depression of the 1890's. For a moment in financial reform history, William Hope Harvey was the star. Then, only a few years later, William Jennings Bryan took the applause with his "Cross of Gold" speech which embodied many of Harvey's ideas.

1894. A stock market panic hit the country, wheat and cotton prices collapsed: bank failures, excessive business bankruptcies, acute unemployment. Jacob Coxey led his "army" to Washington, D.C.; Eugene Victor Debs and the Pullman strikers fought for better working conditions. A solution was necessary so that the country would not be plunged into this depression again.

William Hope Harvey, a young lawyer who had worked in

the silver mines in Colorado and studied their production, came up with a panacea in his book, *Coin's Financial School.*

The book—a phenomenal best-seller for that time—is a fictionalized dialogue between Professor Coin and some of the leading citizens of Chicago. Coin is the mythical young financier who opened a finance school where he taught the rudiments of the nation's monetary system.

Many who read the book at the height of its success believed that such a school did exist and that such prominent citizens of Chicago as Joseph Medill of the *Chicago Tribune*, Lyman Gage, president of a large bank, Marshall Field, Philip D. Armour, and others attended.

In 1895, U.S. Congressman J. C. Catchings (Mississippi) wrote to President Cleveland's Secretary of War, Col. David S. Lamont: "A little free silver book called *Coin's Financial School* is being sold on every railroad train by newsboys and at every cigar store. It is being read by almost everybody."

In his "Introduction" to a reprint of *Coin's Financial School*, Richard Hofstadter described Harvey as "the Tom Paine of the free silver movement." He compared *Coin's Financial School* and its influence on the monetary issues of 1896 to "what *Common Sense* had been to the revolutionaries of 1776."

Born in Buffalo, West Virginia, Harvey went to the county school, attended the Buffalo Academy and Marshall College, West Virginia, "read law" in a lawyer's office, and at the age of nineteen was admitted to the bar. He was lured to the silver mines of Colorado as a result of a trip he made to the territory on behalf of a client. In 1884 Harvey and his family moved to Colorado, where they remained for three years while Harvey worked as a mine supervisor.

But high operational costs were driving the small mine operator out; there was a surplus of workers in the field. Production of silver lost its fascination for Harvey.

He returned to Chicago, where he established the Coin Publishing Company, dedicated to the publication of books on the free coinage of silver. His first publication was a short-lived weekly magazine called *Coin*. Then came Coin's Financial Series, of which *School* was the third. The books were produced on cheap paper, selling four a year for one dollar; single copies twenty-five cents. Clothbound copies were available at one dollar each.

The frontispiece of *School* quoted Matthew 11:25: "I thank thee, O Father, Lord of Heaven and Earth, because thou hast hid these things from the wise and prudent, and hast revealed them unto babes." The dedication followed: "To those . . . trying to locate the seat of the disease that threatens the life of the nation."

Opposition to Harvey's free-silver panacea was immediate. There was an outpouring of such books as H. L. Bliss's *Coin's Financial Fraud*, J. F. Cargell's A *Freak in Finance*, and Henry White's *Coin's Financial Fool*.

Harvey also lectured and organized various "silver clubs." In 1894 he associated himself with the conservative wing of the Chicago Populists; two years later he campaigned for William Jennings Bryan for President. Bryan admitted, "Among the educational influences at work in behalf of bimetallism" during his campaign, "the most potent was *Coin's Financial School*. It is safe to say that no book in recent times has produced so great an effect in the treatment of an economic question."

In 1900 Harvey moved to the Ozark region of Arkansas, where he built the resort town of Monte Ne, promoted a short-line railroad, established briefly another publishing company.

He started to build a pyramid on a peak of the Ozark mountains in Arkansas. Here, he hoped, archeologists would find some of the history of the civilization of the United States and the reasons that Harvey believed would contribute to its downfall. The depression of the 1930's stopped this part of his work.

With the depression came the eighty-year-old Harvey's nomination for President of the United States by a "Prosperity party" meeting in Monte Ne in 1931 and by the Liberty party in 1932. Harvey did not campaign for the office; when the votes were counted, he had received eight hundred. The fervent advocate of bimetallism died at his home in Monte Ne, Arkansas, at the age of eighty-five.

★ COIN'S FINANCIAL SCHOOL

Hard times are with us; the country is distracted; very few things are marketable at a price above the cost of production; tens of thousands are out of employment; the jails, penitentiaries, workhouses, and insane asylums are full; the gold reserve at Washington is sinking; the government is running at a loss with a deficit in every department; a huge debt hangs like an appalling cloud over the country; taxes have assumed the importance of a mortgage, and 50 per cent of the public revenues are likely to go delinquent; hungered and half-starved men are banding into armies and marching toward Washington; the cry of distress is heard on every hand; business is paralyzed; commerce is at a standstill; riots and strikes prevail throughout the land; schemes to remedy our ills when put into execution are smashed like boxcars in a railroad wreck, and Wall Street looks in vain for an excuse to account for the failure of prosperity to return since the repeal of the silver purchase act.

It is a time for wisdom and sound sense to take the helm, and Coin, a young financier living in Chicago, acting upon such a suggestion, established a school of finance to instruct the youths of the nation, with a view to their having a clear understanding of what has been considered an abstruse subject; to lead them out of the labyrinth of falsehoods, heresies and isms that distract the country.

The school opened on the 7th day of May 1894.

There was a good attendance, and the large hall selected in the Art Institute was comfortably filled. Sons of merchants and bankers, in fact all classes of business, were well represented. Journalists, however, predominated. Coin stepped on to the plat-

---

From William Hope Harvey, *Coin's Financial School* (Chicago, 1894).

form, looking the smooth little financier that he is, and said:

"I am pleased to see such a large attendance. It indicates a desire to learn and master a subject that has baffled your fathers. The reins of the government will soon be placed in your hands, and its future will be molded by your honesty and intelligence.

"I ask you to accept nothing from me that does not stand the analysis of reason; that you will freely ask questions and pass criticisms, and if there is any one present who believes that all who differ from *him* are lunatics and fools, he is requested to vacate his seat and leave the room. . . .

"Up to 1873, we were on what was known as a bimetallic basis, but what was in fact a silver basis, with gold as a companion metal enjoying the same privileges as silver, except that silver fixed the unit, and the value of gold was regulated by it. This was bimetallism.

"Our forefathers showed much wisdom in selecting silver, of the two metals, out of which to make the unit. Much depended on this decision. For the one selected to represent the unit would thereafter be unchangeable in value. That is, the metal in it could never be worth less than a dollar, for it would be the unit of value itself. The demand for silver in the arts or for money by other nations might make the quantity of silver in a silver dollar sell for more than a dollar, but it could never be worth less than a dollar. Less than itself.

"In considering which of these two metals they would thus favor by making it the unit, they were led to adopt silver because it was the most reliable. It was the most favored as money by the people. It was scattered among all the people. Men having a design to injure business by making money scarce, could not so easily get hold of all the silver and hide it away, as they could gold. This was the principal reason that led them to the conclusion to select silver, the more stable of the two metals, upon which to fix the unit. It was so much handled by the people and preferred by them, that it was called the people's money.

"Gold was considered the money of the rich. It was owned

principally by that class of people, and the poor people seldom handled it, and the very poor people seldom ever saw any of it. . . .

"It is proposed by the bimetallists to remonetize silver, and add it to the quantity of money that is to be used for measuring the value of all other property.

"In dollars at a ratio to gold of sixteen to one, there are about the same number of dollars of silver in the world as gold. The report of the director of our mint says there was in the world in 1890, in the form of silver coin and bullion used as money, $3,820,571,346.

"A cubic foot of silver weighs 10,474 troy ounces, and using 371¼ grains to each dollar, this will make a cubic foot of cast silver worth $13,544.

"You get this by multiplying the 10,474 by 480, the number of grains in an ounce, and dividing the result by 371¼, the number of grains in a dollar. You then want to divide the $3,820,571-346, the silver of the world, by 13,544, the number of dollars in a cubic foot. It gives 282,085 cubic feet of silver in the world.

"Can you comprehend what a quantity of silver this is? I will tell you how. It will make a block of silver sixty-six feet wide, sixty-six feet long, and sixty-six feet high.

"You can put it all—all the silver of the world—in one of the rooms of this building, and anyone entering at the main entrance on Michigan Avenue would have to inquire in which room of the building the silver of the world was, before he could find it.

"It will go in the Board of Trade room and still leave sufficient space, I imagine, for you gentlemen to do some business on dull days."

Coin now had the teller of the Metropolitan National Bank hand him a satchel containing one hundred and fourteen silver dollars. With these he showed that sixty-four silver dollars would lay down in eight rows, of eight each in a square foot, and that one hundred and fourteen laid one upon the other measured a foot in height; that a cubic foot would therefore contain 7,296 silver dollars.

He then explained that the alloy (one-tenth), and the space between the sixty-four stacks of silver dollars, would hold the other $6,248 of the $13,544 in a solid cast cubic foot of pure silver.

He also stated that the gold and silver of the world obtainable for use as money, when mixed with its alloy and coined, could be stacked up in less than double the space it would occupy in solid cast blocks.

The little economist then continued: "All the silver in the world available for money can be stored in the room of the First National Bank of this city and the basement thereunder.

"This is the quantity of silver in the world, and it will be well for you to remember it when you hear someone talking about a flood of silver.

"We have heard a good deal about the treasury vaults at Washington groaning with silver, and more talk of enlarging them.

"The vaults under our treasury building can easily be arranged to hold all of the silver in all of the countries of the world used as money, either in coins, bars or bullion.

"You can empty all of the pockets of the people of the world of their silver, the bank vaults, the merchants' money drawers, the sub-treasuries, the children's safes, all India, Mexico, South America, England, France, Germany, Russia, Italy, Austria, the Netherlands, British America, China, Japan, and the islands, big and little, of the oceans, and you can put it all into this room, or in the basement of the Treasury building of the United States. [Applause]

"It is a matter of mathematical calculation and no intelligent citizen need be either alarmed or deceived."

With this statement Coin paused a moment, while people looked into each other's faces and back again at the speaker. . . .

"The money lenders in the United States, who own substantially all of our money, have a selfish interest in maintaining the gold standard. They, too, will not yield. They believe that if the gold standard can survive for a few years longer, the people will get used to it—get used to their poverty—and quietly submit.

"To that end they organize international bimetallic committees and say, 'Wait on England, she will be forced to give us bimetallism.' Vain hope! Deception on this subject has been practiced long enough upon a patient and outraged people.

"With silver remonetized, and gold at a premium, not one-tenth the hardships could result that now afflict us. Why? First: it would double the value of all property. Second: only 4 per cent of the business of the people of this nation is carried on with foreign countries; and a part of this 4 per cent would be transactions with silver-using nations; while 96 per cent of the business of our people is domestic transactions, Home business. Is it not better to legislate in the interest of 96 per cent of our business, than the remaining 4 per cent? . . .

"In the impending struggle for the mastery of the commerce of the world, the financial combat between England and the United States cannot be avoided if we are to retain our self-respect, and our people their freedom and prosperity. [Applause]

"The gold standard will give England the commerce and wealth of the world. The bimetallic standard will make the United States the most prosperous nation on the globe." [Applause]

WILLIAM JENNINGS BRYAN, 1860–1925

☆ Free Silver

WILLIAM JENNINGS BRYAN, like William Hope Harvey, considered free silver *the* economic panacea.

Born only a few years after Harvey, in Salem, Illinois, Bryan, after graduating from law school, became associated with the law firm of Lyman Trumbull, a former U. S. Senator. In 1867 Bryan moved to Lincoln, Nebraska, where he not only practiced law but became active in the Democratic party.

In July 1890 Bryan was nominated for Congress by the Democratic party in a strongly Republican district where it was believed no Democrat could win. The nominating convention adopted a silver plank which Bryan had written and in which he expressed his views: "We demand the free coinage of silver on equal terms with gold and denounce the effort of the Republican party to serve the interests of Wall Street as against the rights of the people."

Bryan won the seat with a plurality of 6,713. He was re-elected for a second term during which he delivered a major speech against the repeal of the silver purchase clause of the Sherman Act. The speech attracted national attention. Bryan concluded by telling his opponents in Congress that they "have laid the free coinage of silver away in a sepulchre. But, sirs, if our cause is just, as I believe it is, your labor has been in vain; no time was ever made so strong that it could imprison a righteous cause. Silver will lay aside its grave clothes and its shroud. It will yet rise and in its rising and its reign will bless mankind."

In 1894 Bryan decided not to seek re-election to the House but to become a candidate for the U.S. Senate from Nebraska. He lost. He then became editor of the *Omaha World-Herald*.

Two years later, as a presidential nominee, Bryan was a "dark horse" at the 1896 Democratic convention. The convention had heard the antagonists of bimetallism. The idea of free silver had been decried by its opponents. Then Bryan asked for recognition to speak, and he delivered his "Cross of Gold" speech.

Bryan described the occasion: "From the first sentence the audience was with me . . . I shall never forget the scene upon which I looked. I believe it unrivaled in any convention ever held in our country. The audience seemed to rise and sit down as one man. . . . The audience acted like a trained choir—in fact, I thought of a choir as I noted how instantaneously and in unison they responded to each point made."

The next day the thirty-six-year-old William Jennings Bryan was nominated on the fifth ballot as the presidential candidate of the Democratic party, the youngest candidate ever nominated. He was also the choice of the National Silver party and the Populist party. Out of a popular vote of over 13.5 million votes, Bryan lost to William McKinley by only 600,000.

At the 1900 Democratic party convention, "about the only

plank that aroused discussion was the plank restating the Chicago platform for the restoration of bimetallism and the opening of the mints to the free coinage of silver at the ratio of sixteen to one."

Bryan told the convention that he would not consent to be a candidate if the silver plank were not reiterated. The convention made imperialism the "paramount" issue, the trust plank second. Bryan observed, "The fact that the platform reiterated the demand for independent bimetallism made it less necessary for me to discuss the question than it would have been had the platform attempted to avoid the subject."

Again he was defeated, this time by a larger vote. He announced he would not be a candidate in 1904. He continued to agitate for bimetallism from the lecture platform and in *The Commoner*, a weekly journal he published. But in 1908 he was again the Democratic presidential nominee. This time he lost to William Howard Taft.

Although not a candidate in 1912, Bryan took part in the convention, where he helped set the general tone and was largely responsible for the nomination of Woodrow Wilson. President Wilson repaid this political debt by naming Bryan his secretary of state, the highest political office Bryan was ever to hold. Bryan then tried unsuccessfully to get a position for William Harvey with the federal government.

Because of a disagreement with President Wilson on foreign affairs prior to the U. S. entry into World War I, Bryan resigned from Wilson's cabinet.

His last public appearance was in Dayton, Tennessee, in the summer of 1925, during the Scopes trial, when he helped to prosecute the school teacher for teaching evolution in the public school of the little town. There Bryan debated evolution with Clarence Darrow. Five days after the close of the trial the "golden-voiced orator," William Jennings Bryan, three-time candidate for President of the United States, died in his sleep.

★ THE CROSS OF GOLD

I would be presumptuous, indeed, to present myself against the distinguished gentlemen to whom you have listened if this were a mere measuring of abilities; but this is not a contest between persons. The humblest citizen in all the land, when clad in the armor of a righteous cause, is stronger than all the hosts of error. I come to speak to you in defense of a cause as holy as the cause of liberty —the cause of humanity.

When this debate is concluded, a motion will be made to lay upon the table the resolution offered in commendation of the administration, and also, the resolution offered in condemnation of the administration. We object to bringing this question down to the level of persons. The individual is but an atom; he is born, he acts, he dies; but principles are eternal; and this has been a contest over a principle.

Never before in the history of this country has there been witnessed such a contest as that through which we have just passed. Never before in the history of American politics has a great issue been fought out as this issue has been, by the voters of a great party. On the fourth of March 1895, a few Democrats, most of them members of Congress, issued an address to the Democrats of the nation, asserting that the money question was the paramount issue of the hour; declaring that a majority of the Democratic party had the right to control the action of the party on this paramount issue; and concluding with the request that the believers in the free coinage of silver in the Democratic party should organize, take charge of, and control the policy of the Democratic party. Three months later, at Memphis, an organization was perfected, and the silver Democrats went forth openly and courageously proclaiming their belief, and declaring that, if successful, they would crystallize into a platform the declaration which they

---

Speech delivered July 9, 1896, at the Democratic convention in Chicago.

had made. Then began the struggle. With a zeal approaching the zeal which inspired the Crusaders who followed Peter the Hermit, our silver Democrats went forth from victory unto victory until they are now assembled, not to discuss, not to debate, but to enter up the judgement already rendered by the plain people of this country. In this contest brother has been arrayed against brother, father against son. The warmest ties of love, acquaintance, and association have been disregarded; old leaders have been cast aside when they have refused to give expression to the sentiments of those whom they would lead, and new leaders have sprung up to give direction to this cause of truth. Thus has the contest been waged, and we have assembled here under as binding and solemn instructions as were ever imposed upon representatives of the people. . . .

When you [turning to the gold delegates] come before us and tell us that we are about to disturb your business interests, we reply that you have disturbed our business interests by your course.

We say to you that you have made the definition of a business man too limited in its application. The man who is employed for wages is as much a business man as his employer; the attorney in a country town is as much a business man as the corporation counsel in a great metropolis; the merchant at the cross-roads store is as much a business man as the merchant of New York; the farmer who goes forth in the morning and toils all day, who begins in the spring and toils all summer, and who by the application of brain and muscle to the natural resources of the country creates wealth, is as much a business man as the man who goes upon the board of trade and bets upon the price of grain; the miners who go down a thousand feet into the earth, or climb two thousand feet upon the cliffs, and bring forth from their hiding places the precious metals to be poured into the channels of trade are as much business men as the few financial magnates who, in a back room, corner the money of the world. We come to speak of this broader class of business men.

Ah, my friends, we say not one word against those who live upon the Atlantic Coast, but the hardy pioneers who have braved all the dangers of the wilderness, who have made the desert to blossom as the rose—the pioneers away out there [pointing to the West] who rear their children near to Nature's heart, where they can mingle their voices with the voices of the birds—out there where they have erected schoolhouses for the education of their young, churches where they praise their Creator, and cemeteries where rest the ashes of their dead—these people, we say, are as deserving of the consideration of our party as any people in this country. It is for these that we speak. We do not come as aggressors. Our war is not a war of conquest; we are fighting in the defense of our homes, our families, and posterity. We have petitioned, and our petitions have been scorned; we have entreated, and our entreaties have been disregarded; we have begged, and they have mocked when our calamity came. We beg no longer; we entreat no more; we petition no more. We defy them! . . .

And now, my friends, let me come to the paramount issue. If they ask us why it is that we say more on the money question than we say upon the tariff question, I reply that, if protection has slain its thousands, the gold standard has slain its tens of thousands. If they ask us why we do not embody in our platform all the things that we believe in, we reply that when we have restored the money of the Constitution, all other necessary reform will be possible; but that until this is done, there is no other reform that can be accomplished. . . .

You come to us and tell us that the great cities are in favor of the gold standard; we reply that the great cities rest upon our broad and fertile prairies. Burn down your cities and leave our farms, and your cities will spring up again as if by magic; but destroy our farms and the grass will grow in the streets of every city in the country. . . .

We care not upon what lines the battle is fought. If they say bimetallism is good, but that we cannot have it until other nations help us, we reply, that instead of having a gold standard because England has, we will restore bimetallism, and then let England have bimetallism because the United States has it. If they dare to come out in the open field and defend the gold standard as a good thing, we will fight them to the uttermost. Having behind us the producing masses of this nation and the world, supported by the commercial interests, the laboring interests and the toilers everywhere, we will answer their demand for a gold standard by saying to them: You shall not press down upon the brow of labor this crown of thorns, you shall not crucify mankind upon a cross of gold.

CARRY A. NATION, 1846–1911
☆ Prohibition

CARRY NATION's panacea was a crusade to save man from the evils of liquor. Claiming to be inspired by the Divine Word, armed with a hatchet and with determination, she marched to her utopia.

"If you would live long," reads one of Carry Nation's "Rules for Longevity," "walk by twenty saloons a day; if you must pour liquor, pour it down the sewer."

Her father, a prosperous slaveholder, trader, and planter, had little education. He wrote his new daughter's name in the family Bible as Carry, and she was so christened. Carry believed the spelling of her name was one of the Lord's mysterious ways of prophecy. "C.A.N. are the initials of my name," she wrote after she had become a nationally known temperance crusader, "and then C. (see?) A. Nation! And, all together, Carry A. Nation! This is no accident, but Providence. This does not mean that I will carry a nation, but that the roused heart and conscience will, as I am the roused heart and conscience of the people."

The "lady with a hatchet" was born on a farm in Garrard county, Kentucky. Early in Carry's childhood, her mother showed the first signs of the mental illness that plagued her the rest of her life. As the disease developed, Mrs. Moore, with grandiose delusions, imagined that she was Queen Victoria. The family humored her, and in this atmosphere of the sick, deluded mother, Carry grew up.

In the fall of 1865, Dr. Charles Gloyd, a young physician, was boarding with the Moores. The nineteen-year-old Carry "stood in awe of him because of his superior education." One evening he "astonished" Carry by kissing her. This was the first time "a gentleman" had taken "such a privilege" and she was shocked, covered her face with her hands and cried, "I am ruined. I am ruined."

Her parents warned her that the doctor was addicted to drink, but "I," Carry said, "had no idea of the curse of rum. . . . I was in love, and doubted him in nothing." They were married in November 1867. Carry did not find the doctor the "lover" she expected.

"I find that drink," she wrote in her autobiography, "causes so much enmity between the sexes. Drinking men neglect their wives. Their wives become jealous. . . . The drink habit destroys in men the appreciation of a home life."

Dr. Gloyd died of alcoholism when their baby was six months old. Carry entered the State Normal School in Warrensburg, Missouri, and in a year received her teaching certificate. For the next four years the young widow taught in a primary school from which she was finally dismissed in an argument over a teaching method.

In 1877 Carry married David Nation, "the husband God selected" for her, a successful lawyer and a minister nineteen years her senior. Her marriage to Nation "was not a happy one." She believed that her "combative nature was largely developed by living with him, for I had to fight for everything that I kept." They were divorced in 1901. He charged her with desertion when she began to leave on her various "hatchetation" campaigns.

Carry confessed that the "bitterest sorrows" of her life came "from not having the love of a husband." Had she married a man she "could have loved, God could never have used me."

Kansas, in 1880, was one of the first states to pass Prohibition. But despite the law, liquor was still available in "joints" and "dives." Carry Nation, remembering the bitterness of her marriage to Dr. Gloyd, joined the crusade against these saloons. She became active in the Women's Christian Temperance Union and, as a jail evangelist, began to have "visions." They told her what to do and where to go. "Go to Kiowa, and I'll stand by you." She knew this was God directing her "to break, or smash the saloons."

And so—with bricks and a hatchet—Carry A. Nation fulfilled "God's will."

She extended her activities. With her group of militant followers, Carry invaded major cities to fight intemperance, using a hatchet in the "destruction of malicious property." Since a saloon was illegal, she reasoned, it had no rights.

Carry's "smashing" career continued for ten years during which she was arrested about thirty times. She paid her fines from fees she received from lectures and stage appearances as well as from the sale of souvenir hatchets.

She built a "Home for Drunkards' Wives and Mothers"; and published several periodicals: *Smasher's Mail, The Hatchet,* and *The Home Defender*. She wrote and published her autobiography. Her letters and editorials were signed "Your Loving Home Defender."

Carry A. Nation, who suffered ridicule and imprisonment during her lifetime, did not live to see the passage of the national Prohibition Law in 1920 and its aftermath: the speakeasy, the hipflask, the gangster; or the repeal of the Eighteenth Amendment in 1933. She died before any of it took place. Her gravestone carries the inscription:

CARRY A. NATION
"Faithful to the Cause of Prohibition."
She hath done what she could.

★ PROHIBITION!

"Carry Nation, what have you in your hand?"

Sometimes a rock; sometimes a hatchet; God told me to use these to smash that which has smashed and will smash hearts and souls. The sound of this loving deed will stir conscience and hearts and while I can not finish the smashing, the voters of this nation will use their ballots that will, and this impulse will Carry A. Nation. . . .

Our Saviour's mission on earth was to "break (smash) every yoke and set the captive free." Upon two occasions he made a scourge of small cords and laid it on the backs of wicked men who were doing unlawful things. He came into this world "to destroy the works of the Devil," to "bruise" or crush the "head of the serpent." We are told to "Abhor that which is evil," to "resist (or fight) the Devil and he will flee." We are not to be "overcome with evil but to overcome evil with good." How? Resist the Devil. God blessed the church at Ephesus, because they "hated the evil workers, tried them, and found them liars." The hatred of sin is one mark of a Christian. Just in proportion to your love for God will be your hatred of evil. . . . The ten plagues of Egypt and the overthrow of Pharaoh, were smashing. The death of the first born also. . . .

If I could I would turn the key on every church in the land, so as to teach some preachers to go out and not stay in, and compel poor sinners to stay out. I yield no territory to the Devil. Let us take every saloon, every house of prostitution of men and women for God. "There shall not a hoof be left behind." "The kingdom of heaven suffereth violence, and the *violent* take it by force," which means that where the evil is aggressive, we must be more so, and take, compelling surrender by the determination never to yield.

From the autobiography, *The Use and Need of the Life of Carry A. Nation* (Topeka, Kans., 1905).

I feel that I have been peculiarly favored to go into these places, to "cry aloud and spare not and show my people their sins." I find this class so hungry for something better. These poor actresses, who dress in tights and sing indecent songs, are a weary, tired, heartsick lot of slaves. I mingle with them as a sister. When I can say a warning word I say it. I call them affectionate names and mean it. God will judge both of us. He knows who loved much; He can forgive much. Christ said to a lot of men who took the amen pews: "The publicans and harlots will go into heaven before you." Why? They "repented when they heard." "How are they to hear without a preacher?" I never see a man or woman so low but as a sculptor said of the marble: "There is an angel there." Oh, God, help me to bring it out!

Jesus received sinners and ate with them. He left a command that Christians should invite these to feasts in their homes. Oh! what a revival of religion there would be if the homes of Christians were opened to the lost and sinful, who are dying for some demonstration of love. If the Son of God, the lovely, the pure, the blessed ate with sinners, ought it not to be a privilege to follow Him? We are commanded to "warn, rebuke, and reprove with all long suffering and doctrine." People will work in a revival to get sinners saved, and will pass them day after day on the street and not a word of Scripture do they use to remind them of God's judgments. Jesus said: "The world hateth Me because I testify that the works thereof are evil." I have had men to swear at me, call me names, and threaten to knock me down. At first this caused me to feel mortified but that passed off. These very men have afterward told me I was right and they were wrong. The Devil "threw some on the ground and they foamed at the mouth" before he was cast out. I have often taken cigars and cigarettes out of men's and boy's mouths. I wished to show them the wrong and that I was a friend. Would you let one you love take a knife to open a vein or cut himself? Oh! the sweetness and force of that promise: "Your *labor* is never in vain in the Lord." This covers all cases, if you, for the love of God, do anything. I often say to myself, after rebuking for sin: "You made a mistake in the way you did this or that, and are you sure it was done for the love of God and your neighbor?" "Yes." Then "your labor is never in vain in the Lord." It is not *what we do* that prospers, but what *God blesses*. "He that planteth is nothing and he that watereth is nothing, but it is God that giveth the increase." And it matters not how awkward the work, if it be done from love of God, it will prosper. Like other things, the more you do, the better you can do. . . .

It is a great blessing to know your mission in life. I know why Christians are waiting with folded hands, not being able to see their mission. They are not willing to pay the great price for their commission. The rich young man could have been a follower of Jesus, the greatest honor in earth or heaven, and could have had eternal treasure in heaven for the transient gain of earth. He would not pay the price. You must give all, to get all. The effect of smashing has always been to cause the people to arouse themselves. The Levite that severed his dead concubine and sent parts of her body to the different tribes of Israel was to cause the people to "consider, take advice, and speak." Then they acted and four hundred thousand men presented themselves to redress this wrong. . . .

Let us consider the character of Moses. It is said this man disobeyed God but once, and he was the "meekest of all men." We are first attracted to him peculiarly because he "refused to be called the son of Pharaoh's daughter, rather suffering afflictions with the people of God than to enjoy the pleasures of sin for a season." Rather be counted with the poor despised, afflicted slaves under the taskmaster's lash than to be a king or an absolute monarch. This brought out his characteristic prohibition of sin—the renouncing of every worldly ambition. He here made the choice, at the time when the temptations were greatest, for all that the world could offer was his. He gave all and paid the price it requires to get all. On the banks of the Nile he sees one man oppressing another. That spirit of prohibition of this great wrong caused him to strike (smash) the oppressor.

Here is a lovable trait of this great man. Moses could not

look on and see the helpless suffer at the hands of another even though it brought death to himself. Forgetful of his own safety, defying the absolute power and authority of this despot, so far as it lay in his power, against all these odds he redressed the wrong of a fellow creature. God saw in Moses a man whom He could use. From the golden throne he sought a retreat, and for forty years was an humble shepherd, learning the lesson of caring for the flocks of Jethro, before he should be called to take the oversight of the flock of God. "He that is faithful in that which is least is faithful also in that which is much." God called this man out of the wilderness to go to the greatest court on earth as His ambassador. Not one compromise would he make, still true to his prohibition principles. God never used or blessed any man or woman that was not a prohibitionist. Eli was one of those conservatives and said only, "Nay, verily my sons." And he got his neck broke and both of his sons killed in one day, because he "restrained (or prohibited) not his sons in the iniquity which he knew." Moses, although the meekest of all men, he said to Pharaoh, "There shall not a hoof be left behind." True to the uncompromising spirit of a great leader. When in the Mount, seeing the idolatry, smashed the two tables of stone. Why? He would not deliver the holy laws to a people who were insulting God. This smashing was a demonstration of Moses' jealousy for his God. After this I can see him striding down to the place of this "ball" or "hugging." The round dance of the present day is but a repetition of those lascivious plays, and with his ax or hatchet he hacked up that malicious property, shaped into a golden calf. This did not belong to Moses. It was very valuable but he smashed it and ground it to powder and then to further humiliate these rebels, he made them drink the dust mixed with water, then to absolutely destroy and stamp with a vengeance this insult to God, he divided the people and those who were "on the Lord's side" fought with these rebels and slew (smashed) three thousand men. In one of the canonical books of the Catholic Bible we have the story of the holy woman Judith who cut off the head of Hollifernese to save God's people. Esther the gentle loving queen had the wicked sons of Haman hanged. Our supremest idea of justice is a reward for the good and a punishment for the wicked. We amputate the arm to save the body. David says: "I will not know a wicked person; he that telleth lies shall not dwell in my sight."

The Devil has his agents in the churches, and among those who are doing his work the best are a class of professors who testify that you must not speak ill of any one, not even the Devil. They are the "non-resistives." The Devil is delighted to be respected and not fought. He gets his work in just as he wants to and he can imitate true conversion, if he can place in the church those who hinder a warfare against sin. Paul said: "I tell you even weeping they are enemies of the cross of Christ." They are the devils in light. "But there must needs be heresies among you that they who are approved may be manifest." Persons often propose to *do* something. I may not see the advisability, but because there is action in it, I never object. Oh! for somebody to "*do* with their might what their hands find to do." "Well *done*" is the best commendation. Faith is like the wind, we cannot see it, but by the quantity of motion and commotion. There are workers, "jerkers," and "shirkers"; but through much tribulation and temptation must we enter into the kingdom of heaven. The counterfeit proves the genuine dollar; counterfeits are not counterfeited. So hypocrites prove the genuine Christians. If there were not a genuine there would not be a hypocrite. Our mothers and grandmothers who went into saloons praying and spilling the poisoned slop of these houses of crime and tears were blessed in their *deeds*. Oh that the W.C.T.U. would do as they did, what a reform would take place. I love the organization of mothers. I love their holy impulses but I am heartsick at their conventionality, their red tape. This organization could put out of existence every drinking hell in the United States if they would demand it and use the power they have even without the ballot.

SIMON W. STRAUS, 1866–1930

☆ Thrift

SIMON W. STRAUS dedicated his book, *History of the Thrift Movement in America*, to his mother and father, "who, by precept and example, gave me, in my early life, a deep appreciation of thrift as a guiding influence in character building and the first requisite of all success; and, in later years, inspired within me the hope that I might be instrumental in imparting these teachings to the people of America."

This the internationally known banker, philanthropist, and financier attempted to do within his own company and also through the American Society for Thrift which he founded in 1914, and of which he was president for several years.

Simon Straus was born at Ligonier, Indiana. His forefathers were bankers. His father, a native of Rhenish Prussia, Germany, came to the United States in 1852. The elder Straus settled in

Auburn, Indiana, lived there for only a short time, moved to Ligonier, founded a bank, then moved to Chicago, where he started a mortgage and loan business.

The young Simon attended elementary school in Chicago and high school in Cincinnati. He entered his father's loan and mortgage business, E. W. Straus and Company, Chicago, at the age of eighteen. When his father retired, Simon Straus became president of the company and later board chairman. He was a pioneer in promoting skyscrapers, and his firm was the first to float a real estate bond to finance a building project. He also opened several banks. Meanwhile, within his own company, Straus encouraged thrift among his employees in various ways, including the addition of bonuses to their savings accounts.

The first meeting of the American Society for Thrift was held in 1914 in Chicago. Simon presided and was elected first president.

"The future of our country," said Straus in accepting the office of president, "depends upon our children, and for the good of our country we must instill in them the precepts of thrift." He spoke of the "waste" of unused school buildings during summer vacations. He advocated encouraging school gardening and domestic science in the summer months, as well as teaching conservation of health and wealth. "Thrift," he said, "will give us sober, thoughtful, and self-respecting citizens." Straus was also active at the International Congress for Thrift at the San Francisco Exposition in 1915.

School gardening became one of the first activities of the movement. "During the two seasons of the war [World War I] the so-called war gardens added $850 million worth of food to our supply," Straus announced.

Thrift became a topic for several years at the annual sessions of the National Education Association with Straus among the speakers. The *Annals* of the American Academy of Political and Social Sciences devoted its January 1920 issue to the "New American Thrift." That same year, Straus wrote his *History of the Thrift Movement in America*. An editor's introduction stressed the point that "no man in our century has done so much [as Straus] toward bringing the people to a realizing sense of the crime of wastefulness, and the absolute necessity for the proper practice of economics."

Straus was also a bitter opponent of tipping, but he found little support for his work in this campaign.

He died at the age of sixty-four. At his funeral, three words were used to describe the philanthropist and banker: "Success, service, and simplicity." Ironically, nothing was said about his Thrift Society. In his obituary in the *New York Times*, there was only a passing mention that he was the founder and for several years president of the American Society for Thrift.

★ THRIFT—AN EDUCATIONAL NECESSITY

In appearing before this audience of men and women who are devoting their lives to the education of our children, I feel that it would be presumption on my part to attempt to give counsel on matters pertaining to the technical work of the schoolroom. My only desire, on this occasion, is to tell you how thoroughly I feel the necessity that some action be taken that will lead to the teachings of thrift to our boys and girls.

A great many years ago Abraham Lincoln said: "Teach economy. That is one of the first and highest virtues; it begins with saving money." Lincoln, with his genius, lived decades ahead of his time, and, in the work we are undertaking now, we are just about catching up with the teachings expounded by this great American more than half a century ago. I want to use this quotation from Abraham Lincoln as the text of my sermon, for I think it embraces the entire philosophy of thrift: "Teach economy. That is one of the first and highest virtues: it begins with saving money."

Two years ago, I dare say, not one of us assembled here tonight had the slightest idea that the late summer of 1914 would mark the beginning of the world's greatest war. How secure, how smug

---

Speech made by Simon Straus before the fifty-fourth annual meeting of the National Education Association, July 1–8, 1916.

many of us fancied ourselves. How often we spoke of the horrors of war as things of the past, as relics of barbarism that civilization had outlived. It is not my desire tonight to shout calamity, but my duty compels me to say that the epochal events of the last eighteen months have brought us face to face tonight with conditions that never before existed in America. I am happy to say that I do not believe we shall be drawn into the present cataclysm. I am strong in my belief that the blessings of peace and prosperity shall continue to be ours, but it would be folly for us blindly to assume that we are indefinitely to continue drifting along in such auspicious circumstances.

We hear much today of national preparedness. There is a great clamor about it. We are told that we must be prepared to defend ourselves against attack from powerful foreign adversaries. But in all this agitation regarding national preparedness, I have failed to find one single word in print, or hear one word spoken in public, concerning what, to my mind, is the most vital question in America today—individual preparedness. Not individual preparedness for war, but individual preparedness for anything that may come; individual preparedness to live useful, steadfast lives for the benefit of humanity and posterity; individual preparedness to withstand the temptations that always come with prolonged prosperity; individual preparedness to meet calamity and adversity in whatever form they may appear. It takes fortitude, stability, manliness, and courage to be a good man in the face of temptations, obstacles, and adverse surroundings. It requires just as much moral stamina to conquer the temptations of opulence as it does to combat the onslaught of calamitous circumstances. Every man who has made a success of life is a soldier of many victories. You all know the fight you must make sometimes to be right and to do right under all circumstances—to live cleanly, honorably, above reproach. There are enemies within and without, and ofttimes the battles one fights with oneself are more bitter and more important fights than those one may wage with any external enemy. The battle, after all, is to the strong, not to the weak.

And what has all this to do with the teachings of thrift? you ask. Simply this: Thrift is the very foundation of individual efficiency, and individual efficiency is the foundation of all success. Thrift is submission to discipline, self-imposed. Thrift is denying oneself present pleasures for future gain. Thrift is the exercise of the will, the development of moral stamina, the steadfast refusal to yield to temptation.

We are a prosperous nation, but individually we are not a prosperous people. We are poor. We have grown rapidly. We have uncovered and developed vast resources. Our people have earned plenteously, but have spent lavishly. We have wasted. Our people have neglected to lay by for the rainy day. Let the wheels of industry stop turning in this nation for thirty days, and the vast majority of our citizens would be paupers. Do you know that one person out of every ten who dies today in our large cities is buried in the Potter's Field?

Statistics show that in the United States there are only 108 who save money out of every thousand population. Compare this with 288 in Italy, 302 in England, 317 in Germany, 346 in France, 386 in Sweden, 397 in Belgium, and 544 in Switzerland. All these figures are for the times prior to the war, of course. Two out of every three persons who die in the United States leave no estate whatever. In view of these facts, what appalling economic conditions would ensue in America were the people of this country suddenly confronted by a condition such as exists across the sea! I tell you, my friends, we have not yet learned to differentiate between prosperity and progress. We have spent as we have earned, bountifully, and our savings have been meager. Our orators have been fond of telling us that this is the most prosperous nation in the world, but they have neglected to tell us what would happen if prosperity ceased. We have been deceiving ourselves.

There was a time when America was a thrifty nation. Those were the days of Benjamin Franklin and our colonial forefathers. Life in this new country made thrift necessary, and it was only through frugal habits that they were successful and laid the foundation of this great nation. But in the days that followed, easier times came. The earning power of the average man gradually increased. Slowly we got away from the rugged habits of the Puritans, and today we are recognized throughout the world as the most thriftless nation among the great powers. What we must do is to get back to the days of Benjamin Franklin. Want and waste, extravagance, debauchery, riotous living, artificial social and business practices must cease—in a word, the nation must be remade, not only by talking thrift, but by teaching thrift.

Looking down the long vista of years ahead of us in America, we are bound to have many prosperous periods. We are so rich, so strong, so young. We have so many advantages over the older nations. Our commercial resistance is so tremendous that periods of depression must be of comparatively short duration. But even with the prospect of a golden era of peace lying before us, with the assumption that the wheels of industry will continue to turn, that we shall be continuously blessed with bountiful crops, that our population will increase, that our cities will build, and will grow even more wonderful, and the barren places be taken up for occupation—even with the assumption of all these things, are we sure tonight that our children, and our children's children will be prepared for the temptations that will come with these unfoldings of time? Weakness is begot of the pamperings of opulence. We need but to read our histories. Babylonia, Greece, and Rome fell because their people were pampered, because debauchery ran riot, and the substance was wasted! Thrift and right living were forgotten.

After the present war in Europe is over, this nation will be the subject of attack, commercially, by every country now at arms. The empires of Europe will lie bleeding in ruin. Prosperous America will be the shining target of attack. We must be prepared for this contest. It may mean a prolonged period of financial depression, or, on the other hand, we may be approaching the greatest era of prosperity America has ever known. Whether fortune has in store for us prosperity or adversity, the necessity for individual preparedness is alike necessary.

And now, what are the deductions? I think you will agree with me that, whether we have prosperity or adversity, it is necessary that we have individual preparedness, through thrift. And what shall we do to bring about individual preparedness? How shall we make this nation thrifty? Surely not alone by preaching to those who are old, surely not only by teaching those who are middle-aged. There is only one right way, and that is to begin at the foundation. The nation of tomorrow will be made up of the children who are in your classrooms today. If this nation, tomorrow, is to be thrifty, if these children are to be men and women equipped with individual preparedness, we must begin teaching them today. We must teach them in the home, we must teach them in the Sunday school, above all things else, we must teach them in the schoolroom. These children, whose faces gaze into yours from day to day, will be the blood and fiber, the bone and sinew, of the United States of America in the next decade or two, and their children will be the nation of the next era. So we can be assured that if we teach these school children the ways of thrift today, when they leave the schoolroom and start out into active life, they will be individually prepared to withstand the temptations of life through the practices of thrift. We can be assured that they will at least not be failures. Those who are thrifty never fail entirely; they may not reach the heights, but they never will reach the depths.

When we preach thrift through the press and through the pulpit, we know that good is being done. When the governors of our several states issue proclamations calling upon their citizens to practice ways of thrift, we know that good is being done. And I want to say here, in passing, that those of us who are engaged in this work owe a mighty debt of gratitude to the governors of the states, to the clergy who are preaching thrift from the pulpits, and to the editors who are teaching thrift through the columns of the press.

And while I am speaking of these things, let me give you a few more statistics so that you will have a better understanding of conditions as they really exist. New York County is the most populous county in America. The records of the surrogate's office of that county for the five years which began January 1, 1901, and ended December 31, 1905, revealed the fact that an average of

27,011 adults died each year of that period. Of these, 23,051, or 85.3 per cent, left no estate at all, 1171, or 4.3 per cent, left estates valued at $300 to $1,000; and 1428, or 5.3 per cent, left estates of more than $1,000 but less than $5,000. There are in the United States 1,250,000 dependent wage-earners, who have failed to save anything for their own support, now costing this country $220 million a year. There are 3,000,127 widows in America over sixty-five years of age, and over 32 per cent of them lack the necessities of life, and 90 per cent lack the comforts. What a sad commentary! This country is supporting about one million delinquents in institutions, yet the wealth of the United States, $150 billion, is nearly double England's $85 billion, Germany's $80 billion, and three times that of France. Incredible as it may seem, in this land of such vast wealth, there are between ten and fifteen million people who are in absolute poverty.

If we do not prepare the children of today for the vicissitudes and temptations of the future, what can we expect of the nation in the years that are to come? Teaching thrift to children will, I grant, have varying results. You students of children's characters are well aware that some are by nature thrifty, others are thriftless. You have noticed how one child will write over an entire sheet of paper, while another will use but half a sheet and save the unused part.

You have noticed how some children are wasteful of such little things as pencils, while others are careful of their little belongings. These are indices of character, as you know, but they would seem to prove a basis on which some start could be made in thrift education. But the benefits of thrift do not come so much from the mere act of saving as from the reflex action on the child's character.

In my life I have made this observation: If a man earns $500 a year and cannot save anything, he will not be able to save when he earns $1,000, or $5,000, or $10,000. On the other hand, if a man does save on $500 a year, his savings will be just as great in proportion when he earns $1,000, $5,000, or $10,000. And to my mind that is the great point in thrift. It is not entirely the amount of money that one saves, but it is the effect that the act of saving has on one's character. And what will be the aggregate moral result on the nation of the future, if each individual child in our schools be taught thrift, with the strengthening of character that will come with it?

Let us remember one thing. By education in thrift we can not only influence the nation of today, but we can revolutionize the nation of tomorrow.

BOOM TO BUST

[IMAGES: 1920–1935]

FLAPPER. *Charleston. F. Scott Fitzgerald. Clara Bow—the "It" girl.*

The "Great Experiment." Palmer "red" raids and Harding's "normalcy." Teapot Dome. Abie's Irish Rose, Babbitt, The Hairy Ape. *The Unknown Soldier.* Yes, We Have No Bananas.

Eugene Victor Debs. H. L. Mencken. "Red" Grange. Barney Google. Jazz. Leopold and Loeb.

Al Capone. Bootlegging. The Scopes Trial. The Jazz Singer. *Sacco and Vanzetti. Lindy. Cal Coolidge: "I do not choose to run for President in 1928." The Model T Ford. Crystal radios.*

"A chicken in every pot. . . . Prosperity is just around the corner." Herbert Hoover.

Black Thursday. Empire State Building. Bonus march. Norman Thomas. Scottsboro. FDR: "The only thing we have to fear is fear itself." Buddy, Can You Spare a Dime? *Century of Prog-*

ress. "Oakies" and "Arkies." Grapes of Wrath, God's Little Acre, Pins and Needles, Tobacco Road. *Dos Passos.*

Will Rogers.

Townsend, Coughlin and Huey Long, EPIC. Technocracy. Committee for Industrial Organization. John L. Lewis. Little Steel. The New Deal's Alphabet soup:

AAA
WPA
NRA
REA
NYA
NIRA
PWA
NLRB
CWA
CCC
TVA

Adolf Hitler.

MARGARET SANGER, 1883–1966

☆ Birth Control

"ANOTHER BABY WILL FINISH ME, I suppose?" asked the twenty-eight-year-old mother who had just been saved from the effects of a self-inflicted abortion. "What can I do to prevent it?"

"Tell Jake," her doctor responded, "to sleep on the roof."

Margaret Sanger, the nurse who was attending the young mother of three when the doctor gave her this advice, was again called to the woman's aid six months later. When Mrs. Sanger arrived the woman was in a coma; ten minutes later she was dead—from a self-inflicted abortion.

"I was finished with palliatives and superficial cures," wrote Margaret Sanger. "I was resolved to seek out the root of evil, to do something to change the destiny of mothers whose miseries were vast as the sky."

Mrs. Sanger was asking: "How are mothers to be saved?"

She spent a year in libraries in search of the answer. She talked to everybody who had an interest in social welfare. At the suggestion of Big Bill Haywood, the I.W.W. labor organizer, Margaret Sanger went to France to study the results of "generations of family limitation in that country."

Margaret Higgins Sanger was born in Corning, New York, the daughter of Michael Hennessy Higgins, philosopher, rebel, artist, and tombstone cutter, and Anne Purcell Higgins, mother of eleven who died at the age of forty-eight.

Margaret taught school in New Jersey for a few years, then studied nursing. She was graduated in 1900 and shortly afterward married William Sanger, by whom she had two sons.

For a time the Sanger home in New York City was a meeting place of liberals, Anarchists, Socialists, and Wobblies. Among Mrs. Sanger's friends were John Reed, Mabel Dodge Luhan, Bill Haywood, Emma Goldman, Alexander Berkman, and Jessie Ashley. During this period Mrs. Sanger worked for the Socialist party. She lectured and wrote for the party's paper—including articles which later were published as books: *What Every Girl Should Know* (1916) and *What Every Mother Should Know* (1917).

Her activities on behalf of birth control started during her nursing career when she saw women old at thirty-five because of bearing too many children and young women dead because of self-induced abortions.

The *Woman Rebel,* a radical magazine she was editing, spearheaded her campaign. It was here she used the phrase "birth control" for the first time. The same periodical carried the slogan "No Gods; no masters" on its masthead. Opposing Mrs. Sanger, however, were not only ignorance, prejudice, and religious tenets, but also the Comstock Act of 1873, which considered information about contraceptives obscene.

In 1914, Margaret Sanger, together with a small group of friends, founded the National Birth Control League. That same year she was charged with sending birth control information through the mails and indicted on seven counts. She faced a forty-five-year prison term.

Margaret Sanger left the United States on the eve of her trial. She returned in 1916 shortly before the indictment was dropped. With the help of her sister, she established a birth control clinic in the Brownsville section of Brooklyn, New York.

Authorities soon closed the clinic, and the sisters were sentenced to thirty days in prison. Their appeal to the United States Court of Appeals resulted in a decision which permitted doctors to give contraceptive advice to women for "cure and prevention of disease."

Mrs. Sanger now began a campaign of education and organization to pressure for legislation. But there were many obstacles. For example, in 1921, at a Town Hall meeting at which the topic of discussion was "Birth Control—Is It Moral?", police intervened and dispersed the audience. The *New York Times* in reporting the meeting pointed out that the police intervention was "brought about at the instance of Archbishop Patrick J. Hayes of this Roman Catholic Archdiocese."

But Mrs. Sanger was a determined woman with a single-minded goal. "When women have raised the standard of sex ideals and purged the human mind of its unclean conception of sex, the fountain of the race will have been cleansed."

Before she died at the age of eighty-three, Mrs. Sanger saw much of the world accept family planning as a basic human right. At her funeral service, an Episcopalian priest eulogized that "all the elements of sainthood were personified many times in her life." She was a "good, fighting saint" who experienced martyrdom.

★ BIRTH CONTROL

This remedy can be applied only by woman and she will apply it. . . .

Woman was and is condemned to a system under which the lawful rapes exceed the unlawful ones a million to one. She has nothing to say as to whether she shall have strength sufficient to

---

From Margaret Sanger, *Woman and the New Race* (New York, 1920).

give a child a fair physical and mental start in life; she has had as little to do with determining whether her own body shall be wrecked by excessive child-bearing. She has been adjured not to complain of the burden of caring for children she has not wanted. Only the married woman who has been constantly loved by the most understanding and considerate of husbands has escaped these horrors. Besides the wrongs done to women in marriage, those involved in promiscuity, infidelities, and rapes become inconsequential in nature and in number.

Out of woman's inner nature, in rebellion against these conditions, is rising the new morality. Let it be realized that this creation of new sex ideals is a challenge to the church. Being a challenge to the church, it is also, in less degree, a challenge to the state. The woman who takes a fearless stand for the incoming sex ideals must expect to be assailed by reactionaries of every kind. Imperialists and exploiters will fight hardest in the open, but the ecclesiastic will fight longest in the dark. He understands the situation best of all; he best knows what reaction he has to fear from the morals of women who have attained liberty. For, be it repeated, the church has always known and feared the spiritual potentialities of woman's freedom.

And in this lies the answer to the question why the opponent of birth control raises the moral issue. Sex morals for women have been one-sided; they have been purely negative, inhibitory, and repressive. They have been fixed by agencies which have sought to keep women enslaved; which have been determined, even as they are now, to use woman solely as an asset to the church, the state, and the man. Any means of freedom which will enable women to live and think for themselves first, will be attacked as immoral by these selfish agencies.

What effect will the practice of birth control have upon woman's moral development? . . . It will break her bonds. It will free her to understand the cravings and soul needs of herself and other women. It will enable her to develop her love nature separate from and independent of her maternal nature.

It goes without saying that the woman whose children are

desired and are of such number that she can not only give them adequate care but keep herself mentally and spiritually alive, as well as physically fit, can discharge her duties to her children much better than the overworked, broken, and querulous mother of a large, unwanted family.

Thus the way is open to her for a twofold development; first, through her own full rounded life, and next, through her loving, unstrained, full-hearted relationship with her offspring. The bloom of mother love will have an opportunity to infuse itself into her soul and make her, indeed, the fond, affectionate guardian of her offspring that sentiment now pictures her but hard facts deny her the privilege of being. She will preserve also her love life with her mate in its ripening perfection. She will want children with deeper passion, and will love them with a far greater love. . . .

The moral force of woman's nature will be unchained—and of its own dynamic power will uplift her to a plane unimagined by those holding fast to the old standards of church morality. Love is the greatest force of the universe; freed of its bonds of submission and unwanted progeny, it will formulate and compel of its own nature observance to standards of purity far beyond the highest conception of the average moralist. The feminine spirit, animated by joyous, triumphant love, will make its own high tenets of morality. Free womanhood, out of the depths of its rich experiences, will observe and comply with the inner demands of its being. The manner in which it learns to do this best may be said to be the moral law of woman's being. So, in whatever words the new morality may ultimately be expressed, we can at least be sure that it will meet certain needs.

First of all, it will meet the physical and psychic requirements of the woman herself, for she cannot adequately perform the feminine functions until these are met. Second, it will meet the needs of the child to be conceived in a love which is eager to bring forth a new life, to be brought into a home where love and harmony prevail, a home in which proper preparation has been made for its coming.

This situation implies in turn a number of conditions. Foremost among them is woman's knowledge of her sexual nature, both in its physiology and its spiritual significance. She must not only know her own body, its care, and its needs, but she must know the power of the sex force, its use, abuse, as well as how to direct it for the benefit of the race. Thus she can transmit to her children an equipment that will enable them to break the bonds that have held humanity enslaved for ages.

To achieve this she must have a knowledge of birth control. She must also assert and maintain her right to refuse the marital embrace except when urged by her inner nature.

The truth makes free. Viewed in its true aspect, the very beauty and wonder of the creative impulse will make evident its essential purity. We will then instinctively idealize and keep holy that physical-spiritual expression which is the foundation of all human life, and in that conception of sex will the race be exalted.

What can we expect of offspring that are the result of "accidents"—who are brought into being undesired and in fear? What can we hope for from a morality that surrounds each physical union, for the woman, with an atmosphere of submission and shame? What can we say for a morality that leaves the husband at liberty to communicate to his wife a venereal disease?

Subversion of the sex urge to ulterior purposes has dragged it to the level of the gutter. Recognition of its true nature and purpose must lift the race to spiritual freedom. Out of our growing knowledge we are evolving new and saner ideas of life in general. Out of our increasing sex knowledge we shall evolve new ideals of sex. These ideals will spring from the innermost needs of women. They will serve these needs and express them. They will be the foundation of a moral code that will tend to make fruitful the impulse which is the source, the soul and the crowning glory of our sexual natures.

When women have raised the standards of sex ideals and purged the human mind of its unclean conception of sex, the fountain of the race will have been cleansed. Mothers will bring forth, in purity and in joy, a race that is morally and spiritually free. . . .

What is the goal of woman's upward struggle? Is it voluntary motherhood? Is it a general freedom? Or is it the birth of a new race? For freedom is not fruitless, but prolific of higher things. Being the most sacred aspect of woman's freedom, voluntary motherhood is motherhood in its highest and holiest form. It is motherhood unchained—motherhood ready to obey its own urge to remake the world.

Voluntary motherhood implies a new morality—a vigorous, constructive, liberated morality. That morality will, first of all, prevent the submergence of womanhood into motherhood. It will set its face against the conversion of women into mechanical maternity and toward the creation of a new race.

Woman's role has been that of an incubator and little more. She has given birth to an incubated race. She has given to her children what little she was permitted to give, but of herself, of her personality, almost nothing. In the mass, she has brought forth quantity, not quality. The requirement of a male-dominated civilization has been numbers. She has not met that requirement.

It is the essential function of voluntary motherhood to choose its own mate, to determine the time of childbearing, and to regulate strictly the number of offspring. Natural affection upon her part, instead of selection dictated by social or economic advantage, will give her a better fatherhood for her children. The exercise of her right to decide how many children she will have and when she will have them will procure for her the time necessary to the development of other faculties than that of reproduction. She will give play to her tastes, her talents and her ambitions. She will become a full-rounded human being.

Thus and only thus will woman be able to transmit to her offspring those qualities which make for a greater race. . . .

Birth control itself, often denounced as a violation of natural law, is nothing more or less than the facilitation of the process of weeding out the unfit, of preventing the birth of defectives or of those who will become defectives. So, in compliance with nature's working plan, we must permit womanhood its full development before we can expect of it efficient motherhood. If we are to make racial progress, this development of womanhood must precede motherhood in every individual woman. Then and then only can the mother cease to be an incubator and be a mother indeed. Then only can she transmit to her sons and daughters the qualities which make strong individuals and, collectively, a strong race.

Voluntary motherhood also implies the right of marriage without maternity. Two utterly different functions are developed in the two relationships. In order to give the mate relationship its full and free play, it is necessary that no woman should be a mother against her will. There are other reasons, of course—reasons more frequently emphasized—but the reason just mentioned should never be overlooked. It is as important to the race as to the woman, for through it is developed that high love impulse which, conveyed to the child, attunes and perfects its being.

Marriage, quite aside from parentage, also gives two people invaluable experience. When parentage follows in its proper time, it is a better parentage because of the mutual adjustment and development—because of the knowledge thus gained. Few couples are fitted to understand the sacred mystery of child life until they have solved some of the problems arising out of their own love lives.

Maternal love, which usually follows upon a happy, satisfying, mate love, becomes a strong and urgent craving. It then exists for two powerful, creative functions. First, for its own sake, and then for the sake of further enriching the conjugal relationship. It is from such soil that the new life should spring. It is the inherent right of the new life to have its inception in such physical ground, in such spiritual atmosphere. The child thus born is indeed a flower of love and tremendous joy. It has within it the seeds of courage and of power. This child will have the greatest strength to surmount hardships, to withstand tyrannies, to set still higher the mark of human achievement. . . .

How narrow, how pitifully puny has become motherhood in its chains! The modern motherhood enfolds one or two adoring children of its own blood, and cherishes, protects and loves them. It does not reach out to all children. When motherhood is a high privilege, not a sordid, slavish requirement, it will encircle all. Its deep, passionate intensity will overflow the limits of blood relationship. Its beauty will shine upon all, for its beauty is of the soul, whose power of enfoldment is unbounded.

When motherhood becomes the fruit of a deep yearning, not the result of ignorance or accident, its children will become the foundation of a new race. There will be no killing of babies in the womb by abortion, nor through neglect in foundling homes, nor will there be infanticide. Neither will children die by inches in mills and factories. No man will dare to break a child's life upon the wheel of toil.

Voluntary motherhood will not be passive, resigned, or weak. Out of its craving will come forth a fierceness of love for its fruits that will make such men as remain unawakened stand aghast at its fury when offended. The tigress is less terrible in defense of her offspring than will be the human mother. The daughters of such women will not be given over to injustice and to prostitution; the sons will not perish in industry nor upon the battlefield. Nor could they meet these all too common fates if an undaunted motherhood were there to defend. Childhood and youth will be too valuable in the eyes of society to waste them in the murderous mills of blind greed and hate.

This is the dawn. Womanhood shakes off its bondage. It asserts its right to be free. In its freedom, its thoughts turn to the race. Like begets like. We gather perfect fruit from perfect trees. The race is but the amplification of its mother body, the multiplication of flesh habitations—beautified and perfected for souls akin to the mother soul.

The relentless efforts of reactionary authority to suppress the message of birth control and of voluntary motherhood are futile. The powers of reaction cannot now prevent the feminine spirit from breaking its bonds. When the last fetter falls the evils that have resulted from the suppression of woman's will to freedom will pass. Child slavery, prostitution, feeblemindedness, physical deterioration, hunger, oppression, and war will disappear from the earth.

In their subjection women have not been brave enough, strong enough, pure enough to bring forth great sons and daughters. Abused soil brings forth stunted growths. An abused motherhood has brought forth a low order of humanity. Great beings come forth at the call of high desire. Fearless motherhood goes out in love and passion for justice to all mankind. It brings forth fruits after its own kind. When the womb becomes fruitful through the desire of an aspiring love, another Newton will come forth to unlock further the secrets of the earth and the stars. There will come forth a Plato who will be understood, a Socrates who will drink no hemlock, and a Jesus who will not die upon the cross. These and the race that is to be in America await upon a motherhood that is to be sacred because it is free.

WILLIAM A. (BILLY) SUNDAY, 1863–1935

☆ Repentance and Faith

"MEASURED IN TERMS of claimed converts and net profits," wrote the *New York Times* in its obituary of William A. (Billy) Sunday, "the Rev. Dr. William Ashley Sunday . . . was the greatest high-pressure and mass-conversion Christian evangelist that America, or the world, has known."

At the peak of his crusade, Sunday claimed an average of forty thousand "conversions" at each revival. His largest meetings were in New York City, where his organization spent $200,000 and emerged with 98,000 "decisions" to accept Jesus Christ.

"Lots of people will acknowledge their sin in the world," Sunday preached, "struggle on without Jesus Christ, and do their best to live honorable, upright lives. Your morality will make you a better man or woman, but it will never save your soul in the world."

That was Sunday's panacea: "You can't do some deed of kindness . . . and substitute that for the necessity of repentance and faith in Jesus Christ."

Sunday was born in Ames, Iowa, the son of a Union soldier who marched off to war and never returned. The young Billy was sent to an orphanage. There, at the soldiers' orphans' home, he started to play baseball.

A natural athlete, Billy played baseball throughout his high school career. He was a semi-professional with a Marshalltown, Iowa, team when he was scouted by the Chicago "White-Stockings" and signed as an outfielder. He played the professional game for eight years and was one of the fastest baserunners of his time.

One afternoon in a baseball off-season, while Billy was "tanked up" and sitting on a curbstone in Chicago's Loop, a wandering group from the Pacific Garden "rescue mission" invited Sunday and his companions to hear some girls tell how they had been "saved from the red light district."

Sunday "accepted Christ as his Savior." He refused to play ball on Sunday, gave up smoking, drinking, and the various other "evils." The baseball star spent his free time speaking at the YMCA on the "Earnestness in Christian Life." It wasn't long before he gave up baseball entirely, its glamour and its money. He went to work as an assistant secretary for the Chicago YMCA, organizing Sunday schools, arranging meetings for prayer, and engaging in the various other mundane activities that fall to a "Jimmie Higgins" of evangelism.

Recommended by the "Y" to assist an evangelist who had come upon the scene, Sunday became the evangelist's advance man, making local arrangements for choirs, putting up tents, and organizing the workers for the crusade. Soon Billy was asked to conduct a revival in a small hamlet in Iowa—population one thousand. He was a success, and that same year—1896—he formed his own organization with advance man, singer, choir, and tents which were not much different from the circus tents except that instead of the three rings there were pews.

Until 1900 Billy Sunday limited most of his evangelistic work to Iowa towns of under two thousand population. Then came the expansion into larger towns and cities. A Sunday campaign aided ministers in increasing their flocks. It was an investment that paid off. Spokane heard him in 1908; Youngstown and Boulder by 1910; Toledo in 1911; Columbus, Wheeling, and Wilkes-Barre in 1913; and Pittsburgh, Baltimore, Boston, Philadelphia, Los Angeles, Detroit, Washington, and New York by 1919.

During this time he was ordained by the Chicago Presbytery and received the honorary degree of Doctor of Divinity from the president of Westminster College at New Wilmington, Pennsylvania.

A Billy Sunday revival started with its advance agents, revival prayer meetings, and the recruiting of a chorus and staff of ushers. On the night of the revival only the choir, the trombone, and the piano shared the limelight with Billy. He was the star. He would shadow-box, skip, run, bounce, slide, pound the pulpit, jump, shed his coat, his vest and tie, and roll up his sleeves, all the while exhorting his listeners to do battle with the devil, with booze, and with tobacco. He defended motherhood, womanhood, God, hard work, cleanliness, and America, all the while urging his audience to accept Jesus Christ.

Sunday always ended his oration with a call for converts to the background music of "Onward, Christian Soldiers" or "Softly and Tenderly Jesus Is Calling."

Wrote the *New York Times*: "The willing came with the merest prompting, fluttering in emotional states of tears or joy, to shake the hands of the evangelist and to sign the convert's card. The indifferent were usually locked in the arms of one or more herders, experts who discharged their duties in the task of swelling the ranks of those who came forward, whether they signed up or not."

No figures are available on how many of the converts

remained converted. Some of the figures prepared by the *Baptist Watchman Examiner* asserted that the Philadelphia revival brought in 41,000 conversions with offerings of $51,000; Boston, 40,000 conversions, $51,000; Buffalo, 34,000 and $42,000; and South Bend, 6,000 who made their decision with $10,000 in offerings.

Sunday's most spectacular campaign was in New York City just as the United States became a participant in World War I. It was also the crusade which culminated revivalism in general, and Billy Sunday specifically.

Post-World War I was a different world. "The war was a sudden dividing line between two centuries," wrote Bernard A. Weisberger in his *They Gathered at the River*. "Within two years after the Armistice, the automobile, the radio, Hollywood, and the triumphant adman swept away most of whatever authority still lingered in the commandments of rural nineteenth-century folkways. Once more a sinful world turned its back on the oldtime religion."

Billy Sunday, evangelist of the old "sawdust trail," died suddenly of a heart attack at the age of seventy-two, in Chicago, the city in which he had first "accepted Christ as his Saviour."

★ HEAVEN

What do I want most of all? A man in Chicago said to me one day, "If I could have all I wanted of any one thing I would take money." He will be a fool, and so would you if you would make a similar choice. There's lots of things money can't do. Money can't buy life; money can't buy health. Andrew Carnegie says, "Anyone who can assure men ten years of life can name his price."

If you should meet with an accident which would require a surgical operation or your life would be despaired of, there is

From William T. Ellis, *"Billy" Sunday, The Man and His Message* (Philadelphia, 1914).

not a man here but would gladly part with all the money he has if that would give him the assurance that he could live twelve months longer.

If you had all the money in the world you couldn't go to the graveyard and put those loved ones back in your arms and have them sit once more in the family circle and hear their voices and listen to their prattle.

A steamer tied up at her wharf, having just returned from an expedition, and as the people walked down the plank their friends met them to congratulate them on their success or encourage them through their defeat. Down came a man I used to know in Fargo, South Dakota. Friends rushed up and said, "Why, we hear that you were very fortunate."

"Yes, wife and I left here six months ago with hardly anything. Now we have $350,000 in gold dust in the hold of the ship."

Then somebody looked around and said, "Mr. L——, where is your little boy?"

The tears rolled down his cheeks and he said, "We left him buried on the banks of the Yukon beneath the snow and ice, and we would gladly part with all the gold, if we only had our boy."

But all the wealth of the Klondike could not open the grave and put that child back in their arms. Money can't buy the peace of God that passeth understanding. Money can't take the sin out of your life.

Is there any particular kind of life you would like? If you could live one hundred years you wouldn't want to die, would you? I wouldn't. I think there is always something the matter with a fellow that wants to die. I want to stay as long as God will let me stay, but when God's time comes for me to go I'm ready, any hour of the day or night. God can waken me at midnight or in the morning and I'm ready to respond. But if I could live a million years I'd like to stay. I don't want to die. I'm having a good time. God made this world for us to have a good time in. It's nothing but sin that has damned the world and brought it to misery and corruption. God wants you to have a good time. Well, then, how can I get this life that you want and everybody wants, eternal life?

If you are ill the most natural thing for you to do is to go for your doctor. You say, "I don't want to die. Can you help me?"

He looks at you and says, "I have a hundred patients on my hands, all asking the same thing. Not one of them wants to die. They ask me to use my skill and bring to bear all I have learned, but I can't fight back death. I can prescribe for your malady, but I can't prevent death."

Well, go to your philosopher. He it is that reasons out the problems and mysteries of life by the application of reason. Say to him, "Good philosopher, I have come to you for help. I want to live forever and you say that you have the touchstone of philosophy and that you can prescribe and solve. Can you help me?"

He says to you, "Young man, my hair and my beard have grown longer and as white as snow, my eyes are dim, my brows are wrinkled, my form bent with the weight of years, my bones are brittle and I am just as far from the solution of that mystery and problem as when I started. I, too, sir, must soon die and sleep beneath the sod."

In my imagination I have stood by the bedside of the dying Pullman-palace-car magnate, George M. Pullman, whose will was probated at $25 million, and I have said, "Oh, Mr. Pullman, you will not die, you can bribe death." And I see the pupils of his eyes dilate, his breast heaves, he gasps—and is no more. The undertaker comes and makes an incision in his left arm, pumps in the embalming fluid, beneath whose mysterious power he turns as rigid as ice, and as white as alabaster, and they put his embalmed body in the rosewood coffin, trimmed with silver and gold, and then they put that in a hermetically sealed casket.

The grave-diggers go to Graceland Cemetery, on the shore of Lake Michigan, and dig his grave in the old family lot, nine feet wide, and they put in there Portland cement four and a half feet thick, while it is yet soft, pliable and plastic. A set of workmen drop down into the grave a steel cage with steel bars one inch apart. They bring his body, in the hermetically sealed casket all wrapped about with cloth, and they lower it into the steel cage, and a set of workmen put steel bars across the top and another put concrete and a solid wall of masonry and they bring it up within eighteen inches of the surface; they put back the black loamy soil, then they roll back the sod and with a whisk broom and dust pan they sweep up the dirt, and you would never know that there sleeps the Pullman-palace-car magnate, waiting for the trumpet of Gabriel to sound; for the powers of God will snap his steel, cemented sarcophagus as though it were made of a shell and he will stand before God as any other man.

What does your money amount to? What does your wealth amount to?

I summon the three electrical wizards of the world to my bedside and I say, "Gentlemen, I want to live and I have sent for you to come," and they say to me, "Mr. Sunday, we will flash messages across the sea without wires; we can illuminate the homes and streets of your city and drive your trolley cars and we can kill men with electricity, but we can't prolong life."

And I summon the great Queen Elizabeth, queen of an empire upon which the sun never sets. Three thousand dresses hung in her wardrobe. Her jewels were measured by the peck. Dukes, kings, earls fought for her smiles. I stand by her bedside and I hear her cry, "All my possessions for one moment of time!"

I go to Alexander the Great, who won his first battle when he was eighteen, and was King of Macedonia when he was twenty. He sat down on the shore of the Ægean sea, wrapped the drapery of his couch about him and lay down to eternal sleep, the conqueror of all the known world, when he was thirty-five years of age.

I go to Napoleon Bonaparte. Victor Hugo called him the archangel of war. He arose in the air of the nineteenth century like a meteor. His sun rose at Austerlitz; it set at Waterloo. He leaped over the slain of his countrymen to be First Consul; and then he vaulted to the throne of the emperor of France. But it was the cruel wanton achievement of insatiate and unsanctified ambition and it led to the barren St. Helena isle. As the storm beat upon the rock, once more he fought at the head of his troops at Austerlitz, at Mt. Tabor, and the Pyramids. Once more he cried, "I'm still the head of the army," and he fell back, and the greatest warrior the world has known since the days of Joshua was no more. Tonight on the banks of the Seine he lies in his magnificent tomb, with his marshals sleeping where he can summon them, and the battle flags he made famous draped around him, and from the four corners of the earth students and travelers turn aside to do homage to the great military genius.

I want to show you the absolute and utter futility of pinning your hope to a lot of fool things that will damn your soul to hell. There is only one way: "As Moses lifted up the serpent in the wilderness, even so must the Son of Man be lifted up, that whosoever believeth in him should not perish, but have eternal life. For God so loved the world that he gave his only begotten Son, that whosoever believeth in him should not perish, but have everlasting life." Search the annals of time and the pages of history and where do you find promises like that? Only upon the pages of the Bible do you find them.

You want to live and so do I. You want eternal life and so do I, and I want you to have it. The next question I want to ask is, how can you get it? You have seen things that won't give it to you. How can you get it? All you have tonight or ever will have you will come into possession of in one of three ways—honestly, dishonestly, or as a gift. Honestly: You will work and sweat and therefore give an honest equivalent for what you get. Dishonestly: You will steal. Third, as a gift, you will inherit it. And eternal life must come to you in one of these three ways.

A great many people believe in a high moral standard. They deal honestly in business and are charitable, but if you think that is going to save you, you are the most mistaken man on God's earth, and you will be the biggest disappointed being that ever lived. You can't hire a substitute in religion. You can't do some deed of kindness or act of philanthropy and substitute that for the necessity of repentance and faith in Jesus Christ. Lots of people will acknowledge their sin in the world, struggle on without Jesus Christ, and do their best to live honorable, upright lives. Your morality will make you a better man or woman, but it will never save your soul in the world.

Supposing you had an apple tree that produced sour apples and you wanted to change the nature of it, and you would ask the advice of people. One would say prune it, and you would buy a pruning hook and cut off the superfluous limbs. You gather the apples and they are still sour. Another man says to fertilize it, and you fertilize it and still it doesn't change the nature of it. Another man says spray it to kill the caterpillars, but the apples are sour just the same. Another man says introduce a graft of another variety.

When I was a little boy, one day my grandfather said to me: "Willie, come on," and he took a ladder, and beeswax, a big jackknife, a saw, and some cloth, and we went into the valley. He leaned the ladder against a sour crabapple tree, climbed up and sawed off some of the limbs, split them and shoved in them some little pear sprouts as big as my finger and twice as long, and around them he tied a string and put in some beeswax. I said, "Grandpa, what are you doing?" He said, "I'm grafting pear sprouts into the sour crab." I said, "What will grow, crabapples or pears?" He said, "Pears; I don't know that I'll ever live to eat the pears—I hope I may—but I know you will." I lived to see those sprouts which were no longer than my finger grow as large as any limb and I climbed the tree and picked and ate the pears. He introduced a graft of another variety and that changed the nature of the tree.

And so you can't change yourself with books. That which is flesh is flesh, no matter whether it is cultivated flesh, or ignorant flesh or common, ordinary flesh. That which is flesh is flesh, and all your lodges, all your money on God Almighty's earth can never change your nature. Never. That's got to come by and through repentance and faith in Jesus Christ. That's the only way you will ever get it changed. We have more people with fool ways trying to get into heaven, and there's only one way to do it and that is by and through repentance and faith in Jesus Christ.

Here are two men. One man born with hereditary tendencies toward bad, a bad father, a bad mother and bad grandparents. He has bad blood in his veins and he turns as naturally to sin as a duck to water. There he is, down and out, a booze fighter and the off-scouring scum of the earth. I go to him in his squalor and want and unhappiness, and say to him: "God has included all that sin that he may have mercy on all. All have sinned and come short of the glory of God. Will you accept Jesus Christ as your Saviour?"

"Whosoever cometh unto me I will in no wise cast out," and that man says to me, "No, I don't want your Christ as my Saviour."

Here is a man with hereditary tendencies toward good, a good father, a good mother, good grandparents, lived in a good neighborhood, was taught to go to Sunday school and has grown up to be a good, earnest, upright, virtuous, responsible business man; his name is synonymous with all that is pure and kind and true. His name is as good as a government bond at any bank for a reasonable amount. Everybody respects him. He is generous, charitable, and kind. I go to your high-toned, cultured, respectable man and say to him: "God hath included all under sin that he might have mercy upon all. All have sinned and come short of the glory of God. Whosoever cometh unto me I will in no wise cast out. Will you accept Jesus Christ as your Saviour? Will you give me your hand?" He says: "No, sir; I don't want your Christ."

What's the difference between those two men? Absolutely none. They are both lost. Both are going to hell. God hasn't one way of saving the one and another way of saving the other fellow. God will save that man if he accepts Christ and he will do the same for the other fellow. That man is a sinner and this man is a sinner. That man is lower in sin than this man, but they both say, "No" to Jesus Christ and they are both lost or God is a liar.

You don't like it? I don't care a rap whether you do or not.

You'll take it or go to hell. Stop doing what you think will save you and do what God says will save you.

Morality doesn't save anybody. Your culture doesn't save you. I don't care who you are or how good you are, if you reject Jesus Christ you are doomed. God hasn't one plan of salvation for the millionaire and another for the hobo. He has the same plan for everybody. God isn't going to ask you whether you like it or not, either. He isn't going to ask you your opinion of his plan. There it is and we'll have to take it as God gives it.

You come across a lot of fools who say there are hypocrites in the Church. What difference does that make? Are you the first person that has found that out and are you fool enough to go to hell because they are going to hell? If you are, don't come to me and expect me to think you have any sense. Not at all. Not for a minute.

A good many people attend church because it adds a little bit to their respectability. That is proof positive to me that the Gospel is a good thing. This is a day when good things are counterfeited. You never saw anybody counterfeiting brown paper. No, it isn't worth it. You have seen them counterfeiting Christians? Yes. You have seen counterfeit money? Yes. You never saw a counterfeit infidel. They counterfeit religion. Certainly. A hypocrite is a counterfeit.

But there is one class of these people that I haven't much respect for. They are so good, so very good, that they are absolutely good for nothing. A woman came to me and said: "Mr. Sunday, I haven't sinned in ten years."

I said: "You lie, I think."

Well, a man says: "Look here, there must be something in morality, because so many people trust in it." Would vice become virtue because more people follow it? Simply because more people follow it doesn't make a wrong right; not at all.

MARCUS GARVEY, 1887–1940

☆ Universal Negro Improvement Association

MARCUS GARVEY dreamed of an "Africa for the Africans," but he never set foot on the soil of that continent.

Born in St. Ann's Bay on the northern coast of Jamaica, Garvey was proud of his "pure" African blood and of his father's intellectualism and courage. "My parents were black Negroes," he wrote. "My father was a man of brilliant intellect and dashing courage. He was unafraid of consequences. He took human chances at the close of his career. . . . My mother was a sober conscientious Christian, too soft and good for the time in which she lived."

Marcus Garvey became a printer's apprentice when he was fourteen. At this age, he said, he "had enough intelligence and experience to manage men. I was strong and manly and I made them respect me. I developed a strong and forceful character."

While he was working as a foreman in a printing plant in Kingston, the workers went out on strike. Garvey joined them and soon became their leader. Eventually, the strike was broken and all except Garvey, who was blacklisted, returned to their jobs. He went to work in the government printing office.

Soon after the strike Garvey helped to form one of the first political clubs in Jamaica. He gave up his job at the government printery to publish *The Watchman*. But he had no funds to sustain either himself or his paper. He decided to go to Costa Rica, where a maternal uncle lived and where Garvey felt he could earn enough money to enable him to return to Jamaica and continue his political work.

He became a timekeeper on a banana plantation in Costa Rica. The plight of the Negro workers there dismayed him. He tried to intercede for them with the British consul, but the official to whom he protested was disinterested.

In 1912 Garvey was in England. He was restless, determined to help his race. There could be no help for the black man, he concluded, as long as he allowed himself to be "kicked about" by all other races. "I saw before me . . . a new world of black men, not peons, serfs, dogs, and slaves, but a nation of sturdy men making their impress upon civilization and causing a new light to dawn upon the human race."

He left London for the island of his birth, Jamaica, arriving there in July 1914. Within five days he had founded the Universal Negro Improvement Association (UNIA) and the African Communities (Imperial) League to assist the Negro race in establishing its own country. In addition, the UNIA looked forward to promoting the "spirit of race pride and love; . . . to administer to and assist the needy; to assist in civilizing the backward tribes of Africa; to strengthen the imperialism of independent African states; . . . to establish universities, colleges, and secondary schools for the further education and culture of the boys and girls of the race."

Garvey decided to start his organizing in the United States; he arrived here in 1916. Negro leadership in the United States generally was hostile to him and to his ideas of Africa for the Africans. But he was a persuasive speaker and organizer, and soon he had a large following among the country's mass Negroes. At the 1920 convention of his association, held in New York's Madison Square Garden, more than 25,000 attended. His official publication had a circulation of 75,000 to 100,000.

In 1922 Garvey appeared before the League of Nations as the representative of "the black people of the world" and urged that international body to heed the Negro voice. "We believe," he insisted, "that as a people we should have a government of our own in our homeland—Africa."

Although Garvey had a large following, many Negroes in Harlem were skeptical of his idea and even resented it. It was not unusual to hear them chant:

"Garvey, Garvey is a big man
To take his folks to monkey-land.
If he does, I'm sure I can
Stay right here with Uncle Sam."

A major project of the UNIA was the Black Star Steamship Line, Negro-owned and Negro-operated. Since Garvey did not make a practice of going to the wealthy Negro for help, his contributions came from the poor Negroes who could make only small investments. The steamship line which promised success for Garvey's project instead was his downfall: he had sold stock; he had made promises which could not be fulfilled; he had allegedly used the mails to solicit funds.

In 1922 the United States government indicted him for using the mails to defraud. Since Garvey had no confidence in Negro attorneys and objected to retaining a white lawyer, he conducted his own defense. His behavior in the courtroom, where he held forth at great length lecturing and belittling witnesses, was enough to prejudice the jury, which found him guilty. The man who had intended to lead his people to freedom was fined $1,000 and given the maximum of five years in jail. Released on bond, Garvey continued with his plans to send Negroes to Africa as colonists.

In 1925 he began to serve his time in the federal penitentiary in Atlanta. Within two years his sentence was commuted by President Coolidge, and Garvey was immediately deported to Jamaica. Without his leadership and organizing capabilities, the UNIA fell apart.

Marcus Garvey, who aspired to be the "Emperor of the Kingdom of Africa," died in London at the age of fifty-three, a bitter, unhappy man. Denounced by many as a "fabulous con-man," his scheme labeled "hopelessly visionary" and his panacea "wild" and "imaginary," Garvey has also been recognized as a "Negro genius," a "martyr," "the greatest organizer." And his dream has been called by some "a tempting legacy for present-day Negro leaders."

★ A NEW WORLD OF BLACK MEN

Some people have misunderstood me. Some don't want to understand me. But I must explain myself for the good of the world and humanity. Those of the Negro race who preach social equality, and who are working for an American race that will, in complexion, be neither white nor black have tried to misinterpret me to the white public and create prejudice against my work. The white public, not stopping to analyze and question the motive behind criticism and attacks aimed against new leaders and their movements, condemn without even giving a chance to the criticized to be heard. Those of my own race who oppose me because I refuse to endorse their program of social arrogance and social equality, gloat over the fact that by their misrepresentation and underhand methods, they were able to discredit me, so as to destroy the movement that I represent, in opposition to their program of a new American race; but we will not now consider the opposition to a programme or a movement; but state the facts as they are, and let deep souled white America pass its own judgment.

In another one hundred years white America will have

From "Appeal to the Soul of White America," *Negro World* (October 1923).

doubled the population; in another two hundred years it will have trebled itself. The keen student must realize that the centuries ahead will bring us an overcrowded country; as the population grows larger, opportunities will be fewer; the competition for bread between the people of their own class will become keener, to such an extent that there will be no room for two competitive races—the one strong and the other weak. To imagine Negroes as district attorneys, judges, senators, congressmen, assemblymen, aldermen, government clerks and officials, artisans, and laborers at work, while millions of white men starve, is to have before you the bloody picture of wholesale mob violence that I fear, and against which I am working. No preaching, no praying, no presidential edict will control the passion of hungry, unreasoning men of prejudice when the hour comes. It will not come, I pray, in our generation, but it is of the future that I think, and for which I work.

A generation of ambitious Negro men and women, out from the best colleges, universities and institutions, capable of filling the highest and best positions in the nation, in industry, commerce, society and politics! Can you keep them back? If you do, they will agitate and throw your constitution in your faces. Can you stand before civilization and deny the truth of your constitution? What are you going to do then? You who are just will open the door of opportunity and say to all and sundry, "enter in." But, ladies and gentlemen, what about the mob, that starving mob of your own race? Will they stand by, suffer and starve, and allow an opposite, competitive race to prosper in the midst of their distress? If you can conjure these things up in your mind, then you have the vision of the race problem of the future in America.

There is but one solution, and that is to provide an outlet for Negro energy, ambition and passion, away from the attractiveness of white opportunity, and surround the race with opportunities of its own. If this is not done, and if the foundation for same is not laid now, then the consequences will be sorrowful for the weaker race, and disgraceful to our ideals of justice and shocking to our civilization.

The Negro must have a country and a nation of his own. If you laugh at the idea, then you are selfish and wicked, for you and your children do not intend that the Negro shall discommode you in yours. If you do not want him to have a country and a nation of his own; if you do not intend to give him equal opportunities in yours, then it is plain to see that you mean that he must die, even as the Indian, to make room for your generations.

Why should the Negro die? Has he not served America and the world? Has he not borne the burden of civilization in this Western world for three hundred years? Has he not contributed of his best to America? Surely all this stands to his credit. But there will not be enough room, and the one answer is, find a place. We have found a place; it is Africa, and as black men for three centuries have helped white men build America, surely generous and grateful white men will help black men build Africa.

And why shouldn't Africa and America travel down the ages as protectors of human rights and guardians of democracy? Why shouldn't black men help white men secure and establish universal peace? We can only have peace when we are just to all mankind; and for that peace, and for that reign of universal love, I now appeal to the soul of white America. Let the Negroes have a government of their own. Don't encourage them to believe that they will become social equals and leaders of the whites in America, without first on their own account proving to the world that they are capable of evolving a civilization of their own. The white race can best help the Negro by telling him the truth, and not by flattering him into believing that he is as good as any white man without first proving the racial, national, constructive mettle of which he is made. Stop flattering the Negro about social equality, stop appealing to his vanity, and not to his good common sense; tell him to go to work and build for himself. Help him in the direction of doing for himself, and let him know that self-progress brings its own reward.

I appeal to the considerate and thoughtful conscience of white America not to condemn the cry of the Universal Negro

Improvement Association for a nation in Africa for Negroes, but to give us a chance to explain ourselves to the world. White America is too big, and when informed and touched, too liberal, to turn down the cry of the awakened Negro for "a place in the sun."

The Universal Negro Improvement Association teaches our race self-help and self-reliance, not only in one essential, but in all those things which contribute to human happiness and well-being. The disposition of the many to depend upon the other races for a kindly and sympathetic consideration of their needs, without making the effort to do for themselves, has been the race's standing disgrace, by which we have been judged, and through which we have created the strongest prejudice against ourselves.

There is no force like success, and that is why the individual makes all efforts to surround himself throughout life with the evidence of it. As of the individual, so should it be of the race and nation. The glittering success of Rockefeller makes him a power in the American nation; the success of Henry Ford suggests him as an object of universal respect, but no one knows and cares about the bum or hobo who is Rockefeller's or Ford's neighbour. So, also is the world attracted by the glittering success of races and nations, and pays absolutely no attention to the bum or hobo race that lingers by the wayside. The Negro must be up and doing if he will break down the prejudices of the rest of the world. Prayer alone is not going to improve our conditions, nor can the policy of watchful waiting. We must strike out for ourselves in the course of material achievement and by our own effort and energy present to the world those forces by which the progress of man is judged.

The Negro needs a nation and a country of his own, where he can best show evidence of his own ability in the art of human progress. Scattered as an unmixed and unrecognized part of alien nations and civilizations is but to demonstrate his imbecility, and point him out as an unworthy derelict, fit neither for the society of Greek, Jew, or Gentile. It is unfortunate that we should so drift apart, as a race, as not to see that we are but perpetuating our own sorrow and disgrace in failing to appreciate the first requisite of all peoples—organization.

Organization is a great power in directing the affairs of a race or a nation toward a given goal. To properly develop the desires that are uppermost, we must first concentrate through some system or method, and there is none better than organization. Hence the Universal Negro Improvement Association appeals to each and every Negro to throw in his lot with those of us who, through organization, are working for the universal emancipation of our race and the redemption of our common country—Africa.

No Negro, let him be American, European, West Indian, or African, shall be truly respected until the race as a whole has emancipated itself, through self-achievement and progress, from universal prejudice. The Negro will have to build his own government, industry, art, science, literature and culture, before the world will stop to consider him. Until then, we are but wards of a superior race and civilization, and the outcasts of a standard social system. The race needs workers at this time, not plagiarists, copyists, and mere imitators, but men and women who are able to create, to originate and improve, and thus make an independent racial contribution to the world and civilization.

The unfortunate thing about it is that we take the monkey apings of our so-called "leading men" for progress. There is no real progress in Negroes aping white people and telling us that they represent the best in the race, for in that respect any dressed monkey would represent the best of its species, irrespective of the creative matter of the monkey instinct. The best in a race is not reflected through or by the action of its apes, but by its ability to create of and by itself. It is such creation that our organization seeks. Let us not try to be the best or the worst of others, but let us make the effort to be the best of ourselves. Our own racial critics criticize us as dreamers and fanatics, and call us benighted and ignorant, because they lack backbone. They are unable to see themselves creators of their own needs. The slave instinct has not yet departed from them. They still believe that they can only live or exist through the good graces of their "masters." The good slaves have not yet thrown off their shackles; thus to them, the UNIA is an "impossibility."

It is the slave spirit of dependence that causes our so-called leading men to seek the shelter, leadership, protection and patronage of "the master" in their organization and so-called advancement work. It is the spirit of feeling secured as good servants of the master, rather than as independents, why our modern Uncle Toms take pride in laboring under alien leadership and becoming surprised at the audacity of our organization in proclaiming for racial liberty and independence. But the world of white, and other men, deep down in their hearts, have much more respect for those of us who work for our racial salvation under the banner of the UNIA than they could ever have, in all eternity, for a group of helpless apes and beggars who make a monopoly of undermining their own race and belittling themselves in the eyes of self-respecting people, by being "good boys," rather than able men. Let the white race of America and the world be informed that the best in the Negro race is not the class of beggars who send out to other races piteous appeals annually for donations to maintain their coterie, but the groups within us that are honestly striving to do for themselves with the voluntary help and appreciation of that class of other races that is reasonable, just and liberal enough to give to each and every man a fair chance in the promotion of those ideals that tend to greater human progress and human love. There is no desire for hate or malice, but every wish to see all mankind linked into a common fraternity of progress and achievement, that will wipe away the odour of prejudice, and elevate the human race to the height of real Godly love and peace.

BENJAMIN B. LINDSEY, 1869–1943

☆ Companionate Marriage

IT WAS DECRIED by many as "free love," but to Judge Benjamin B. Lindsey "companionate marriage" was "a solution to the problem of free love now rampant in the country."

H. G. Wells saw companionate marriage as an "opening" in "a very wide and far reaching movement for the courageous revision and modernization of marriage." Jane Addams, on the other hand, said she never believed in companionate marriage. "Young people should be taught self-control."

Benjamin B. Lindsey—lawyer, judge, and social reformer—was born in Jackson, Tennessee, but it was in Denver that he studied law, began to practice, and entered politics.

In 1900, as a delegate to the Democratic party convention, Lindsey was chairman of the credentials committee. Because he was too radical in his general political views he was not nominated at this time for an elective office; sometime later, however, he was named to fill a vacancy on the county court.

Lindsey was one of the first American judges to establish a juvenile court system. Because of his work with young people, he was known as "the kids' judge." He also received national attention with his book *The Beast and the Jungle* in which he muckraked political conditions in Colorado.

For more than four decades Judge Lindsey was the center of controversy. In 1927 he was disbarred, charged with accepting a gift in a case where he acted as the official mediator for the rights of two children. That same year he published his 396-page book, *The Companionate Marriage,* in which he suggested that legal marriage be dissolved at any time in cases where there were no children. He also proposed legalized birth control. Both were radical proposals, even in the era of the flapper and the jazz age.

Judge Lindsey explained that his advocacy of the companionate marriage was based on his intimate study of family life during his time as a judge. In what was described as a "companionate ceremony," Judge Lindsey advised a young couple: "Make your partnership a 'go' for life if you can. That is the way to the greatest happiness, and remember happiness is relative, made of joys and sorrows. . . . Do not feel that you really own each other without the other's full and free consent or you will encounter the green eye of jealousy. . . . If with such an honest effort your marriage should fail . . . insist in your honesty upon a divorce by mutual consent."

Judge Lindsey moved to California, where he was elected a judge in Los Angeles by the largest vote ever cast in a similar election. In 1933 the Supreme Court of Colorado offered to reinstate him if he would apologize for charges made in his book *The Beast* about the court. He refused.

His campaign for companionate marriage outraged conventional people. Preachers launched sermons against him; the press attacked him. In December 1930 Bishop Manning announced he would preach on the judge. In his sermon the bishop accused

Lindsey of breaking down "the moral defense of the young" as well as "trying to destroy the moral foundations of our life." Just as the bishop was going to lead his congregation in prayer, the judge, who was at the service, shouted from his seat: "Bishop Manning, you have lied about me." Ushers pulled him out of the church, but not before angry voices of the membership shouted, "Kick him . . . punch him . . . throw him out."

Police arrested Lindsey, who was charged with disorderly conduct. The complaint was dismissed on the ground that it had not been drawn up properly. The magistrate then wanted to charge Judge Lindsey with interrupting a meeting in a house of worship, but since there was no one to sign this complaint, it, too, was dismissed.

The famed jurist died at the age of seventy-three in Los Angeles. "If I've worn myself out, I've done it for children," he told his wife shortly before he died.

★ COMPANIONATE MARRIAGE

Companionate marriage is legal marriage, with legalized birth control, and with the right to divorce by mutual consent for childless couples, usually without payment of alimony.

Companionate marriage is already an established social fact in this country. It is conventionally respectable. Sophisticated people are, without incurring social reproach, everywhere practicing birth control and are also obtaining collusive divorce, outside the law, whenever they want it. They will continue the practice, and no amount of prohibitive legislation can stop them.

My thought is that we should put an end to this hypocritical pretense, under which we profess one thing and do another; that the companionate marriage, now largely monopolized by educated people who understand scientific contraception, and who can employ skilled lawyers in the obtaining of collusive divorces, ought to

---

From Benjamin B. Lindsey, *The Companionate Marriage* (New York, 1927).

be made legally and openly available to all people—particularly to the poor and the socially unfit, who need it most.

Scientific contraception promises what may develop into the most revolutionary change in human affairs that history has ever recorded. It would be difficult to overstate the economic, the eugenic, the broad social significance of a discovery which is even today changing marriage in some of its most fundamental aspects. Birth control has brought the companionate into existence. It has made possible between men and women a relationship which has never before in the history of the world been practicable for multitudes of people.

To protest against this colossal phenomenon is like trying to stop the tide by scolding it. I suggest that if we rationalize this new thing and use it intelligently, we may be able to derive from it a degree of social and spiritual power capable of creating for our descendants a better world than we have been able to fashion for our own use and happiness. . . .

I want, so far as possible, to forestall misunderstanding and prejudice on the part of readers who have been told by ill-informed critics of my views that I advocate men and women living together in free love unions, without marriage, and that they should remain in that unmarried status till the birth of a child.

Another version is that I advocate "trial marriage." What these critics mean by "trial marriage," apparently, is a technically legal marriage which is entered with the intention that it shall be, not an enduring union, but merely a temporary sex episode, similar in spirit to what we commonly call the "unmarried union." The parties to a "trial marriage" would be marrying, that is to say, strictly on a basis which would emphasize the "trial" element in the union, and create in it a psychology of impermanence. The very name "trial marriage" indicates this; and it suggests to those who believe that marriage should be as permanent as possible the thought that persons so doubtful as that of their ability to remain married had better not marry in the first place. An unmarried union would suit the needs of such couples better than any sort of legal union, one would think. The fact is that the distinction between "trial marriage" and free love is nominal. A trial marriage is really a free love union which avails itself of a legal form. I am not here concerned to criticize it. I merely insist on this identity between free love and trial marriage; and I further insist that free love and trial marriage are by no means to be confused with companionate marriage.

Technically the companionate and trial marriage have certain features in common but *one* is not the *other*. Both would normally avail themselves of birth control and divorce by mutual consent. Both would place a minimum of obstruction in the way of childless couples wishing a divorce. And both recognize the fact that when men and women marry they can never be perfectly certain that their marriage will turn out to be a permanent success. But there the similarity ends.

For the emphasis—the psychological emphasis—is altogether different. All men and women who are sensible and honest know when they marry that there is at least a possibility of failure ahead. But they assume that the chance is remote. They have confidence in their ability to weather all storms and make port. It is their intention to do that, and to make such adjustments as may be necessary to that end. That is *marriage*. That is the spirit of marriage. It involves the same recognition of risk that goes into trial marriage, but it stoutly proposes to overcome and nullify that risk. It emphatically does not propose to seek divorce the moment the flame of romantic passion begins to cool.

Now the trouble with this attitude in ordinary marriage is that not enough account is taken of the risk. If the trial marriage psychology puts too much emphasis on the risk, the psychology of traditional marriage bullheadedly ignores it altogether. The result is that couples who make a mistake in their choice of each other find that in getting into marriage they have walked into a trap.

There is room for sane compromise between these two extremes. Men and women who enter marriage should be encouraged to do it under conditions that would best insure the success and permanence of the marriage, but which would also afford a line of retreat in case the marriage failed. They should not have children, for instance, till they have been married long enough to be reasonably sure of their ability to carry on together; and they should not have them till they can afford them. This is common sense. It is not free love or trial marriage at all. It may, as I have indicated, have a technical similarity to trial marriage, but legal technicalities are not what make a marriage. What makes a marriage is the spirit and intent of it.

I do not deny that it would be possible for people to enter the companionate with a trial marriage psychology. But so is it possible for them to enter traditional marriage with a trial marriage psychology. Some do it; but they are not many. For such persons the unmarried union, achieved secretly, is easier, and involves less responsibility before society. The companionate would not invite many such persons. Nor, since it would offer small hope of alimony, would it attract ladies of the "gold-digger" type. It would give marriage a chance to breathe and live; it would give it room in which to grow; it would give it soil in which to put forth roots; and it would establish it on a better basis than it has yet known.

HOWARD SCOTT

☆ Technocracy

WILL ROGERS, writing in 1933 at the ebbtide of Technocracy, observed that America, "sorely pressed economically" and with its sense of humor "lost in a mad whirl of grabbing at anything offering relief, took two events seriously, a thing called Technocracy and a thing called a lame-duck Congress. . . . Both tried to save the country by a confusion of words, words, words."

In August 1932 newspapers first carried the story of Technocracy, a group that had undertaken an "Energy Survey" of North America and through charts planned to present the country's history from 1830 to 1930. Three thousand of the country's leading industrial and agricultural products were to be surveyed. Already 150 charts had been completed, including those of the steel and cement industries. Technocracy was housed at Columbia University and was jointly sponsored by the university's industrial engineering department and the Architects Emergency Committee of New York.

The man who sparked Technocracy was Howard Scott. The Columbia University announcement listed Scott as consultant technologist and said he was being assisted by thirty-six unemployed architectural draftsmen and engineers.

A familiar personality in New York's Greenwich Village, Scott was articulate and impressive, but little was known about him. Reportedly he was a wax producer with a small factory in New Jersey—but was more interested in economics than in making wax. He conducted some research for the Industrial Workers of the World but "never was active in the I.W.W. or in any organization, labor union, or political party, nor was I ever a member."

On January 24, 1933, the *New York Times* reported that Scott, in response to a question regarding his educational background, said: "I don't care to discuss my educational qualifications. My past does not matter as far as technocracy is concerned. The idea is bigger than the individual."

In a letter dated April 14, 1967, to the editors of this volume, Scott wrote: "As for a personal biography, may I say that we have never had the time nor inclination to go in for it."

The forerunner of Technocracy was the Technical Alliance, organized in 1918 with Scott as chief engineer. Among those on the temporary organizing committee were Stuart Chase, Thorstein Veblen, and Charles P. Steinmetz.

The Alliance was formed to collect data "for the purpose of designing or coordinating the system, and to give progressive bodies the plans and data of the present mechanism of industry." Its prospectus stated: "Engineering is the science of planning and utilizing natural resources and human effort for the satisfaction of the wants of man. . . . The solution of the industrial problem is primarily an engineering one; therefore it is essential that an alliance of technicians . . . [be] formed to ascertain and present the results of the present non-technical control of industry . . ."

Scott proclaimed that "there are no physical factors in existence which would prevent the efficient operation of this continent on an energy basis." He insisted that "the only thing that does prevent it is our devotion to a Shibboleth—price." The administration of the country, he contended, should be in the hands of the engineers, and the monetary system would be based on the measurement of energy.

The Alliance was short-lived, but in the early 1930's, when economic crises were again rampant and again there were predictions of the collapse of capitalism, Technocracy came into being.

Soon after Columbia University announced the Energy Survey, Scott became a popular speaker at various dinners and meetings which were attended not only by influential bankers and industrialists but by liberals, radicals, and representatives of labor and various dissident groups.

So widespread was the interest in Technocracy in its early days that the *Wilson Library Bulletin* rushed into print—"in response to scores of feverish requests from libraries"—a selected bibliography of eleven books and thirty-four articles "on the surprising phenomenon—Technocracy—an economic theory that is sweeping over the bridge tables."

Upton Sinclair called Technocracy "the most important movement which has shown its head in our time." To Stuart Chase it was "perhaps the most arresting challenge which the American industrial system has ever faced."

Scott was honored at a dinner in January 1933 by the Society of Arts and Sciences. He spoke to the four hundred dinner guests—capitalists, bankers, industrialists, writers, artists, economists—as well as to a nationwide radio network audience on "The Place of Science and Technology in Modern Civilization." In his talk he predicted that if present trends continued, the country could expect more than twenty million unemployed within eighteen months.

Audience reaction to the speech was mixed; applause at the end was "modest."

Ten days after the dinner, four of the eight members of the Committee on Technocracy—including Professor Walter Rautenstrauch of Columbia and Leon Henderson of the Russell Sage

Foundation—resigned because they were "not in accord with some of the statements and attitudes expressed by Mr. Howard Scott."

Newspapers reported that the research had been "formally taken over" by Columbia University's Department of Engineering "as a scholarly enterprise of the University." At the same time, Scott accepted the resignations and said that the research of Technocracy would continue outside the university.

Technocracy, which had created such sudden excitement and hope in the winter of 1932-1933, just as quickly faded away.

In 1964 Scott, still determined, wrote: "Technocracy has prepared the design of almost every component of a large scale social system."

As with Henry George's Single Tax movement, there are still today individuals who espouse Howard Scott's ideal. They wear "Great Monad" buttons, the sign of Technocracy. Scattered groups in the United States publish a variety of periodicals on the subject.

How large was the membership of Technocracy during the 1930's? How large is it in 1968? There are no official figures. Scott says the bylaws and general regulations of Technocracy, Inc., and its policies generally "prevent us from giving . . . any figures on membership of any period of Technocracy's history. This has always been the policy of Technocracy."

Al Smith, former governor of New York and 1928 presidential candidate opposing engineer Herbert Hoover, commented during the 1932 presidential campaign: "As for substituting engineers for political leaders in running the country, I cannot refrain from mentioning the fact that we have finished an era of government by engineers in Washington."

★ ENERGY VERSUS MONEY

Under a technological system, money would no longer exist. Debt could not be created. There would be a medium of *distribution*

From Howard Scott, *Science versus Chaos* (New York, 1933).

but not one of debt, value, or exchange. This medium of distribution would have to satisfy the following conditions:

a. It would designate by functional number the goods or services purchased.

b. It would designate the purchaser by function and by sex, and show whether the purchase was made prior to, during, or after the fulfillment of his energy contract (service period with the Technate).

c. The point of origin and point of consumption of the goods or services would be shown numerically.

d. It must be non-exchangeable between individuals and consequently not susceptible to being lost, stolen, or bestowed as charity.

e. It will be valid only for the time period for which issued, a period determined by the time required to make one complete industrial cycle (for the North American continent this period is about two years). One's income, being valid only for the time period for which issued, can not be saved. It can only be spent or forfeited.

The purchasing power of the individual would depend upon the operation of the physical equipment and would be a prorated division of the energy consumed in the given area during the given time period, after the deduction of that part of the total energy spent in the construction of plants, etc., and fixed charges for such other items as are not directly distributable to individuals. Thus the income of the individual can be altered only by a change in the rate of expenditure of energy by the social mechanism as a whole.

The only way for an individual under Technocracy not to participate in this income would be:

a. To leave the continent permanently.

b. To commit suicide.

c. To induce the Technate to execute him.

These Energy Certificates, issued to individuals, would resemble somewhat a cross between a traveler's check and an ordinary bank check. They would be similar to a bank check in that they would represent no denomination until a purchase of goods or services had been made. (The denomination, or the cost of that particular transaction, would be indicated on the certificate surrendered in the process.) They would resemble a traveler's check in that they would be issued to a particular individual and would not be valid except as identified by that individual. Hence they could not be stolen, exchanged, or given away, and would be useless in the hands of any other person.

On this certificate would be a number, according to a system similar to the library cataloging system, identifying the person to whom issued by function and geographical position.

A color band would cross the certificate diagonally, one direction to designate a male, the opposite a female. The holder of a male certificate would not be allowed to purchase female apparel, and vice versa. Thus one's relationship to the opposite sex would depend entirely on personal merits, because for the first time it would be impossible to purchase favors.

The background of this certificate would be one of three colors. If the first, it would signify that the holder had not yet begun the fulfillment of his or her energy contract for services to the Technate. If a second color, it would signify that the holder was engaged in the fulfillment of such an energy contract. If a third color, it would signify that such fulfillment had been completed and the holder had retired.

The income of the individual would continue until death. This income is not in any manner a payment or reward for services done. True, the individual is expected and required to fulfill a period of service according to his capacity and ability during his lifetime; but the income is a per capita share of the net available energy and is not allotted on a man-hour participation basis or because of his social contribution.

Once such a system was beyond the preliminary stages of reconstruction, such a period of service should not exceed four hours per day, four consecutive days at a shift, and 165 days per year. For a period of about twenty years, from the ages of twenty-five to forty-five, this period of service would cover the fulfillment of the energy contract. The income, in terms of physical goods and services made possible by virtue of our possession of energy reserves, would be several times the present average income in this country, and many times greater than any possible contribution of services by any individual.

Purchasing would be effected by means of surrendering the energy certificates properly identified in return for goods and services. The cost of any particular commodity would be determined entirely by the energy consumed in the process of its production and delivery to the point of consumption. There would be no profits. The entire physical equipment of this continent would, of course, be operated by the Technate. Every item of goods or services would, in the functional numeration system mentioned above, bear its own particular catalog number. Should an energy certificate be surrendered in payment for any commodity or service, it would be canceled by having punched through its face the functional number of the item purchased. It would then be pushed through photo-electric control recording machines which would deduct from the inventory the item purchased, and simultaneously, from the purchaser's account, the "amount" of the item purchased.

Since the system of certificates and accounting used would be uniform throughout the Continent, all inventories and accounts would be relayed continuously by wire to a central headquarters, where a complete and up-to-the-minute inventory of the physical operation of the entire Continent as to rates of production, stocks on hand, and rates of consumption would be automatically maintained.

The rates of consumption would be ascertained by sorting the energy certificates canceled—such sorting to be done photoelectrically according to the status of the purchaser, the geographical division, and the item purchased—which would provide the maintenance of a complete statistical tabulation of every significant physical and social operation down to minute details.

The operational as well as the sociological implications and possibilities of such a controlled system are astounding. The quality of goods to be produced would no longer be the cheap and shoddy variety turned out at present. Instead, the criterion by which goods would be judged would be the energy cost per unit of service; and those goods would be produced which by experimental test were found to cost the least energy expenditure per unit of service.

The Technate would not be interested in the expansion of consumption for its own sake, since no profits can accrue. On the contrary, the need of conserving our raw materials would discourage wasteful practices of all kinds. There would be no advertising or salesmanship. But for such practices the present consumption of goods would be considerably reduced, as any large retailer or advertising concern now knows very well. It follows that in a Technocracy, where a very ample variety and quantity of only the best goods would be available for all, the rate of consumption, instead of expanding ad infinitum, would probably tend to contract, or at least reach a state of equilibrium at a moderately simple mode of living.

Thorstein Veblen, in *The Theory of the Leisure Class,* ably discussed the " 'canons of conspicuous waste' and the 'pecuniary canons of taste,' " as induced by the existence of a Price System. Once revoked, as they would be under a non-Price System of equal income for all, it follows that social rivalry, which seems an inherent characteristic of the human species, would have to find other means of expressing itself. Consequently, if one found it impossible to display one's superiority to the Joneses by virtue of being able to live more pretentiously, one would be obliged to find some more substantial manner of self-expression. The chief channel for that would be the performance in the social system of a more important or responsible task than that of Jones.

In matters of design of equipment practically nothing would be left unaffected. It goes without saying that the most efficient and automatic processes that could be devised would be used wherever possible. Under such a control the use of automatic machinery would not, as now, result in the evils of unemployment, but instead would lighten the *burden* of all by equal amounts. All industry, all social functions, would be conceived and operated on a Continental scale. This again is not a philosophic premise but is based on the fact that, under a high-energy system, every individual piece of equipment is dependent for its own operation upon the operation of the system as a whole. Since this is so, it is imperative that the considerations concerning single units be secondary to the prime consideration of the operation of the complete mechanism.

A homely illustration may suffice to make this clear. Suppose that a group of designing engineers is assigned the task of designing an automobile. One, shall we say, is a carburetor expert; a second, an ignition expert; a third, a transmission expert, etc. Now it would be possible for each of these men to focus his attention on his own particular specialty and create that part as a separate entity with a high degree of perfection; yet the complete car, while composed of perfect parts, when assembled would perform very imperfectly. This might be due, for instance, to the fact that the carburetor was of a capacity sufficient for a small car, whereas the designer of the chassis called for a car twice that size; and to other similar types of misfits.

If, however, the procedure had been reversed and it had been specified that the car should carry a given number of passengers, should perform at a given speed with a gasoline consumption of a certain number of miles per gallon, then in order to meet these specifications the separate parts may vary in pattern only within strict limitations. In other words, it is not possible by haphazard integration of perfect parts to achieve a perfected whole. Conversely, however, if the performance of the whole is specified, the limitations of the parts are automatically determined.

The whole, in the case under consideration, is of course the entire social mechanism. The specifications are that it shall perform in such a manner as to provide economic security with equal income from birth until death at a high energy standard of living for each and every member thereof, at the lowest necessary expenditure of human effort and non-recurrent natural resources. The fulfillment of these specifications automatically affects every functional sequence within that social mechanism. As a convenient illustration on this greater scale, we may consider the problem of housing 150 million people at a minimum standard of housing per person.

This [scientific housing] is not a problem in architecture. It is a problem of construction and maintenance of buildings. It involves a consideration of materials. Materials must be chosen of which there are ample quantities, eliminating from serious consideration the so-called metal houses talked of by some of the modern architects. It demands material much more durable than used in houses of today. Since a house is an operating mechanism and therefore an energy-consuming device, in order to keep the energy cost at a minimum, insulation must be carefully considered. This and many more conditions are implied as a consequence of the requirement that housing 150 million people shall, when operated as a whole, fall within given operating specifications.

Attacking the problem of housing in the converse sense, as has been customary and is still the basis of most of our current architecture, it may be remarked that there is no design or composite of designs in existence in the past or present of architecture adequate to meet the above requirements. Architecture, as it is now practiced, occupies exactly the same role with regard to the problem of housing as did the various experts in the case of the automobile mentioned above. When housing is viewed as a problem of construction, operation, and maintenance at a basic minimum standard for 150 million people, architecture as it is now constituted—essentially individualistic and anarchic—will cease to exist.

Exactly the same line of reasoning applies to every necessary functional sequence from agriculture to education, communication, or public health.

I have attempted to point out something of the evolution and the rate of acceleration in the immediate past in the technique of the means whereby we live. I have indicated that, due to the introduction of technological procedures which are totally without historic precedent, we are witnessing the initiation of a social change which is unidirectional and irreversible. I have shown that, due to these technological processes under a Price System, unemployment has resulted and will continue to increase; that the growth curves of industry during the fifty years from 1870 to 1920 were expanding at a compound interest rate, that they have been flattening out, and that this process started prior to 1920. This is evidence of industrial growth maturation. As a consequence, unemployment will be even more highly accelerated and the interest rate will tend to approach zero, due to the inability to create further debt. The total consequence of these simultaneous trends will be an unprecedented social impasse as long as operation is continued in accordance with the rules of the game of a Price System.

On the other hand, I have pointed out that, with the greatest array of productive equipment on the earth's surface, with the lion's share of the earth's natural resources, and with the largest technically trained and functionally competent personnel in existence, this Continent stands ready to move from an economy of scarcity and poverty into an era of peace and plenty.

I have indicated a few of the details of what such a system would be like. I have not inquired as to whether you do or do not like the idea. The events that are going to occur in this area within the very near future are not going to be respecters of human likes or dislikes. The problem of operating any existing complex of industrial equipment is not and can not be solved by a democratic social organization. The executive of the telephone company is not consulted as to whether he likes the design of the telephone, nor is the general public. With few exceptions, you know nothing at all about a telephone except that by following a certain routine someone answers at the other end of the line. That is all you need and, for the most part, all that you want to know.

The problem of operating the entire industrial equipment of

this Continent is a technical problem so far transcending any other technical problem man has yet solved that many individuals would probably never understand why most of the details must be one way and not another; yet the services of everyone, in the highest capacity at which he can perform, will be needed.

Fortunately, it has been demonstrated that once the basic necessities of economic security have been achieved at a not uncomfortable expenditure of personal effort on our part, we are so constituted physiologically that, by a rapid process of habituation, we find and pronounce such circumstances to be good.

WALTER C. TEAGLE, 1878–1962

☆ Share the Work

"SPURRED BY A DECLARATION FROM President Hoover that the 'major financial crisis' had been successfully overcome, business and industrial leaders called together from over the nation set up a central council of war today for a vigorous new attack on what remains of the Depression."

So reported the *New York Times* in a front-page story on August 22, 1932.

The "vigorous new attack" was the "share-the-work" movement, with Walter C. Teagle, president of the Standard Oil Company of New Jersey, as the campaign's chairman and L. C. Walker, president of the Shaw-Walker Company, as its vice-chairman.

President Hoover in his speech before the conference which officially initiated the movement said that it was "doubtful whether any action we could take at this time would so greatly accelerate our progress, save the welfare of our unemployed millions, or so quickly give us as a nation the benefit of widespread spending power as a further spread of equitable plans of sharing available work."

Walter Teagle was born into the oil business. His father, John, was a partner in Scofield, Shurmer, and Teagle, an independent oil firm; his mother was a daughter of Maurice B. Clark, the first business partner of John D. Rockefeller. The young Teagle attended Cornell University, where he was active in student affairs. He was assistant manager of the football team and business manager of the *Cornell Widow*. He majored in chemistry and wrote his thesis on oil.

In 1900, graduating with a B.S. degree, he went to work for his father. He donned a pair of overalls and started by shoveling coal and driving tankwagons. The same year that his father's firm merged with the Republic Oil Corporation, Walter Teagle was made a vice-president. In 1903 he joined the export department of the Standard Oil Company, became president of that company in 1917, and chairman of the board in 1937.

It was in 1932 that President Hoover called upon the Standard Oil executive to head the "share-the-work" movement. Teagle left his office for six months to devote all his time to the project.

At the time of his appointment, *Business Week* described Teagle as "a staunch minimum-hour man, an endowment insurance man, a paid vacation man, a sick leave champion, no wage cutter, a laborer-stockholder doctrinaire, a stagger-plan master, an arbitrator, about every human thing."

"Share-the-work" did not originate with the conference. It was already in existence as early as 1930 in many industrial plants, particularly on the West Coast. Thousands of jobs had already been found for the unemployed on the West Coast by spreading employment. Proponents of the share-the-work movement felt that a similar program could be put into effect in other parts of the country, specifically in the industrial states where unemployment was most acute.

Standard Oil had already incorporated a similar plan. Teagle pointed out that his company had added three thousand additional workers to the 23,000 already employed by reducing hours of labor and spreading the jobs.

The slogan of the campaign was "Job Security by Job Sharing." To Teagle, share-the-work was "a proved remedy immediately available for a severe unemployment crisis." The movement was supported by industrialists and labor. William Green, president of the American Federation of Labor, hailed the work-spreading panacea and urged employer and employe to support it. But there were still opposition and complaints. To these, Mr. Teagle responded that "the fellow who stands on a sidewalk finding fault with men who are trying to rescue persons involved in a street accident is not contributing anything helpful to the situation."

When the National Recovery Act was set up, President Franklin D. Roosevelt invited Teagle to organize the National Industrial Advisory Board, of which he became chairman. But the industrialist was not sympathetic to the New Deal. He insisted that "government should not write the rules, name the umpire, and then enter the field as one of the players in the business game."

Teagle retired as board chairman and a director of Standard Oil in 1942, after thirty-nine years with the company. He died twenty years later, at the age of eighty-four, after a long illness.

"He put into force liberal and enlightened labor policies at a time when welfare and pension funds were almost unknown," observed the *New York Times* upon his death.

★ YOUR JOB—WILL YOU SHARE IT?

Some time after the cataclysm of 1929, business leaders were invited to Washington to discuss ways and means of stabilizing prosperity. As the first step to this end, it was thought that there

---

From Walter C. Teagle, *Review of Reviews and World's Work*, November 1932.

should be no reduction in wages. Suppose those present had been gifted with telescopic sight, which would have permitted them to look ahead to 1932. In that event, instead of the suggestion that the 1929 level of wages be maintained, they might well have decided to cooperate as large employers to use their efforts to retain their forces intact, come what may in the way of business contraction, by dividing work to keep all workers on the payroll.

So many new factors complicated the business situation that no one had such a vision of the slump ahead. With certain exceptions the old method was followed, of laying off men as fast as the need for their services disappeared. The largest surplus of idle workers in history was built up.

When the first group of men and women were released from steady employment, prosperity began to wane. The purchasing power of this group was eliminated; its members had that much less buying power for the products of their neighbors, and as a result others were made idle. For fear that they too might be thrown out of work, those still employed cast about for things to do without, in order that their savings might not be impaired. In this way the spread of enforced idleness was launched; and each plant, store, and office which further reduced the number on its payroll widened the circle of unemployment and decreased purchasing.

Building an organization of trained and efficient workers is one of the principal tests of management. It was therefore only natural that when declining volume of business made it necessary to reduce staffs, some executives recognized what it had cost them in time and money to get together their organizations, and they were loath to follow the general practice and lay off workers. Another difficulty was that in many companies the seniority right is generally recognized; and to have confined discharges to the younger men, or those most recently engaged, would not only have reduced efficiency but would have seriously affected the company's future, since it is from the younger men that management must select its successors. The management of some companies put the problem up to their workers for decision. They were asked whether they thought it better to keep part of the force on full time and lay off the remainder, or to keep everybody and shorten the number of hours worked. Unanimously the employees voted to share the work. Without knowledge of this action, other companies found they could close their plants entirely for part of the week and retain all of their employees. All over the country various devices were adopted by sympathetic, but hard-headed executives, to keep their forces intact so far as possible.

And so, without any heaven-sent vision, without any attempt then at cooperative action, nearly two years ago Share-the-Work began to be a real factor in our employment situation.

Few people realize how the various forms of Share-the-Work have kept the unemployment situation from being worse. An estimate shows that three and one-half million people who were employed when the Washington meeting was held would have been off the payrolls but for workspreading. The American Telephone and Telegraph Company alone has today 48,600 names on its payrolls which would not be there if employees had been dropped as rapidly as the decline in business warranted.

We all know that the country has passed through a severe crisis, the potentialities of which fortunately were known to few. The more pressing problems were handled by the administration, by Congress, and by the different groups called in for consultation. We reached the point where there was no longer any question of the ship keeping afloat. The storm had abated, the hold had been cleared of water, and repairs were well under way.

At the end of August 1932, even though the skies were lifting, President Hoover summoned to Washington bankers and industrialists from all over the United States, for a discussion of such other measures as might be taken to hasten the revival of trade and industry. These men who assembled in the national capital agreed that we could not have prosperity while some ten million usually gainfully employed are without means of livelihood. These idle workers, with those depending upon them, represent nearly 20 per cent of our entire population. For the most part they are unable to purchase anything but the barest requirements in the way of food and shelter. Business of every character feels the loss of their patronage.

But the effect of the withdrawal of this group did not stop with the curtailment of their buying. Those who still had jobs became fearful lest another week see them added to the widening circle of unemployed. So they too stopped avoidable expenditures. They kept their old automobiles. They postponed painting their houses. They clung to clothes that should have been given to the Salvation Army. Caution walked by their side every time they started for the shopping centers.

With sentiment and business looking up, there remains this problem of finding jobs for as many as possible through the coming winter. Nothing is more important to stimulate business and increase buying. With the President's endorsement, the banking and industrial committees of the twelve Federal Reserve districts have undertaken to further what had already been done by more than 3,500 firms and companies in the way of reducing the time worked per individual, in order to give that extra time to someone else.

Share-the-Work is not a five-day-week movement, nor a thirty-hour-week movement. All these plans are excellent where they apply; but the Share-the-Work plan is broader in conception than any of these movements, though it embraces them all.

It can be described as the application of flexibility to the working period—whether it be a working day, a week, a month, or a season—and to the working organization, or particular parts of it. How the work schedule is arranged is unimportant. Days may be shortened, vacations without pay lengthened, or working weeks or months alternated. The point is to provide work and livelihood for an increasing number of workers.

An immediately helpful feature of the Share-the-Work movement is that as soon as it is put into operation it gives the worker a feeling of assurance of steady—if somewhat curtailed—employment. Thus fear is routed, and a sense of confidence and hope takes its place. Restoring the confidence of the wage-earner tends to restore his customary mode of living and his normal consumption of commodities.

Share-the-Work is a measure to relieve unemployment and give the worker that sense of security in his job to which he is entitled. If American business can abolish the worker's fear of loss of a job, it will put wages back into the stream of business, and normal buying will gradually be restored. This in turn will make for more employment and greater security for the worker, and greater stability for business.

Shared work in a crisis like this is comparable to the practice of civilized peoples in a famine situation. If there is but a limited amount of food, no one would suggest feeding two-thirds of the distressed people fully and letting the other third starve. The available food is rationed. That is what we are now doing with work, because there is a partial famine in work. . . .

The movement so far has developed itself on sheer merit, as a logical and fair way of protecting interests of both employer and employee. Now it seems worthwhile to try to put the force of public sentiment behind it, to make acceptance of work-sharing general in all lines of business. . . .

We are not fanatically wedded to some new theory of business conduct. When, in the future, work-sharing becomes a thing of the past through a recovery in business and other forms of income production, which will make the worker sought after rather than the job, we can say good-bye to it without a qualm.

UPTON SINCLAIR, 1878–

☆ End Poverty in California

IN 1933 UPTON SINCLAIR, veteran socialist, author, and muckraker, changed his voting registration from Socialist to Democrat, a move which was to create an upheaval in California Democratic party politics.

The proprietor of a small hotel in Santa Monica, California, invited Sinclair to meet with a group of his political friends. The purpose of the session was to urge Sinclair to permit these men to nominate him as a gubernatorial candidate in the Democratic primaries. They felt that if this author of forty-seven books and hundreds of articles of social significance could come up with a practical program, he could sweep the primaries and win the governor's office in November 1934.

Reluctant at first, Sinclair soon found himself lured by the idea. He outlined his program in a story in which he imagined himself the governor of California. He told how he would conduct himself in office and how he would run the state. The sixty-four-page booklet was titled, *I, Governor of California, and How I Ended Poverty*. It was published in October 1933; hundreds of thousands of copies were sold. Other booklets followed during the campaign: *Epic Answers, The Lie Factory Starts,* and *Immediate Epic.*

To Sinclair, the remedy to the Depression in which the country found itself—and in which the State of California alone, out of a population of seven million, had a million unemployed—was "obvious." It could only be a remedy based on "production for use."

The slogan for Sinclair's campaign: "End Poverty in California" (EPIC). The emblem: a bee. ("I like the bee; she not only works hard but has the means to defend herself and is willing to use them on behalf of the young.") The motto: "I produce, I defend."

In the primaries Sinclair received 436,000 votes, a majority of the total votes cast for the half-dozen candidates.

The campaign for governor was bitter; the opposition spent millions of dollars to defeat Sinclair. The movie industry and the press combined in attacking the Democratic nominee. They pinned "horns and a tail on me," Sinclair recalled. He was accused of being "an agent of Moscow," "a fascist"; of carrying on "amatory monkeyshines" and a "fly-by-night, will-o'-the-wisp, utopian campaign."

During the campaign, Dr. Francis Townsend, the old-age pension advocate, came to see Sinclair. The doctor wanted Sinclair to endorse his program. "I could not," Sinclair related. "It had no constructive qualities; it only had a pension for old age. I was interested in production. Production comes before distribution."

About a month before the election, Sinclair visited with President Franklin D. Roosevelt, to whom he outlined his program. "The President told me he would come out in a talk in favor of production for use." But President Roosevelt never did.

If he had, Sinclair feels, "I would have been elected Governor of California."

Sinclair lost the election by 1,138,620 votes to 879,537. "I was lucky to have lost," Sinclair said. "A businessman had made his will, got a gun, and made plans to shoot me if I were elected. The furor of that campaign was extraordinary."

Upton Sinclair was born in Baltimore in 1878, the scion of a proud but no longer prosperous southern family. His great-grandfather who commanded the first frigate built by the United States government was one of the founders of the Annapolis Naval Academy. His grandfather was a commander of the U.S. Navy and later of the Confederate Navy.

Sinclair was twenty-one when he started "serious writing" and began what he hoped would be the great American novel. But he found socialism, and he turned to writing about social and economic injustice. *The Jungle* in 1905 exposed the plight of workers in the Chicago stockyards and spotlighted the filth and dirt there. The book resulted in the passage of the Pure Food and Drug law. He commented then: "I aimed at the public's heart, and by accident I hit it in the stomach."

All of Sinclair's books which followed had social justice as the theme: *The Brass Check, King Coal, Oil, The Goose-Step, Boston.* The Lanny Budd novels—a series of eleven books, one of which, *Dragon's Teeth,* won the Pulitzer prize in 1943—interpret contemporary history through Budd's position as an insider in the high councils of government.

Ninety books later, at the age of ninety, Sinclair is no longer writing. "I am written out . . . I have done my job," he says.

★ END POVERTY IN CALIFORNIA

I have the program clearly in mind . . . I have summed it up in a slogan: End Poverty in California.

From Upton Sinclair, *I, Governor of California, and How I Ended Poverty* (Los Angeles, 1933).

We confront a real crisis in this state, and I see no prospect of things getting better. Like all good Americans I am giving my support to the NRA, but I cannot shut my eyes to its failures. The figures which the Government has collected indicate that production has been boosted to the 1926 level, but employment is only 70 per cent of that level and wages only 50 per cent. In other words, under the stress of competition we have so perfected processes that we can turn out the same amount of goods with two-thirds as many workers and one-half the payroll. This means that the people will be able to buy only half of what they were buying in 1926—and their lack of buying power then was what brought on the Depression. Very soon our warehouses are going to be crammed with goods for which there is no market. Our manufacturers have borrowed money from the banks to finance new production, expecting inflation and a rise in prices. They will not be able to meet their notes and so there will be another bank crisis.

As a matter of fact, the NRA program admits its own inadequacy. We are told that the hope is to put six million men to work this fall, but we had fifteen million unemployed when we started, so nine million are left hopeless. My studies of the problem have convinced me that at least one-half the people who are out of work in the United States will never again have work under the profit system. They have built such a perfect machine of production that it can run without them. They have completed the upbuilding of the country, and it is time for them to move on to some other planet.

Consider the situation here in Los Angeles County. We have more than half a million people getting public relief. We repudiate the British idea of a "dole," and say that we are going to preserve the self-respect of our people by giving them work; but we have no real work, so we take them down into the bed of the Los Angeles River and set them to shoveling sand, making a channel. Of course the river fills it up again in a few days. The work is a farce, and the workers know it is a farce, and it does not do much to keep up their morale.

And meanwhile the county is going bankrupt. Mobs of irate taxpayers besiege the supervisors, and these poor fellows do not know which side to favor—the unemployed whose families are starving, or the taxpayers who are about to lose their homes. The county relief officials starting cutting down on jobs; men may no longer shovel sand six hours per day, but only four hours. A man is told that he can no longer have his $29 a month relief, because his daughter has a job which pays $50 a month, and a family of half a dozen people are supposed to get along on that. We try to economize in the cost of government, which means that more people are thrown out of jobs and get a dole instead of a salary. In the first four months of this year Los Angeles County took on 63,000 new persons as objects of charity; and in the months of May, June, and July there were added 322,500. This sounds incredible, but it stands in the County records: 75,000 new charity "cases" in three months, each "case" involving 4.3 persons.

It is manifest that this cannot go on. If it continues for the next fourteen months, I will find myself elected Governor of a bankrupt state with fifty-eight bankrupt counties and a hundred bankrupt cities and towns. The first plank of a political platform today must be to give the unemployed productive work and make them self-supporting. Why is this not done? Why has not every taxpayer demanded that the destitute shall no longer be fed out of the tax funds, but shall be set to work raising their own food and making their own shoes and clothing and shelter?

The answer is obvious. It is not the taxpayers who govern the State of California; it is the profit-takers represented by the heads of great corporations and banks. When the state buys goods for the unemployed, it buys them from private manufacturers, and that means profits. When the state gives money to the unemployed, the unemployed spend it in the channels of our profit system, and again we are subsidizing private industry. But if the state should put the unemployed to work, they would be entering into private competition with private industry. If the unemployed were to raise their own wheat, it would reduce the profits of the great feudal wheat-ranchers of our state. If they ground their own grain, it would interfere with the profits of the milling-trusts. If they baked their own bread, it would cut the profits of the baking trust—and all these operations would hurt the bankers who have the bonds of these corporations in their vaults. We are held tight in the grip of a system, which decrees that a million of our citizens shall suffer slow starvation, rather than let the stranglehold of Big Business slip.

So I say that the first essential of our new political program is a change of mind toward this problem. We must summon the courage to take the wild beast of greed by the beard. We have to say that human lives and human welfare are first. We have to recognize and proclaim the right of all human beings in this state to own or have access to the land and the means of production; the right to labor and produce the necessities of existence for themselves and their loved ones. We have to say it, and mean it, and act upon it, regardless of whatever it may do to any vested right of exploitation. Do you agree with me in that statement?

Very well then, we know what we are going to do: to return the unemployed to the land. That does not mean to dump them out on the desert without tools or training; still less does it mean to turn them over to real estate speculators. All over California today are thousands of our best ranches which have been sold to the state for taxes. There are counties in which more than 50 per cent of taxes are delinquent. A very slight change in the law will enable the state to keep and utilize the land which it is forced to acquire for taxes. Another law would enable the state to bid for and acquire land sold under foreclosure proceedings. For a very small outlay we can have the best agricultural land in the state, already under cultivation and equipped with machinery for operation.

My proposition is that we establish land colonies for the unemployed. These colonies will be run by the state under expert supervision. We have two kinds of agriculture in California at present: small-scale individualist ranching, in which the ranchers are in bondage to the banks, and large-scale operations, in which great land corporations work Chinese, Japanese, Hindus,

Filipinos, Mexicans, and other kinds of foreigners, under what amounts to peonage. I propose a third kind of agriculture. The state will set up colonies managed by trained men. It will provide adequate housing for workers, cooperative kitchens and cafeterias, and rooms for social purposes. It will guarantee a living at the outset, and when the colonies have got fairly under way, it will guarantee comfort. It will offer to every unemployed man and woman in the state a chance to become completely self-supporting. Can you approve that program?

[To the objection that many people had lost contact with the land and if put back on it would not know what to do, Sinclair responded:]

The answer is that great numbers of agricultural workers are now out of work, and also many ranchers are losing their land. Moreover, modern large-scale farming, such as we have on our bean, wheat, and rice ranches, is largely a proposition for mechanics. Again, we do not have to assume that all our colonies will be remote from cities and towns. There are tracts of valuable land held by speculators on the outskirts of all our cities, and here we can have our scientific horticulture, and grow for our own use every kind of vegetable and fruit. There are useful and beautiful plants that can be grown in California.

Do not assume that our land colonies will be bare and unattractive. If you elect a true Christian like myself as Governor, we shall remember that "Man does not live by bread alone." Every land colony will become a cultural center, with a branch library, a motion picture theatre, a lecture hall where we can explain the principles of cooperation. Our present class system takes it for granted that the workers have to live in squalid surroundings and be ignorant and dirty. If I am Governor of California, every man, woman and child will have opportunities of self-development, not merely physical but intellectual, moral and aesthetic. Does that meet your objections? . . .

["How will you provide for other kinds of unemployment besides that of farm-workers?" Sinclair was asked.] . . .

If a man knows how to make shoes or shirts or clothing, it

would be foolish to put him on the land. Let him stay in the city where he has a home, and produce for the landworkers who grow his food. In our state at the present time are thousands of factories which are idle, or half idle, and we shall immediately acquire them and start them up. A simple enabling act by the Legislature would give us the right to do this. Many factories are in the hands of the bankers who do not know what to do with them and would be glad to sell them for the amount of the bonds. We shall need a public corporation to handle our land colony development and another to handle our industrial production.

Let us begin with the absolute necessities, of course. Let us take laundries, bakeries, canneries, clothing, and shoe factories, cement plants, brick-yards, lumber-yards. Let us construct a complete industrial system, a new and self-maintaining world for our unemployed, in which they will live, having as few dealings as possible with our present world of speculators and exploiters. Every land colony will have its store where the products of the factory are sold. Every factory will have its kitchen and cafeteria, and its market where the products of the land are sold. Our system will maintain a trucking service to take the products of the cities to the land colonies and bring the food products to the factories. No middleman will get a finger into our pie.

[A realtor commented: "It seems to me that you will want a separate money system for such an organization. That is what I am interested in, having believed all my life in a commodity dollar."]

That is what we shall have in fact. Our workers will be paid mainly in scrip, which will be good for all the products of the system based upon cost. By this means the unemployed will be providing themselves with all the necessities of life, and our taxpayers will escape the burden which is breaking their backs."

["Will you permit the products of the system to be sold outside the system?" asked another realtor.]

You touch on a crucial point there, because that would be permitting the system to enter into competition with private producers, not merely for the support of the unemployed but for the making of profits. It seems to me that at the outset we will have our hands full to produce enough for the million unemployed and dependents of the unemployed in our state. As a matter of fact, of course, we shall be undermining private industry, by withdrawing the hundred million dollars a year which the state is now paying the unemployed, and which they are spending for goods. The present system is like a row of tin soldiers: when you permit the first to fall, he knocks down the second, which in turn knocks down the third. That is the terror which confronts Big Business today, and the reason we see the government propping up the railroads, propping up the insurance companies, propping up banks—not daring to let anything fail, until the whole thing fails at once.

[A law student asked how this plan would be financed, and the answer was:]

It appears that there are federal banking laws, passed in the money trust, to discourage states from engaging in banking. I propose that the State of California shall issue bonds of denominations as low as ten dollars, these bonds to bear low interest; some to be long term bonds, others to be redeemable at thirty days notice. This would practically be the same thing as a public savings bank, and the bonds would serve as a state currency. My campaign for office will be a crusade to persuade the people to withdraw their savings from private banks, and turn them over to the state to be used for the development of a state system of industrial production. "Lend your money to California and not to the bankers; let your money work for you and not against you." It would not be very long, I think, before the private bankers would be begging the state to buy their beautiful marble palaces at cost, and we should put an end to the private control of credit, which is the taproot of our troubles. Could the Democratic party of California be won to that program? . . .

The cause of our present Depression is the concentration of wealth in the hands of a small class. Income is going to be redistributed in the United States by one of two methods, either by legal enactments or by violent revolution; and we have not much longer in which to make the choice. I do not need to point out to you the situation today. We have passed a sales tax which puts the burden of the support of the state upon the poor. Governor Rolph signed that bill and vetoed the income tax bill. He is beginning to realize what a blunder he made, and is trying to put the blame off on others. . . .

If I beat him, I will kill the sales tax and substitute a tax on stock exchange transactions. Let Wall Street pay the sales tax! Also, a state income tax which will take at least 30 per cent of all incomes beyond $50,000. They take that much in England. And let any person who inherits more than $50,000 pay 50 per cent to the State.

["Won't that drive capital out of the State?" Sinclair was asked.] It will drive money out, of course, but it won't drive the land out and it won't drive the factories out, and we do not have to worry about the cash, because if we put our people at productive labor they will soon create plenty of wealth in California, and we can cheerfully do without the parasites and speculators. When word goes over the country what we are up to, there will be tens of thousands of able-bodied workers coming in our direction, and under the new system we can put them to work and they will add to our wealth and taxing power. When we make the unemployed self-supporting, we no longer have to be afraid of them.

Of course, for the starting of our land colonies we shall need a great deal of money. If we issue bonds, we have to provide for the interest and a sinking fund. Let us reform our tax system, and put the burden of supporting the state upon those who can afford to carry it. I propose that all homes assessed at less than $3,000 shall be exempt from taxation. Anybody who lives in that poor a home in these times needs help and not taxing. Homes of from $3,000 to $5,000 pay a normal rate, and for each additional $5,000 we add one-half of 1 per cent. That means that if you live in a $100,000 home you will pay a tax of about 11 per cent, and if you don't care to pay that, the state will take over your mansion and turn it into a public institution for orphan children, or for the aged, or for those who have acquired tuberculosis by slaving twelve hours a day in a department store or a restaurant kitchen.

There should be a graduated tax on all idle and unused land. That will put the speculators out of business, and provide us with the land for our colonies, and with sites for our factories and workers' homes. In addition, we shall boost the tax on public utilities and on the banks. From these sources we will get money for old age pensions, and pensions for the support of widows and orphans and the sick and incapacitated. Thus, you see, our program is completed, and there can be no more poverty in California. . . .

That is the Two-Year-Plan for California. . . . If I am your candidate for Governor it will be for the purpose of putting that across. Let me make plain that being Governor means nothing to me personally. I do not need fame; I get that by writing books, which are being translated into some fifty languages all over the world. I do not need money, for during these years of Depression I have been able to earn somewhat more with my pen than the State of California pays to its governor. But I cannot enjoy the comforts of home, and the freedom of work and recreation which I have been able to earn somewhat more with my pen than the me suffering for lack of the common necessities. That is why I am here tonight—to find out what is the reaction of a group of Democratic Party workers to this Plan. . . .

I am ready to go ahead with you. I repeat the slogan for our campaign:

END POVERTY IN CALIFORNIA.

HUEY LONG, 1893–1935

☆ Every Man a King: Share Our Wealth

THE LAST TWO LINES OF HUEY LONG's favorite poem read:

> "I am the master of my fate,
> I am the captain of my soul."

But while he may have been captain of his soul enough to become virtual dictator of the state of Louisiana, Huey Long was not master of his fate enough to prevent an assassin's bullet from cutting him down at the age of forty-two, just as he was thinking of running for the office of President of the United States.

Huey Long was born in a four-room log house on a 320-acre tract in Winn Parish, Louisiana. He was the seventh of nine children. Winn was a center of Populism in Louisiana; at one time the town had elected a Socialist slate. But although the Longs were radical, they were not Socialists.

Huey bragged that he was "behind the plow" from an early age until he was thirteen, when he became a printer, then a book salesman. At fifteen he represented his high school at a debating rally where he received honorable mention; a year later he won third place and a scholarship to Louisiana State University. He was not able to take advantage of the scholarship because it did not include living expenses and books. He became a house-to-house salesman, a traveling salesman. After seven months of intensive study at Tulane, he was admitted to the bar in 1915.

He was an effective orator, and his reputation as a lawyer spread. At the age of twenty-five Long ran for his first public office. He was elected to the State Railroad Commission, where he began his attack on the utilities, calling them "Lords of Wall Street."

In 1924, at the age of thirty-one, he was a candidate for governor of Louisiana but was defeated by a few thousand votes. Four years later he campaigned again with a phrase adapted from William Jennings Bryan: "Every man a King but no one wears a crown." He was elected. No one wore a crown—except Huey Long.

The new governor was not so much interested in money as he was in power, and he immediately began to push his legislation—a massive highway program including new bridges, increased school appropriations and free text books, and charity hospitals, all of which had been neglected by the previous administrations. He replaced anti-Long men with his own.

His was the power. He called a special session of the legislature to pass an occupation tax on refined crude oil. The opposition objected; they saw this as part of Long's dictatorship. They demanded his impeachment, charging him with various impeachable acts including plotting the assassination of a political foe. The procedure was dropped when it became apparent that no two-thirds vote would be obtained, and the Senate adjourned *sine die*.

He nicknamed himself "Kingfish" during one of his political

battles. The name came from the then popular "Amos 'n' Andy" radio show in which one of the characters was "Kingfish of the Mystic Knights of the Sea." Long was sitting in on one of the hearings of the Highway Commission regarding awards, when it was pointed out that the commission must make the awards and not the governor. "I am participating here anyway, gentlemen," Governor Long said. "For the present you can call me the 'Kingfish.' " It was an appellation that stuck.

In 1930 the governor was elected to the United States Senate, but he did not take his seat until a year and a half later. He remained in Louisiana because he feared that once he left the governor's office it would be taken over by his political enemy, the lieutenant-governor. During this period, the president pro tem of the Senate ruled the state.

Long's nostrum was "Share the Wealth."

"I had come to the U.S. Senate," he wrote, "with only one project in mind, which was that by every means of action and persuasion I might do something to spread the wealth of the land among all of the people."

In 1932, during a pending tax-bill hearing, he proposed a resolution which provided "that the tax bills should be so revamped that no one should be allowed to have an income of more than a million dollars; that no person should inherit in a lifetime more than four million dollars without working for it."

Long was friendly to President Franklin D. Roosevelt and his administration during its early days, but he soon became disenchanted. He was suspicious of some of the President's associates, he disliked what he considered the conservatism of some of the President's proposals, and he felt that many of the same bankers who had dominated President Hoover were also playing important roles with the new President. By 1934 he began to break with the Roosevelt administration. He staged one-man filibusters; he held up appropriations for what the administration considered important measures.

There was talk of a third party. Long admitted he was a candidate for the presidency of the United States.

While in the U.S. Senate, Huey Long wrote a book in which he outlined his plans, aspirations, and actions during his imaginary first days in the White House. The book was published posthumously. Titled *My First Days in the White House,* Long named his cabinet: Franklin D. Roosevelt, Secretary of the Navy; Herbert Hoover, Secretary of Commerce; Senator Borah of Idaho, Secretary of State; General Smedley D. Butler, Secretary of War; former Governor Alfred Smith, Director of the Budget.

The day he was shot, Senator Long was directing the passage of several bills in the Louisiana House of Representatives building. The bills were directed at strengthening his hold on the state's politics as well as doing battle with the New Deal. His assassin, killed by the state police, was the son-in-law of a leader in the Long opposition. The Senator had sponsored a bill to gerrymander the district boundaries from which his political enemy was elected to reassure his defeat in the next election.

When informed of the shooting, and before the Senator died, President Roosevelt commented: "I regret the attempt made upon the life of Senator Long of Louisiana. The spirit of violence is un-American."

Socialist Norman Thomas: "It is too early to speculate confidently on the significance of Huey Long's work and the manner of his death. It is a tragedy that his dictatorship was not corrected by orderly processes of political education but that a dictator was killed by an assassin. . . . The ablest and most colorful forerunner of American fascism is dead."

Publisher Frank E. Gannett: "I recognized that he was one of the ablest men in the Senate and a dynamic force in America. This fact made him a menacing figure. If he had achieved his ambition, all America would be ruled by a dictator."

In his eulogy at Senator Long's funeral, the Rev. Gerald L. K. Smith, a Long enthusiast, said the Senator would be remembered "as long as hungry bodies cry for food."

★ SHARE-THE-WEALTH

I had been in the United States Senate only a few days when I began my effort to make the battle for a distribution of wealth among all the people a national issue for the coming elections. On July 2, 1932, pursuant to a promise made, I heard Franklin Delano Roosevelt, accepting the nomination of the Democratic party at the Chicago convention for President of the United States, use the following words:

"Throughout the nation, men and women, forgotten in the political philosophy of the government for the last years, look to us here for guidance and for a more equitable opportunity to share in the distribution of the national wealth."

It therefore seemed that all we had to do was to elect our candidate, and that then my object in public life would be accomplished.

But, a few nights before the presidential election, I listened to Mr. Herbert Hoover deliver his speech in Madison Square Garden, and he used these words:

"My conception of America is a land where men and women may walk in ordered liberty, where they may enjoy the advantages of wealth, not concentrated in the hands of a few, but diffused through the lives of all."

So it seemed that so popular had become the demand for a redistribution of wealth in America, that Mr. Hoover had been compelled to somewhat yield to that for which Mr. Roosevelt had previously declared without reservation.

It is not out of place for me to say that the support which I brought to Mr. Roosevelt to secure his nomination and election as President (and without which it is hardly probable he would ever have been nominated), was on the assurances which I had that he would take the proper stand for the redistribution of wealth in the campaign. He did that much, in the *campaign*;

From Forrest Davis, *Huey Long* (New York, 1935).

but after his election, what then? I need not tell you the story. We have not time to cry over our disappointments, over promises which others did not keep, and over pledges which were broken.

Even after the present President of the United States had thrown down the pledge which he had made time after time, and rather indicated the desire, instead, to have all the common people of America fed from a half starvation dole, while the plutocrats of the United States were allowed to wax richer and richer—even after that, I made the public proposition that if he would return to his promise, and carry out the pledge given to the people and to me, that regardless of all that had passed, I would again support his administration to the limit of my ability.

Of course, however, I was not blind; I had long since come to the understanding that he was chained to other purposes and to other interests which made impossible his keeping the words which he uttered to the people.

I delayed using this form of call to the members and well-wishers of the Share Our Wealth Society until we had progressed so far as to convince me that we could succeed either before or in the next national election of November 1936. Until I became certain that the spirit of the people could be aroused throughout the United States, and that, without any money (because I have none, except such little as I am given), the people could be persuaded to perfect organizations throughout the counties and communities of the country, I did not want to give false hopes to any of those engaged with me in this noble work. But I have seen and checked back enough, based upon the experiences which I have had in my public career, to know that we can, with much more ease, win the present fight, either between now and the next national campaign, or else in the next national campaign—I say with much more ease than many other battles which I have won in the past, but which did not mean near so much.

It is impossible for the United States to preserve itself as a republic or as a democracy, when six hundred families own more of this nation's wealth—in fact, twice as much—as all the balance of the people put together. Ninety-six per cent of our people live below the poverty line, while 4 per cent own 87 per cent of the wealth. America can have enough for all to live in comfort and still permit millionaires to own more than they can ever spend, and to have more than they can ever use; but America cannot allow the multi-millionaires and the billionaires, a mere handful of them, to own everything unless we are willing to inflict starvation upon 125 million people.

We looked upon the year 1929 as the year when too much was produced for the people to consume. We were told, and we believed, that the farmers raised too much cotton and wool for the people to wear, and too much food for the people to eat. Therefore, much of it went to waste, some rotted, and much of it was burned or thrown into the river or into the ocean. But, when we picked up the bulletin of the Department of Agriculture for that year 1929, we found that, according to the diet which they said everyone should eat in order to be healthy, multiplying it by 120 million, the number of people we had in 1929, had all of our people had the things which the Government said they should eat in order to live well, we did not have enough even in 1929 to feed the people. In fact, these statistics show that in some instances we had from one-third to one-half less than the people needed, particularly of milk, eggs, butter, and dried fruits.

But why in the year 1929 did it appear we had too much? Because the people could not buy the things they wanted to eat, and needed to eat. That showed the need for and duty of the Government then and there, to have forced a sharing of our wealth, and a redistribution, and Roosevelt was elected on the pledge to do that very thing.

But what was done? Cotton was plowed under the ground. Hogs and cattle were burned by the millions. The same was done to wheat and corn, and farmers were paid starvation money not to raise and not to plant because of the fact that we did not want so much because of people having no money with which to buy. Less and less was produced, when already there was less produced than the people needed if they ate what the Government said they needed to sustain life. God forgive those rulers who burned hogs, threw milk in the river, and plowed under cotton while little children cried for meat and milk and something to put on their naked backs! . . .

And now, what of America? Will we allow the political sports, the high-heelers, the wiseacres, and those who ridicule us in our misery and poverty to keep us from organizing these societies in every hamlet so that they may bring back to life this law and custom of God and of this country? Is there a man or woman with a child born on the earth, or who expects ever to have a child born on earth, who is willing to have it raised under the present-day practices of piracy, where it comes into life burdened with debt, condemned to a system of slavery by which the sweat of its brow throughout its existence must go to satisfy the vanity and the luxury of a leisurely few, who can never be made to see that they are destroying the root and branch of the greatest country ever to have risen? Our country is calling; the laws of the Lord are calling; the graves of our forefathers would open today if their occupants could see the bloom and flower of their creation withering and dying because the greed of the financial masters of this country has starved and withheld from mankind those things produced by his own labor. To hell with the ridicule of the wise street-corner politician! Pay no attention to any newspaper or magazine that has sold its columns to perpetuate this crime against the people of America! Save this country! Save mankind! Who can be wrong in such a work, and who cares what consequences may come following the mandates of the Lord of the Pilgrims, of Jefferson, Webster, and Lincoln? He who falls in this fight falls in the radiance of the future. Better to make this fight and lose than to be a party to a system that strangles humanity.

It took the genius of labor and the lives of all Americans to produce the wealth of this land. If any man, or one hundred men, wind up with all that has been produced by 125 million people, that does not mean that those one hundred men produced the wealth of the country: it means that those one hundred men stole, directly or indirectly, what 125 million people produced. Let no one tell you that the money masters made this country. They did no such thing. Very few of them ever hewed the forest; very few ever hacked a cross-tie; very few ever nailed a board; fewer of them ever laid a brick. Their fortunes came from manipulated finance, control of government, rigging of markets, the spider webs that have grabbed all businesses; they grab the fruits of the land, the conveniences and the luxuries that are intended for 125 million people, and run their heelers to our meetings to set up the cry, "We earned it honestly." The Lord says they did no such thing. The voices of our forefathers say they did no such thing. In this land of abundance, they have no right to impose starvation, misery and pestilence for the purpose of vaunting their own pride and greed.

Whenever any newspaper or person, whether he be a private individual or an officer of the government, says that our effort to limit the size of fortunes is contrary to the principles of our government, he is too ignorant to deserve attention. Either he knows that what he says is untrue, or else he is too ignorant to know what the truth is. . . .

We are calling upon people whose souls cannot be cankered by the lure of wealth and corruption. Fear of ridicule? Fear of reprisal? Fear of being taken off of the starvation dole? It is too late for our people to have such fears. I have undergone them all. There is nothing under the canopy of heaven which has not been sent to ridicule and embarrass my efforts in this work. And yet, despite such ridicule, face to face in any argument I have yet to see the one of them who dares to gainsay the principle to share our wealth. On the contrary, when their feet are put to the fire, each and every one of them declare that they are in favor of sharing the wealth and the redistribution of wealth. But then some get suddenly ignorant and say they do not know how to do it. Oh, ye of little faith! God told them how. Apparently they are too lazy in mind or body to want to learn, so long as their ignorance is for the benefit of the six hundred ruling families of America who have forged chains of slavery around the wrists and ankles of 125 million free-born citizens. Lincoln freed the black man, but today the white and the black are shackled far worse than any colored person in 1860.

The debt structure alone has condemned the American people to bondage worse than the Egyptians ever forged upon the Israelites. Right now, America's debts, public and private, are $262 billion, and nearly all of it has been laid on the shoulders of those who have nothing. It is a debt of more than $2,000 to every man, woman, or child. They can never pay it. They never have paid such debts. No one expects them to pay it. But such is the new form of slavery imposed upon the civilization of America; and the street-corner sports and hired political tricksters, with the newspapers whom they have perverted, undertake to laugh to scorn the efforts of the people to throw off this yoke and bondage; but we were told to do so by the Lord, we were told to do so by the Pilgrim fathers, we were guaranteed such should be done by our Declaration of Independence and by the Constitution of the United States.

Here is the whole sum and substance of the Share Our Wealth movement:

1. Every family to be furnished by the government a homestead allowance, free of debt, of not less than one-third the average family wealth of the country, which means, at the lowest, that every family shall have the reasonable comforts of life up to a value of from $5,000 to $6,000. No person to have a fortune, of more than one hundred to three hundred times the average family fortune, which means that the limit to fortunes is between $1.5 million and $5 million with annual capital levy taxes imposed on all above $1 million.

2. The yearly income of every family shall be not less than one-third of the average family income, which means that, according to the estimates of the statisticians of the U.S. government and Wall Street, no family's annual income would be less than from $2,000 to $2,500. No yearly income shall be allowed to any person larger than from one hundred to three hundred times the size of the average family income, which means that no person would be allowed to earn in any year more than from

$600,000 to $1.8 million, all to be subject to present income tax laws.

3. To limit or regulate the hours of work to such an extent as to prevent over-production; the most modern and efficient machinery would be encouraged so that as much would be produced as possible so as to satisfy all demands of the people, but to also allow the maximum time to the workers for recreation, convenience, education, and luxuries of life.

4. An old age pension to the persons over sixty.

5. To balance agricultural production with what can be consumed according to the laws of God, which includes the preserving and storing of surplus commodities to be paid for and held by the Government for the emergencies when such are needed. Please bear in mind, however, that when the people of America have had money to buy things they needed, we have never had a surplus of any commodity. This plan of God does not call for destroying any of the things raised to eat or wear, nor does it countenance wholesale destruction of hogs, cattle, or milk.

6. To pay the veterans of our wars what we owe them and to care for their disabled.

7. Education and training for all children to be equal in opportunity in all schools, colleges, universities, and other institutions for training in the professions and vocations of life; to be regulated on the capacity of children to learn, and not on the ability of parents to pay the costs. Training for life's work to be as much universal and thorough for all walks of life as has been the training in the arts of killing.

8. The raising of revenue and taxes for the support of this program to come from the reduction of swollen fortunes from the top, as well as for the support of public works to give employment whenever there may be any slackening necessary in private enterprise.

Let everyone who feels he wishes to help in our work start right out and go ahead. . . . The reward and compensation is the salvation of humanity. Fear no opposition.

FATHER CHARLES E. COUGHLIN 1891–

☆ The National Union for Social Justice

"I AM NOT FORGETFUL that the path of my pilgrimage is both treacherous and narrow," orated Father Charles E. Coughlin in a radio broadcast of his "Golden Hour of the Little Flower" series during the 1930-31 season.

"On the one side there are the quicksands of idealism, of radical socialism, in whose depths there are buried both the dreams of the poet and the ravings of the revolutionist. On the pathway's other side there are the smiling acres of Lotus Land where it is always afternoon, always springtime, always inactivity."

This was the radio priest's opening salvo to a nation in the midst of economic depression.

Father Coughlin was born in Hamilton, Ontario. His father was American, his mother Canadian. At the age of twenty he received an honors degree in philosophy from the University of Toronto. Three careers lured him—religion, politics, and sociology. He was to gain notoriety in two of these—the church and politics.

Ordained a priest in 1915, Father Coughlin was assigned to assist at several parishes around Detroit. Ten years later he was named pastor of a parish serving twenty-five families in Royal Oak, Michigan, a small community outside Detroit. That same year, 1925, he met a Detroit radio station manager to whom he confided the difficulties of raising money for a small parish. He added that there was antagonism in the community, too, as shown by the cross that had been burned on the lawn of the church by the Ku Klux Klan.

In the course of the conversation the station manager agreed to give the young priest free radio time to help him raise funds and alleviate community hostilities.

The first program was broadcast on October 3, 1926. In the beginning, he aimed his sermons primarily at children, with periodic comments on the political and economic scene. Father Coughlin, with a resonant brogue and a colorful vocabulary, soon had a national radio network program on Sundays. The polls showed he had a wider listening audience than such then-popular radio programs as "Amos 'n' Andy," Ed Wynn, and "Dr. Fu Manchu." He began to speak out against the dangers of communism. He urged American capitalists to provide the American worker with a decent standard of living so he would not be lured into the communist camp. When the House Committee to Investigate Communist Activities, chaired by Congressman Hamilton Fish, held hearings in Detroit, the Catholic priest was a star witness. He called himself a "religious Walter Winchell."

As the Depression grew more acute, the radio priest accelerated his attack on the ills which permeated the nation. He urged a return to the Christian principles of charity. His views on social justice were in line with the *Rerum Novarum* of Pope Leo XIII.

The Royal Oak priest was one of the first supporters of President Franklin D. Roosevelt and referred to him as a "President who thinks right, who lives for the common man."

As Father Coughlin saw it, the major problem facing the country was a monetary one, and many of his sermons touched on the money question. In his broadcasts he praised the New Deal, although he was critical of some elements in it. He hoped that FDR would extend his economic reforms.

In his loyalty to President Roosevelt, Coughlin coined such phrases as "Roosevelt or Ruin" and, later, "Roosevelt and Recovery." His sermons were punctured with such phrases as "international bankers," "Wall Street," "money changers."

"It is still impossible to assess Coughlin's role in the first fourteen months of the New Deal," observes Charles J. Tull in his *Father Coughlin and the New Deal.* Yet, he asserts, "It is clear that the priest at first considered himself an unofficial partner and spokesman of the administration, a delusion that Roosevelt deliberately chose to foster until November of 1933."

"More than ever I am in favor of the New Deal," the Reverend told his followers. But letters from his millions of listeners—sometimes at the rate of twenty thousand a day—continued to complain of economic plights.

It was not long before Father Coughlin's disillusionment with the Roosevelt administration began. Soon the priest proclaimed that the old parties are all but dead and suggested that "the skeletons of their putrefying carcasses" be relinquished "to the halls of a historical museum." The breaking point was the Roosevelt administration's support of the World Court. "I will not support a New Deal which protects plutocrats and comforts communists," he cried.

On the domestic scene, Father Coughlin did not feel the administration was doing enough, and on the foreign scene he felt it was doing too much. Though he objected to government "going into business," he demanded government "ownership of the banks."

In November 1934, Father Coughlin announced the formation of the National Union for Social Justice, with a platform of sixteen points, six of which dealt with monetary policy. He insisted that it was not his intention to create a third party. The function of the National Union would be to act as a pressure group. Soon, however, it was endorsing congressional candidates, and in the 1936 election Father Coughlin joined with Dr. Francis Townsend, Gerald L. K. Smith, and Congressman Walter Lemke of North Dakota to support Representative Lemke for President on the new Union party ticket.

The Detroit priest observed bitterly, "It is not pleasant for me who coined the phrase 'Roosevelt or Ruin'—a phrase based on promises—to voice such passionate words. But I am constrained to admit that 'Roosevelt' and 'Ruin' is the order of the day because the money changers have not been driven from the temple." At the same time he described the Republicans as "Punch and Judy Republicans, whose actions and words were dominated by the ventriloquists of Wall Street."

The Lemke national ticket did not cull even a million votes, although Lemke was re-elected to his congressional seat on the Republican ticket. Coughlin had promised to go off the air if his candidate did not get nine million votes for President. He did not keep his promise. Nor did he step out of the public eye. His activities expanded into other areas. His magazine *Social Justice,* for instance, started to print the discredited anti-Semitic "Protocols of Zion." He associated with the Christian Front. He accused the Jews of starting World War II. He turned his attention to blocking the revision of the Neutrality Act of 1937. He was an active isolationist.

In 1940 the late Archbishop Mooney forced Father Coughlin to abandon his radio programs. Two years later his magazine was barred from the mails, charged with violation of the sedition law. Father Coughlin remained the parish priest until May 1966, when the Roman Catholic Archbishop of Detroit announced that Father Coughlin had asked to be relieved of his duties because of "impaired health."

★ IDLE CREDIT

It is evident to any thinking citizen that the economic breakdown which we have experienced cannot be cured by a single remedy. Our national ailments are too numerous and diverse. Finance, industry, labor, agriculture and politics, like five different organs of the economic body, are afflicted all at one time. In one sense, our national sickness is similar to a patient whose heart, lungs, spine, stomach and brains have suffered from the ravages of specifically different diseases. When planning for the patient's recovery, it is necessary, first, to place him in the environment of the hospital of good morals. Once situated there, it is then scientific to ascertain the causes which produced the diseases. This progressive step is followed by the skillful application of medicine and surgery.

There is no candy-coated pill which will cure a broken spine and heal a diseased heart. There is no panacea or nostrum which will restore America to prosperity.

With this homely metaphor in mind, may I partially develop for you the thought that the National Union for Social Justice, while abhorring all panaceas, is dedicated to the theory that afflicted America cannot be restored to healthful prosperity unless it submits to a program that is designed to cure its various major ailments.

That is why our prescriptions, as it were, could not be compounded in one bottle. That is why sixteen different treatments, each designed for a specific ailment, were incorporated in our program for social justice. . . .

From "A Series of Lectures on Social Justice," by the Rev. Chas. E. Coughlin, published by the Radio League of the Little Flower, Royal Oak, Michigan, 1935.

I

Relative to the disease of unprofitable unemployment and a just, living annual wage for all citizens willing and able to work, it is well to recapitulate the following points.

It is certain beyond dispute that while production has increased, employment decreased. It is likewise certain that the laborer has been laboring at a loss. According to the American Federation of Labor's survey, a family of five required, in 1934, $1,912 to live and meet the necessary humble expenses. The actual average wage which approximately fourteen million laborers received was $1,120.36½. Thus, our laboring class, who were fortunate enough to secure employment, were living and working at a loss of $792 per year. Disregarding for the moment the eleven million unemployed, the National Union realizes that the unhealthy condition of low wages which has been prevalent for many years must be rectified. It views with concern the ever-increasing profits gained by the industrialist and the stockholders in mass production corporations. Therefore, unafraid to face realities and deeming it entirely radical to nurse the exorbitant concentration of wealth resulting from an age that is dedicated to mass productionism, we set down the principle that the profits accruing to industry must be more equitably divided with the laborer. The laborer is justified in demanding a just and living annual wage if, through no fault of his own, he is forced to spend a portion of his time in idleness.

The acceptance of this principle is advantageous to both the laborer and to the industrialist. Without purchasing power in the hands of the laborer, profits will cease flowing into the purses of the industrialist.

II

It is evident to every observing person that agriculture is suffering as much, if not more, than labor. Therefore, the National Union, realizing how imperative it is to cure this economic ill, prescribed the principle that the American farmer must receive for his efforts the cost of production plus a fair profit. If one diagnoses the agricultural disease he will discover some alarming facts. In 1920 the value of farm property in America was $78.5 billion. In the ten prosperous years immediately following, this value depreciated to $58 billion—a loss of $20 billion! . . .

Forty billion dollars, or more than 50 per cent, has been wiped away from the value of American farms in a period of fourteen years!

This serious economic ailment becomes more alarming when we learn from official figures that the cash income to farmers has been decreasing with a rapidity that is startling. In 1929 the farmers' financial receipts amounted to $10.5 billion. Last year, despite the agricultural doles administered by the AAA, the American farmer received only $6 billion. His revenue had decreased by 40 per cent!

Here we have one-third of our population suffering from an economic malady that will be fatal to our national life unless it is cured immediately. Does any fair-minded critic discover the taint of radicalism in our principle which prescribes not only the cost of production but also a fair profit for the farmer?

III

When I speak of the American farmer and laborer I am speaking of those persons who are responsible for carrying the major portion of our nation's tax burden. Forced in common by social injustice to eke out a profitless existence, how can these persons hope to meet the exorbitant demands of taxation?

Does not this aggravated situation claim our common attention? Its analysis shows that we have one federal government and forty-eight state governments each supreme in its proper sphere. Under the forty-eight states there are 3,070 counties, 16,000 cities, towns and villages, 128,000 school districts, 19,000 townships, and more than 14,000 special assessment districts. In all there are

182,658 governments or agencies or districts each with its own power to levy and assess taxes.

The National Union, believing in the simplification of government, prescribes that, at least in part, the burden of taxation should be lifted from the slender revenues of those laborers and farmers who pay the major portion of this bill. With this principle in mind, we suggest that thousands of our present taxing governments and agencies be coordinated or abolished. For the alleviation of the poor and the security of the wealthy we advocate that taxation should be organized upon the theory of the ownership of wealth and according to one's capacity to pay. To encourage private ownership, we advocate that the first $5,000 of real property wealth possessed by an individual should be exempted from taxation. The iniquitous sales tax whose burden rests upon the great mass of people living below the American standard of decency should be abolished. The excise taxes on tobacco and on gasoline, both of which bear more heavily upon the shoulders of the poor than upon those of the rich, should be eliminated.

If the perfection of citizenship is related to property ownership, why not encourage this by deed as well as by word? "Every man a citizen in deed as well as in name" should be our common ambition.

Thus it is in keeping with the philosophy of social justice to substitute for the multitude of taxes now being levied a simplified system of equitable taxation. Basing the rule for assessment upon one's wealth, the National Union prescribes that those who possess less than $5,000 of real wealth should be exempt from any federal, state, or land tax. From this point forward, all owners would be obliged to pay their proportionate land tax.

Over and above this land tax, those possessing between $5,000 and $10,000 worth of any wealth should be assessed 1 per cent for state and federal purposes; 2 per cent for those in the $25,000 classification; 3 per cent for those in the $50,000 classification—and upwards, by graduation, until 10 per cent would be levied on those whose capacity to pay is so limitless that this assessment in no way would injure their personal fortune. . . .

IV

While dwelling upon this subject of taxation let me clarify the attitude of the National Union on those bonds which are classified as non-productive and which, under our present system, are generally free from taxation. Most bonds have been issued for productive purposes such as school bonds, highway bonds, railroad bonds. Others were issued to supply money for digging shell holes, for filling hospitals with cripples, for destroying cities and fertilizing the fields of France with the corpses of young men. Is it patriotic to profiteer upon bloodshed? Is it just to profit upon human misery? The National Union prescribes that all these non-productive bonds should be recalled. It does not advocate that currency be traded for these bonds, but it does suggest that the coupons on these interest-bearing bonds be reduced to a minimum and subjected to taxation. Many billions of dollars of our wealth is represented by these bonds which, under modern capitalism, permit their holders to escape taxation. This burden, then, is, at present, borne by the poor—who were not able to indulge in the purchase of such choice and unjust profit-making securities. All bonds should be taxed.

V

Pursuing our principles in the program for social justice, permit me to refer to the attitude of the National Union toward public and private property. In diagnosing the economic ills of America we are convinced that there is a growing tendency to diminish the ownership of private property. In one sense, there is too little of private ownership. This is caused, first, by an economic system which persistently tends to concentrate wealth in the hands of a few, and, second, by an obnoxious system of taxation which discourages private ownership.

On the other hand, there are some things which, by their nature, should be owned nationally or publicly. Among these things there are listed the Central Bank which will have the sole right of issuing, coining, and regulating the value of money be it currency or credit. In no sense does the National Union propose to nationalize any other bank. The local banking system must be kept intact. Its functions of safeguarding depositors' money and of extending local loans upon a reasonable basis must not be destroyed. It is regrettable that more than $773 million, or 23 per cent of the capital stock in these banks, is now owned by the government. It would be a benediction, however, if the government nationalized the Federal Reserve Bank, whose capital stock is valued at approximately $140 million.

Then there are the natural resources scattered throughout the nation. The ownership and development of Niagara Falls, of the St. Lawrence Waterway, which is capable of generating 1,200,000 horsepower, of Boulder Dam, of the Tennessee Valley project, of the Grand Coulee on the Colorado—these and other natural resources should be owned and developed by the nation. In no sense should they be farmed out for private exploitation. The National Union further subscribes in its principles to a permanent public works program of reforestation, of land reclamation, of slum clearance, of national highway building, and of other public activities whereat the idle factory workers may be employed during slack industrial seasons.

Relative to the many public utilities, the National Union regards the great majority of their holding companies as economic maladies. In many cases these holding companies were born in iniquity. By their nature they deceived the investing public. By their desire for greedy gain, oftentimes they marked up their values three, four, and five times the tangible value of their physical properties. On this false basis they sold their securities to an unsuspecting public.

However, the National Union is not convinced that the ownership and the operation of public utilities should be nationalized. We prescribe that these should be kept in private hands subject to governmental supervision. At all times we must avoid the communistic tendency to sovietize industry or public service enterprises. Two extremes confront us: the one is advocating the national ownership of those things which should be retained in private hands; the other is advocating and supporting the private ownership of those things which should be owned in public.

Thus, while we cling to this twofold principle of ownership—one public, the other private—let it also be noted that even private ownership must be subject to public regulation for the public good.

Relying upon that principle, the theory is sustained that, for the public welfare, the government may enact salutary laws to regulate not only personal liberties but also property and industrial liberties. Private ownership must be protected against corporate ownership. Small business must be safeguarded reasonably against monopolistic business. Were we to permit private ownership and small business gradually to be assimilated by corporate and monopolistic creations, then we are only preparing the way either for state capitalism or for communism.

VI

In the rapid resume of the economic ills of America and the citation of remedial principles which the National Union suggests as guides for treatment, I am well aware that the observant critic will suggest the question relative to unemployment, to the living annual wage, to a profitless farming, and to the program for public works: "What will we use for money?" Although he accepts the other principles and subscribes to their adoptions insofar as they are practical, he seriously doubts if the spine, which is labor, and the stomach, which is agriculture, can be cured.

It is readily admitted that these cannot be cured unless, first of all, the heart of the patient is cured so that it can supply the entire body with an abundant flow of healthy blood.

By the heart, I refer to banking. By the blood, I refer to money—both currency and credit.

Before I forsake the metaphor permit me to observe that the patient's heart is sorely misplaced and, as a result, the blood flow is totally inefficient. This organic ailment must be rectified immediately before we can discuss realistically a permanent public works program and profitable farming for the unemployed and the underpaid citizens of our nation.

In the United States there are more than fifteen thousand privately owned local banks. These banks are controlled either directly or indirectly, in matters of extending loans to industry, to commerce, or to individuals, by the gigantic bank known as the Federal Reserve Banking System, which is not owned in any shape, form, or manner by the government. It is purely a private corporation owned by a group of private bankers.

When we consider that at least 90 per cent of our money is credit money or check book money, it follows that, if the Federal Reserve Bank controls the credit policies of local banks, it controls 90 per cent of the nation's money. This was totally true until the Reconstruction Finance Corporation was established and is true, in a great degree, at the present moment.

The Constitution of our country explicitly states that Congress has the right to coin and regulate the value of money. Here, then, when confronted with the private ownership and control of money, is an organic misplacement of the heart upon which depends all of our economic activities.

In the cure of our financial ailments, the National Union prescribes the establishment of a government-owned Central Bank, subject to Congress, to replace the Federal Reserve Banking System. . . . This is an absolutely essential prescription which must be compounded and administered immediately before we can entertain valid hope for the patient's survival. . . .

My friends, our beloved nation is neither bankrupt nor verging upon bankruptcy, as the Federal Reservists intimate. According to the National Industrial Conference Board, there are approximately $200 billion of actual wealth and immediate potential wealth within our confines.

Credit, I repeat, represents at least 90 per cent of the money which we use in our daily domestic, commercial, and industrial lives. Under our present system where does this credit money originate? Briefly, the banks create credit. On the dollar you deposit, bankers were accustomed to lend ten credit dollars. Against the valuable stocks, bonds, and securities in their vaults they issued more credit. The total amount of credit, therefore, could never be more than ten times the actual money or wealth owned by the bankers. Today there is scarcely more than $30 billion of credit available under our present banking system because the theory of modern banking which operates on issuing credit against its privately owned property does not permit a further extension of credit. I repeat that the present actual wealth of the nation is practically $200 billion, although in 1920 it was estimated to be $488 billion. Thus, of this stupendous amount, at least $170 billion of credit is unattachable and therefore unusable by the Federal Reserve private banking system. Let me stress that point: the usable credit of this nation is, at present, limited and measured by the actual wealth owned and controlled by the bankers. It is not limited by the vast amount of wealth which is over and above what the bankers own. With this new viewpoint we discover that here is a new, uncharted ocean of available credit which, by its constituted authority, Congress may utilize, if it restores to itself its original right of coining and regulating the value of money for the benefit of the nation at large instead of permitting the ship of State to rust and rot upon the dry bottom of a private financial mud pond which has been drained dry. . . .

Idle factories and a population hungry for the goods which could be produced; unused wheat and pork and a hungry population suffering from undernourishment. Yes! Idle credit—and we fear to reach out and use it!

Last Sunday, my friends, I developed for you the fact that the United States government already owns 23 per cent of the capital stock of 13,896 banks, including 5,400-odd national banks, 958 state banks in the Federal Reserve System, 7,459 state banks not in the Federal Reserve System, and a few Morris Plan and industrial banks. By the investment of $773,344,000 of R.F.C. money belonging to the people of the United States, we already have secured a 23 per cent interest in the $3,319,000,000 total capital stock of 13,896 private banks. The figures I have quoted you are taken from a combined statement of the condition of all banks in the Federal Deposit Insurance Corporation, and the figures were as of June 30, 1934.

We are in the banking business today, but we are playing the game according to the bankers' rules. Instead of utilizing the power of eminent domain to extend the credit of the nation, we are content to piddle with the policies of utilizing the meager credit created by the bankers! However, I want to carry that thought one step further. I want to show you how far the United States government is in the business of bankers' banking today. When the financial system of the United States failed in 1929 and brought upon us one of those periodic depressions which has been our lot for over a century, the greatest bank in the world was formed. . . .

After 1929 the United States of America went into the banking business. The largest bank in the world has become the R.F.C., the Reconstruction Finance Corporation. Private credit collapsed; so the government of the United States started a bank to make loans and subscriptions to those institutions which the private banks of America could not handle. The banks themselves came to the R.F.C. for loans of $591 million, the railroads for $343 million, mortgage loan companies for $160 million, the Federal Land Bank for $116 million, the insurance companies for $30 million, the building and loan associations for $28 million, the Joint Stock Land Banks for $7.6 million, the Regional Agricultural Credit Corporation for $4.3 million—so that the total in loans and subscriptions outstanding on a single day, June 30, 1934, was $1,287,000,000. But all this time the government was in the old-fashioned banking business, content to use as a base of credit the privately owned loans which it borrowed from the banks. Although this appears to be contradictory and an insult to your intelligence, nevertheless it is the truth.

FATHER DIVINE, *ca.* 1865–1965

☆ Peace

FATHER DIVINE was "God" to members of the Peace Mission, and when he died on September 10, 1965, his death was seen as "only the throwing off of the physical body."

"I don't have to say I'm God," Father Divine would explain, "and I don't have to say I'm not God. I said there are thousands of people call me God. Millions of them. And there are millions of them call me the Devil, and I don't say I'm God and I don't say I am the Devil. But I produce God and shake the world with it."

He claimed to have transferred the spirit of his dead first wife, a Negro, into the body of his second wife, a twenty-one-year-old white girl from Canada. They had been married secretly for three months before he introduced her to the "angels" as "the Spotless Virgin Bride," claiming that she and his first wife were the same.

Although he did not say, "I'm God," Father Divine inferred that he had the power and the wrath of God. He gave as an example the judge who had sentenced him to six months in jail and imposed a $500 fine for Father Divine's disturbing the peace and making a public nuisance of one of his first "heavens" in Sayville, Long Island. When the judge dropped dead several days after the trial, Father Divine told his following: "I hated to do it."

Father Divine's nostrum was a mass cooperative based on the banquet table. It offered security not only in such physical necessities as food and shelter but in the ego; it offered social status and an escape from the realities of life.

Father Divine provided equality, grace, food, and shelter. The bywords were:

"Peace, it's wonderful!"

"Peace"—the greeting between members.

"Father will provide. Thank you, Father. Thank you."

"The story of Father Divine," reported the Associated Press, "marred by legal troubles and once interrupted by jail, is one of belief mixed with superstition, of faith and the filling of an empty stomach."

The movement was given impetus by the Depression of the 1930's after Father Divine came to Harlem.

Who was Father Divine? Where was he born? When? These questions remain unanswered. His age at his death was reported to be about one hundred. He answered all questions as to when he was born with: "Before Abraham was." Several biographers said he was George Baker from Georgia, but this Father Divine denied.

His first "inspiration" was a Negro Holy Roller, Father Jehovia. Father Divine began to think of himself as God and preached this. He was arrested in Valdosta, Georgia, and declared insane. When he was released he came to New York. Father's first "heaven" was in Manhattan; then it moved to Brooklyn. In 1919, as Major Morgan J. Divine, he purchased a home in Sayville, Long Island. This home, which was operated jointly with Mother Divine, opened its doors to all. Father found jobs for his followers. "Angels" joined the "heaven," many coming from Harlem. The banquets were happy events, with shouts of joy, singing, and praying.

But the citizens of Sayville did not take kindly to the turmoil. Father Divine was arrested and charged with violating the peace.

The "heaven" was moved to Harlem, where Father Divine's movement grew rapidly. Followers came to live at the "heaven." When they joined, they deposited all their earthly possessions—money, property, insurance—with the Kingdom. Those who lived outside the "heaven" but were members gave the Kingdom their money after having provided minimum requirements for themselves.

Father Divine enjoyed the good life—from a second-hand Rolls Royce to $500 silk suits. Yet he had no personal estate and paid no income tax.

When they entered the "heaven" to live, husbands and wives, parents and children were separated. Father Divine preached that, once having joined the Peace Mission Movement, the "angels" entered a new life. As part of this, his followers assumed new names such as Miss Charity, Job Patience, Angel Flash, Peach Samuel, Bunch of Love. His second wife's name is Sweet Angel.

Although Father Divine promised security and faith, illness had no place in the Kingdom; those who became ill were considered not to be true believers and were dropped. Many of these died in hospitals and state institutions. The "angels" accepted a code when they joined: no smoking or drinking, no obscenity, no vulgarity, no profanity, no undue mixing of the sexes, no accepting of gifts, tips, or bribes.

"When I have sex relations with you," Father Divine reportedly told an "angel," one of his secretaries, "I am bringing your desire to the surface so that I can eliminate it."

Father Divine also insisted that his followers pay back debts—both old and new. Issue after issue of his newspaper *New Day* carried letters from lenders who reported a debt paid by an "angel." Typical was a letter in the July 7, 1945 issue, from the acting director, Bureau of Public Welfare, town of Montclair, New Jersey, telling Father Divine that "Star Hope of 2783 Eighth Avenue, N.Y.C., has completed repaying financial assistance given her some years ago."

During the 1930's Father Divine participated in parades and demonstrations in New York City for the relief of certain ills during the Depression. His "angels" even marched in a Communist May Day Parade. In 1936 the Peace Mission Movement held the International Righteous Government convention in New York City and adopted the Righteous Government platform.

When Father Divine died in 1965 in his thirty-two room French Gothic mansion in Woodmount, near Philadelphia, the movement controlled properties estimated at $10 million. Attending physicians said Father Divine's death was caused by lung congestion. But Sweet Angel insists that Father has just "gone away for a spell, that he will come back to earth in bodily form and not reincarnated either."

"Father did give me a position alongside him that he has given to no other one," Sweet Angel told a *New York Times* reporter, and she is now "the center of attraction."

★ FATHER DIVINE'S PEACE MISSION

Peace to all! We, the inter-racial, international, inter-religious, interdenominational and non-partisan coworkers of Father Divine's Peace Mission and its Department of Righteous Government, greet all mankind with Peace in the light of this new day and dispensation in which we are now living since the advent of Father Divine—Whom twenty-two million have recognized as their Savior come to earth again in bodily form—we are advocating

---

Platform of Father Divine's Peace Mission Movement as adopted by the International Righteous Government Convention, New York City, July 10–12, 1936.

Righteousness, Justice, and Truth in every walk of life. Therefore, we request the cooperation of all governments in legalizing these qualities, and the participation of all right-thinking people in universalizing a righteous government.

For this cause we are assembled in a great International Righteous Government convention in New York City these three days, the tenth, eleventh, and twelfth of January, 1936, A. D. F. D., with delegates from many different countries and states. The Righteous Government Department of Father Divine's Peace Mission Movement has adopted a platform embodying some of the more important issues of its Righteous Stand. This platform, which has been verified and endorsed by Father Divine, with his personal signature, we are privileged to present to you as follows: . . .

PRINCIPLES

That the whole human race is essentially one, and 'of one blood God formed all nations,' has been attested both by Scripture and by science. The Righteous Government of Father Divine's Peace Mission stands for and actually produces such an organization of society. It is founded upon the recognition of the brotherhood of man and the fatherhood of God. Its watchword is peace, and it actually establishes peace among the nations by eradicating prejudice, segregation, and division from among the people and promoting the welfare of every living creature. From this angle we emphatically protest against the persecution of the Jews in Germany and all other countries, and the oppression of all minorities.

This movement stands for and demands an equal opportunity for every individual without regard to race, creed, or color, in accordance with the declaration made in the Constitution of the United States, that all men are created equal. It stands for the life and teaching of Jesus the Christ exactly as He lived it. . . .

The Righteous Government Department of Father Divine's Peace Mission bases its plan for universalizing prosperity upon the fundamental principle personified in Father Divine, that has made millions prosperous. It has taken his followers off the relief and made them independent, thus saving the government millions. Not one of his true followers would accept relief in any form, or even so much as go on the relief rolls, in order to get a job. We demand the abandonment of the government regulation requiring the people of America to declare themselves destitute and go on the relief rolls, in order to get jobs.

The Divine plan calls for equal distribution of opportunity, and giving every man a chance to be independent, but not so much charity. In the experience of millions who have accepted Father Divine, all economic and unemployment problems have been solved, and they are actually enjoying the ideal conditions others are striving for. He has made it possible for those who are cooperative and meek, especially in this country, to live well on five dollars a week or less. He has further supplied them with part-time jobs at least, to earn an independent living, while causing them to desire to serve their fellowmen in all their waking hours. Speaking of his personal activities in New York, Father said:

"I have been feeding the unemployed in a number around about from 2,500 to three thousand a day, but this is not my great aim in life. This is not the greatest expression. The great expression according to my version, is to help you to be independent. I will cut out so much feeding of the unemployed as I have been. I have opened ways and means whereby you can get jobs, whereby you can be independent, self-supporting and self-respecting. That is what I am desiring to see you all do and be.

"Therefore I have made the way possible for the last three years or more, in the City of New York and elsewhere, that you might be able to get by, at from four to five dollars a week and be independent. If you come here, or go any place and get a meal for ten or fifteen cents, you do not have to feel as a beggar. You can feel independent, for that is the price, or those are the prices for the meals in all of our connections, not only here in New York City but all the way across the country in all of the places fifteen cents is the maximum fee for a meal. I wish to further announce . . . hereafter our barber shops will not charge but ten cents for a haircut for men, and five cents for a shave . . . We shall make similar cuts in the dress shops in proportion, and in the grocery stores, and other expressions of our industries."

Naturally the cost of these facilities is greater than the income from them, and no man could continue indefinitely to carry them on, but as they are the gift of God to mankind they are amply provided for. Father Divine takes no collections, accepts no donations or financial support whatsoever, and has never been known to do so. On the contrary, he is constantly giving.

Another of his personal activities for the benefit of the masses has been a free employment agency. After operating his own private agency free for many years, he recently opened up a public agency to get at the intolerable conditions in the employment field.

Regarding these conditions, he recently spoke as follows:

"I call your attention to an incident just happening now here in your midst which I am in, and that is this: I took over and opened up 'The Busy Bee Employment Agency.' The law has been for years that the employees and the employers are supposed to pay 10 per cent to the agency . . . but I learned since I have been in it, that the employers will not pay a penny. They have been forcing the employees to pay their 10 per cent and the employers not paying anything. It is indeed wonderful! But I will not have it that way longer."

"That is one of the outrages that has been manifested or concealed here . . . where they would force the employees to pay their fees, but would not force the employers who have millions, to pay a fee. Many of the employees did not have bread to eat, neither a place to sleep, seeking work to be honest, competent, and true, and yet if they got a chance to get a position, they could not have it unless they paid their fees, yet the millionaire that was hiring them as the employer—they would not charge him a penny. It is indeed wonderful!

"In every little simple expression, you can see the outward expression of the oppression of those who are as the hireling and the fatherless, the poor and the needy, the laboring class of people.

It is indeed wonderful! As I said some time ago, when I am participating with my comrades, the Communists, whether they know it or not, I know they are fulfilling the Scriptures more than many of the preachers and those that are called religious . . . I will get you positions if you are competent. If you have good references I will get you positions, free of charge. I will let you go free—the employee—but the employers can pay their fee."

Following Father's example, others of Father's movement endeavored to open licensed employment agencies and cooperate in the same work of helping the masses, but the commissioners showed every evidence of a desire to uphold and perpetuate the old system of squeezing small sums out of the poor and letting the employers go free, and they would not grant licenses. Father spoke in this regard as follows:

"It has been distinctly discerned that wheresoever there is an application put in for an employment agency, the prejudicial officials in connection with the administration, are trying to keep my co-workers or anyone who is connected with me, from having an employment agency. It is because they know within themselves, I will cut the cost of living. They know I am here as a help for the meek and lowly. They know that I came as a swift witness against those who will oppress the widow and the fatherless, and will not come nigh me. That is why they are trying to keep my connection out of it. I will put it through if I have to put them out of office! That is what I will do! Everyone who comes in opposition, everyone who will rise in an endeavor to oppose my endeavors, I shall put them to an open shame. Every prejudicial official who is in the commission, and connected in any way in this administration, who desires to prohibit me from having an employment agency personally, I shall put him out of office. There are thousands of people out of work, without food and shelter and I can see the oppressed—the widows and the orphans, the hireling and his wages, and I will bring swift judgment to the offender."

Unlike other plans that have been declared economically unsound and impractical on account of the tremendous expenditures involved, the Divine plan requires nothing that is not already available. It is based on cooperation, equal opportunity, and the recognition of the brotherhood of man and the fatherhood of God. Wealth, if it is to continue to exist and prosper in this new day, must be continually used for the benefit of humanity, and not for selfish gains. If all idle plants and machinery, and available lands now costing billions in taxes and upkeep, were immediately made available to the workers, they would soon become profitable, and the eleven millions now said to be unemployed in the United States, would soon be employed. The Divine plan means work, and more work, with prices of commodities reduced to a minimum.

As a sample and an example of how wealth should be used, Father is buying large tracts of land in one of the best parts of the state of New York and making homesites available to the people free. Speaking along this line at his Righteous Government Forum in New York City recently, Father spoke the following words to the masses assembled:

"The earth is the Lord's and the fullness thereof, but yet He does not claim everything personally. The communistic idea must be endorsed—I mean to say, many of them. At the Day of Pentecost, they had all things in common, did they not? I am not asking you all to buy, neither to help me buy a piece of property. I have purchased the property—several places—and they are all free and clear. If perchance you have the means, or will have the means to build a home, the ground, the land, the lots, will be given to you free of cost, and you will have your deeds for them without a string tied to them. This is an abstract expression of the communistic idea, making all things common, claiming nothing for yourself as an individual, refusing to hoard up riches for yourselves for a selfish purpose, but give everybody a chance to enjoy some of it."

The followers of Father Divine in every community, state, province, colony, and nation have the opportunity of becoming an example for all governments, by co-operative living and a universal pooling of all of their interests. They can become an independent unit even as these in New York City, according to the example set by Father's personal activities. He has made living accommodations of the best available in the world's most expensive city, for from one to two dollars a week; bountiful meals of high quality for ten and fifteen cents, with dress shops, tailor shops, grocery stores, bus lines, boat excursions, special trains, and other facilities available at similarly low prices.

Advocating equal distribution of opportunity; a chance for every man; plenty of work with good wages; prices reduced to a minimum, and all of the advantages for the masses, we are now enjoying these things and we know they can be enjoyed by all. Therefore, we request the following:

NECESSARY LEGISLATION

1. Legislation prohibiting employment agencies from collecting fees or remuneration in any form from employees, but authorizing them to collect the present legal fees in full from the employers; also the establishment of a minimum wage scale prohibiting agencies from sending out workers for less than their respective minimum rates.

2. Governmental control of all idle plants and machinery, tools and equipment, where owners are unwilling to operate them at full capacity; such facilities to be made available to workers on a co-operative, non-profit basis under supervision of government experts, with temporary provision for materials; workers to be paid a living wage until income exceeds expenses, then the wage scale to be increased and maintained at as high a rate as conditions permit. The owners would have the privilege of operating the plants at any time they are willing and able to operate them at full capacity, until some arrangement is made for change of ownership.

3. Immediate abandonment of the government regulation requiring individuals to be on the relief rolls in order to get work on relief projects.

4. Immediate provision, under government supervision, of

work on useful projects, for every unemployed worker according to his qualifications, with suitable pay for amount of work accomplished. Expenditures for many such projects, such as high speed tunnels, express highways, or whatsoever it might be, could quickly be regained by tolls, as in the case of the Holland tunnel in New York City.

5. Immediate abandonment by all states and counties, of government crop control, destruction of foodstuffs and other products, and the establishment of an efficient and equitable distribution system. The spectacle of hungry people in a land of plenty is worse than uncivilized.

6. Laws to be altered so that equal opportunity is allowed to all, that every worker be allowed access to the land, to the tools and materials needed for the carrying out of his individual talent, for the welfare of himself and of society.

7. Abolition of all tariff schedules and obstacles to free trade among the nations. Trade among all the peoples of the earth should be left as free as is now the trade among the various states of the American union.

8. Legislation limiting the amount of profit to be made on any article or product, but leaving the individual free to sell it for as little as he chooses.

9. Government to print its own money and make it illegal to hoard it. Government to redeem all its bonded debts and to lend the money to the co-operative non-profit enterprises; abolish all interest and make it a criminal offence to take usury or interest, or to receive dividends that exceed 3.5 per cent, or money without labor performed or practical service rendered.

10. Government ownership and operation of the financial system.

11. Legislation making it a criminal offence for any individual to spend money except for necessities of life, while he owes a just debt to any other individual or organization.

The followers of Father Divine will not owe another, and will not buy on the installment plan.

12. Immediate destruction of all counterfeit money, by those

who have acquired it, rather than attempting to pass it on; and a change in the currency to eliminate all counterfeits in circulation. The followers of Father Divine destroy all counterfeit money they find in circulation, at their own expense, rather than pass it on to another.

Father said in a recent message:

"Now in reference to counterfeit money: whensoever one has a counterfeit dollar, a counterfeit fifty-dollar bill, or counterfeit of any denomination of a bill or money, it matters not what it is, if it would be a thousand dollars, if you find out that it is counterfeit, this counterfeit expression should be destroyed. If someone else happens to pass a counterfeit dollar on you, destroy it immediately. If you find that it is a counterfeit dollar, and you are convinced that it is counterfeit, you should destroy it, for it is false; therefore, you should destroy the false."

It is not claimed that the recommendation contained in this platform will solve every economic problem of the world at large, but the fundamental principle will. In Father Divine is found the solution of every problem that may arise. Neither is it claimed that legislation alone can solve the problem, but as we have already stated, righteousness, justice, and truth must be legalized, and all unrighteousness, injustice and untruth, outlawed.

The principles advocated are just a few of those that Father Divine has established in the lives of millions. They have changed underworld characters into upright citizens. They have changed dishonesty and good-for-nothingness into honesty, competence, and truth; making millions prosperous and independent of relief, causing them to return stolen goods and pay old bills they never intended to pay. Thus Father has saved the government, public utilities companies, department stores, and business as a whole, millions of dollars annually, and caused millions to seek justice through righteousness, when they might have sought it in unrighteousness, through force of arms.

DR. FRANCIS E. TOWNSEND, 1867–1960

☆ Old-Age Pension

DR. FRANCIS E. TOWNSEND looked out of his bathroom window in Long Beach, California, while shaving one morning in 1933 and saw three old women scavenging in a garbage can.

The sixty-six-year-old physician shouted a "torrent of invectives . . . the big blast of all the bitterness that had been building in me for years. I swore and I ranted, and I let my voice bellow with the wild hatred I had for things as they were."

His wife tried to soothe him. "Doctor, you mustn't shout like that. All the neighbors will hear you!"

"I want all the neighbors to hear me," the doctor retorted. "I want God Almighty to hear me! I'm going to shout till the whole country hears."

This is the legend of Dr. Townsend's inspiration which led to his old-age pension plan.

A letter in the *Long Beach Press Telegram* on September 30, 1933, was the doctor's initial step in his campaign to alert the country to the problem of its old people. The letter was titled "Cure for Depression." In it, Dr. Townsend proposed a national sales tax to raise pensions of $150 a month for everyone over sixty years of age, the money to be given with the stipulation that it be spent immediately. A few weeks later the Long Beach paper devoted a full page to letters from readers, discussing, arguing, and debating over the doctor's plan.

Soon, however, Dr. Townsend came out with a revision: the $150 per month was to be increased to $200 per month, the money to be raised by a two percent "transaction sales tax."

Why $200 a month? To the author of a sympathetic biography—*That Man Townsend,* by Richard Milne—the doctor explained: "There are two other points we must bear in mind . . . First, the glamour of a $200 pension. It will compel attention, and has great psychological value. Second, with our figure set as high as $200 we can feel reasonably sure that no one will bring out a pension plan with a higher amount."

Francis E. Townsend, a farmer's son, born in Fairbury in northern Illinois, was educated in the rural school and in a Congregational academy. Before he entered the Omaha Medical School at the age of thirty-one, he held numerous jobs—as salesman, teacher, ranch hand, farm laborer, and homesteader.

The oldest member of his class, Townsend worked his way through medical school. Until World War I, when he enlisted in the army, Francis Townsend was a country doctor in the Black Hills of South Dakota. In 1919, because of ill health, he moved to Long Beach, California, with his wife and son, and here he built up a small practice. Real estate investments supplemented his income. During the early years of the "Great Depression" the doctor was a medical officer for the indigents of the city.

Then he wrote his letter to the newspaper offering a cure

for the depression, and a new career opened up for him. He became an actor on the national stage.

Reaction to the publication of his letter was immediate. With the aid of a former employer, a real estate promoter, the idea began to be merchandised and promoted. Townsend clubs were formed: three thousand clubs in six months. The movement had a successful and profitable newspaper. In the mid-thirties it claimed a membership of more than two million in about seven thousand clubs.

The Townsend Plan became a crusade with the zeal and emotionalism of evangelism. Each meeting concluded with a song and a pledge:

"Onward Townsend soldiers,
Marching as to war,
With the Townsend banner
Going on before.
Our devoted leader
Big Depression go;
Join them in the battle
Help them fight the foe."

The pledge: "The Townsend plan will succeed. I therefore pledge my allegiance to its principles, to its founder, Dr. Francis E. Townsend, to its leaders, and to all loyal members."

The Townsend Movement became an important force in many states; in some it "unsettled the political balance of power." It helped move Congress into the Social Security Act.

In his historical study, *The Townsend Movement*, Abraham Holtzman observed: "The Townsend Plan and the Social Security Act are inextricably linked together, the inclusion of an old-age provision within the Act represents a direct response to Townsend pressure. The Townsend Movement must be credited with having crystallized tremendous popular sentiment in favor of old-age security."

To Dr. Townsend, the federal Social Security program was "wholly unfair, inadequate, and unjust." He waited until he was eighty-three years of age before he applied for his own Social Security.

Though it was the pressure from the Townsend Movement that moved the Roosevelt administration toward old-age insurance, Dr. Townsend never met with the President. President Roosevelt refused to grant him an interview in 1934.

The doctor never forgave the President for this rebuff. He looked upon the President as a personal "devil." The Townsend Movement weekly editorialized: "We have aristocracy in the White House—not democracy."

In 1937 the select committee to investigate old-age pension organizations was established in the House of Representatives with an eye to destroying the political strength of the Townsend Movement. Its purpose was to investigate the financial transaction of the movement's leaders and promoters, particularly their records and methods of collecting and spending money.

"The immediate goal of the investigation was to smear," wrote Professor Holtzman in his book, "to insinuate, if possible to prove the movement a racket operated for personal gain at the expense of the faith and pennies of the aged."

After three days of testimony in which he was ruthlessly questioned and his words, he felt, misconstrued, Dr. Townsend refused to answer further questions of the committee. He was cited for contempt, tried, sentenced to one year of imprisonment and fined $100. When the doctor's appeal was turned down by the U.S. Supreme Court, President Roosevelt granted him a pardon.

During the 1936 presidential election, Dr. Townsend joined forces with the Rev. Gerald L. K. Smith, who, since Huey Long's assassination, had been out of the political machine in Louisiana, and Father Charles E. Coughlin, the Detroit priest, to support a third-party candidate, William Lemke, on the new Union party ticket. But Townsend urged his followers in states where Congressman Lemke was not on the ballot to vote for the Republican candidate, Alfred Landon. In the election, Lemke received fewer than 900,000 votes.

To the doctor, the Townsend Plan was "only incidentally a pension plan; the old people are simply to be used as a means by which prosperity will be returned to all of us."

To some people, the Townsend Plan was a "utopian pipe dream." "Big Bill" Thompson, Chicago's mayor of the prosperous 1920's, thought it was "the most Christ-like plan that has been conceived since the Crucifixion."

★ OLD-AGE REVOLVING PENSIONS

The Townsend plan proposes a pension from the Federal government of $200 a month for every person more than sixty years old, the money to be spent each month before another $200 can be received. It means that where a man and wife both were sixty or more the combined pension would be $400 a month and that they would have to spend it to receive more.

The immediate placing of nearly $2 billion into trade channels as a revolving fund, to be turned over and renewed each month, would put the United States back on its feet through the stimulation of industry and commerce—through the immediately increased demand for all commodities and the resultant increase in employment.

"Why make it $200 a month? That is more than most of the employed are earning now. Why not $100 a month?"

Because, to cut it in two would be to cut its economic benefits in two. Please understand this: the persons more than sixty who receive the pension will be performing a task and a duty when they spend their pensions. The chief purpose is to get someone to spend money, to increase the buying power of the nation. The more that is put into circulation the better off we will be as a nation.

"But the average old couple couldn't spend $400 a month, could it?"

F. E. Townsend, "Is the Townsend Plan for 'Old-Age Revolving Pensions' Sound?", *Congressional Digest,* March 1935.

There is where you are mistaken. Most of those who would benefit have been pinched by the lack of sufficient money most of their lives. They never have had all they desired of anything.

All that would be putting money into circulation, and that is the objective. There would be no particular economic benefit in distributing "pork and bean" money. That has been done through other pensions and through present relief work and it doesn't get us anywhere.

"Wouldn't the operation of the plan place an enormous additional tax burden on those who are doing the country's work?"

No, not an enormous burden. Suppose the first cost was two billion dollars to put the pension in the hands of from the six million to eight million persons more than sixty years old. That would be returned to the government monthly through the collection of a tax on all business transactions. In the first place there would be immediately an amazing increase in the number of business transactions, and the number would increase as the pensioned persons learned better how to spend money. The tax would be reduced as the volume of business increased.

It would increase the cost of living, and isn't that what President Roosevelt has been trying vainly to do; to raise the market prices of commodities? But don't forget the primary purpose is to stimulate business and employment. What benefit is there to an unemployed man in low prices if he doesn't have the money with which to buy? And isn't he immeasurably better off with higher prices and a job? Isn't every one better off when the nation is busy, when business and industry are humming? Does anyone worry about high prices then? No, high prices are the accompaniment of prosperity.

No one has to retire unless he desires. Let the man who desires go ahead with his work, but not a great number will do so.

It would be just as easy to select some other group to spend the pension money, but I believe the selection of that group past sixty would solve both a social and an economic problem.

Certainly it would be a wonderful prospect for the aged to have the fear and doubt of their last years removed and there could be no fear of weakening the fiber of our ambitious people through providing for those who have lived their most useful years.

Here they are either working and competing with young men and women striving to get a start in life, or they are competing at a great disadvantage with the young for jobs. This plan certainly would take out of business and industry millions of persons who have served their time and served their nation well.

And that is where the benefits to those under sixty would come in.

Take out of competition those who have served their time and are willing to retire and enjoy themselves and you have opened up the millions of places vacated to the younger and more ambitious.

But that is only a part of the benefits for those under sixty. The forced circulation of $2 billion a month through every line of business would open up millions of new jobs for those under sixty.

Think what it would mean to remove fear from the lives of the old, to create places for the young as they step out into life and to give assurance to the middle-aged that they could do their best without fear, because when they reached sixty they at least would be sure of a comfortable living. No cold chills in the night over the thought of the poorhouse or the "old folks' home."

More efficiency in productive years is destroyed by worry over old age than any that would be lost through a feeling of security. Ambition, the desire to accomplish, is inborn in the American. You couldn't destroy that in those years when his blood runs fast and his brain works quickly.

It is just as natural for man or woman in the energetic years to desire to do things in their respective lines as it is for a child to take its own exercise.

BIBLIOGRAPHY

GENERAL

Aaron, Daniel. *America in Crisis: Fourteen Crucial Episodes in American History*. New York, Alfred A. Knopf, 1952.

———. *Men of Good Hope: A Story of American Progressives*. New York, Oxford University Press, 1951.

Adams, Ephraim D. *The Power of Ideals in American History*. New Haven, Yale University Press, 1913.

Adams, Frederick B., Jr. *Radical Literature in America*. Stamford, Conn., Printed at the Overbrook Press, 1939.

Adams, Henry. *History of the United States of America*. New York, Scribner's, 1889–91.

Adams, James T. *The Epic of America*. Boston, Little, Brown, 1931.

Adams, Samuel H. *Incredible Era: The Life and Times of Warren Gamaliel Harding*. Boston, Houghton Mifflin, 1939.

Allen, E. A. *Life and Public Services of James Baird Weaver*. No city, People's Party Publishing Co., 1892.

Allen, Frederick Lewis. *The Big Change: America Transforms Itself, 1900–1950*. New York, Harper, 1952.

———. *Only Yesterday: An Informal History of the Nineteen-Twenties*. New York, Harper, 1931.

American Messiahs, by the Unofficial Observer. New York, Simon and Schuster, 1935.

Andrews, Stephen Pearl. *The Basic Outline of Universology*. New York, Dion Thomas, 1872.

———. *The Science of Society (No. 1)*. Boston, Sarah E. Holmes, 1888.

Arnold, Thurman W. *The Folklore of Capitalism*. New Haven, Yale University Press, 1938.

Bacon, Leonard. *Slavery and Colonization*. New Haven, A. K. Maltby, 1833.

Ballard, G. W. *Unveiled Mysteries*. Chicago, Saint Germain Press, 1934–35.

Banning, M. C. "Shopping for Utopia," *Saturday Evening Post,* CCVII (January 19, 1935).

Bartlett, David W. *Modern Agitators; or, Pen Portraits of Living American Reformers*. New York, Miller, Orton & Mulligan, 1855.

Bascom, John. *Protection and Patriotism*. Boston, American Free Trade League, 1901.

Beard, Charles A., ed. *America Faces the Future*. Boston, Houghton Mifflin, 1932.

———. *Economic Origins of Jeffersonian Democracy*. New York, Macmillan, 1915.

———, and Mary R. *America in Midpassage*. New York, Macmillan, 1939.

———, and Mary R. *The American Spirit: A Study of the Idea of Civilization in the United States*. New York, Macmillan, 1942.

———, and Mary R. *The Rise of American Civilization*. New York, Macmillan, 1927.

Beard, Charles A., and George H. E. Smith. *The Future Comes: A Study of the New Deal*. New York, Macmillan, 1933.

Beardsley, Harry M. *Joseph Smith and his Mormon Empire*. Boston, Houghton Mifflin, 1931.

Bennett, D. M. *The World's Sages, Infidels and Thinkers; Being Biographical Sketches of Leading Philosophers, Teachers, Reformers, Innovators, Founders of New Schools of Thought, Eminent Scientists, Etc*. New York, D. M. Bennett Liberal and Scientific Publishing House, 1876.

Bentley, Wilder. *The Communication of Utopian Thought: Its History, Forms, and Use*. San Francisco, San Francisco State College Bookstore, 1959.

Berens, Lewis Henry. *The Story of My Dictatorship*. Cincinnati, J. Fels Fund of America, no date.

Bestor, Arthur. *Backwoods Utopias: The Sectarian and Owenite Phases of Communitarian Socialism in America, 1663–1829*. Philadelphia, University of Pennsylvania Press, 1950.

Billington, Ray Allen. *The Protestant Crusade, 1800–1860: A Study of the Origins of American Nativism*. New York, Macmillan, 1938.

Bingham, Alfred. *Insurgent America: Revolt of the Middle Classes*. New York, Harper, 1935.

Bliss, William D. P., ed. and prop. *The Dawn* (a journal of Christian Socialism), Vol. 3. Boston, 1890–92.

———, ed. *The Encyclopedia of Social Reforms*. 2d ed. New York, Funk and Wagnalls, 1898.

———. "Union Reform League Activities," *Arena*, July 1899.

———. "The Social Reform Union," *Arena*, July 1899.

Bontemps, Arna, and Jack Conroy. *Anyplace But Here*. New York, Hill & Wang, 1966.

Boorstin, Daniel J. *The Americans: The National Experience*. New York, Random House, 1965.

Braden, Charles Samuel. *These Also Believe: A Study of Modern American Cults and Minority Religious Movements*. New York, Macmillan, 1949.

Braeman, John. "Seven Progressives," *Business History Review*, XXXV (Winter 1961).

Brewton, William W. *The Life of Thomas E. Watson*. Atlanta, Published by the Author, 1926.

Brisbane, Albert. *Social Destiny of Man; or, Association and Reorganization of Industry*. Philadelphia, C. F. Stollmeyer, 1840.

Brown, Anna B. A. "A Dream of Emancipation," *New England Magazine*, XXX (June 1904).

Broyles, J. Allen. *The John Birch Society: Anatomy of a Protest*. Boston, Beacon Press, 1964.

Buck, Solon J. *The Agrarian Crusade: A Chronicle of the Farmer in Politics*. New Haven, Yale University Press, 1920.

Calverton, Victor Francis. *Where Angels Dared to Tread*. Indianapolis, Bobbs-Merrill, 1941.

Cantril, Hadley. *The Psychology of Social Movements*. New York, John Wiley & Sons, 1941.

Cargill, Oscar. *Intellectual America: Ideas on the March*. New York, Macmillan, 1941.

Carnegie, Andrew. *Triumphant Democracy; or, Fifty Years' March of the Republic*. New York, Scribner's, 1887.

Carroll, Anna Ella. *The Great American Battle; or, the Contest Between Christianity and Political Romanism*. New York, Miller, Orton & Mulligan, 1856.

Caryl, Chas. W. *New Era. Presenting the Plans for the New Era Union to Help Develop and Utilize the Best Resources of this Country*. Denver, New Era Union, no date.

Chamberlain, John. *Farewell to Reform: The Rise, Life and Decay of the*

Progressive Mind in America. 2d ed., paperback. Chicago, Quadrangle, 1965.
———. "Panaceas for the Depression," *New Republic*.
I. "Solving It with a Thirty-Hour Week" (March 29, 1933).
II. "The Rorty Plan for a Federal Subsidy to Business" (April 5, 1933).
III. "The Crusoe Economics of Exchange by Barter" (April 26, 1933).
IV. "Gold, Prices and Inflation" (May 3, 1933).
Clark, Elmer T. *The Small Sects in America*. Nashville, Cokesbury Press, 1937.
Cluskey, M. W., ed. *The Political Text-Book, or Encyclopedia*. Philadelphia, Jas. B. Smith, 1860.
Cole, Arthur Charles. *The Irrepressible Conflict, 1850–1865*. New York, Macmillan, 1934.
Commager, Henry Steele. *The American Mind*. New Haven, Yale University Press, 1950.
———. *The Era of Reform, 1830–1860*. Princeton, Van Nostrand, 1960.
———, ed. *Living Ideas in America*. New York, Harper, 1951.
———. *Theodore Parker, Yankee Crusader*. Boston, Little, Brown, 1936.
Commons, John R., *et al*. *A Documentary History of American Industrial Society*. Vols. 1–10. Cleveland, Arthur H. Clark, 1910–11.
———. *History of Labour in the United States*. Vols. 1–4. New York, Macmillan, 1918–35.
Conway, Moncure D. *Autobiography*. Boston, Houghton Mifflin, 1904.
Cooper, Peter. *Ideas for a Science of Good Government*. New York, Trow's Printing & Bookbinding Co., 1883.
———. *The Political and Financial Opinions of . . . With an Autobiography of His Early Life*. New York, Trow's Printing & Bookbinding Co., 1877.
Curti, Merle. *The Growth of American Thought*. 3rd ed. New York, Harper, 1964.

Davenport, C. B. *Eugenics, the Science of Human Improvement by Better Breeding*. New York, Holt, 1910.
Davis, Andrew Jackson. *Free Thoughts Concerning Religion; or, Nature versus Theology*. Boston, Bela Marsh, 1854.
———. *The Harmonial Man; or, Thoughts for the Age*. Boston, Bela Marsh, 1853.
———. *The Magic Staff: An Autobiography of Andrew Jackson Davis*. New York, A. J. Davis & Co., 1876.
———. *The Principles of Nature, Her Divine Revelations and a Voice to Mankind*. New York, S. S. Lyon & Wm. Fishbough, 1852.
Davis, Jerome. *Contemporary Social Movements*. New York, The Century Co., 1930.
DeLeon, Daniel. *Flashlights of the Amsterdam International Socialist Congress, 1904*. New York, New York Labor News Co., 1904.
———. *Socialist Landmarks*. New York, New York Labor News Co., 1952.

———. *Two Pages from Roman History*. New York, New York Labor News Co., 1903.

Destler, Chester McArthur. *American Radicalism, 1865–1901: Essays and Documents*. New London, Conn., Connecticut College, 1946.

Dixon, William Hepworth. *Spiritual Wives*. Philadelphia, Lippincott, 1868.

Dodd, Mrs. Anna Bowman. *The Republic of the Future; or, Socialism a Reality*. New York, Cassell, c. 1887.

Dohrman, H. T. *California Cult: The Story of "Mankind United."* Boston, Beacon Press, 1958.

Dombrowski, James. *The Early Days of Christian Socialism in America*. New York, Columbia University Press, 1936.

Donnelly, Ignatius. *The American People's Money*. Chicago, Laird & Lee, 1895.

Dorfman, Joseph. *The Economic Mind in American Civilization*. New York, Viking, I, II (1606–1865), 1946; III (1865–1918), 1949; IV, V (1918–33), 1959.

———. *Thorstein Veblen and His America*. New York, Viking, 1934.

Ellis, John B. *Free Love and Its Voltaires, or, American Socialism Unmasked*. New York, United States Publishing Co., 1870.

Ely, Richard T. *The Labor Movement in America*. New York, Crowell, 1886.

———. *Recent American Socialism*. Johns Hopkins University Studies in Historical and Political Science. Third series, IV. Baltimore, Johns Hopkins University, 1885.

———. *Socialism and Social Reform*. New York, Crowell, 1894.

———. *Socialism: An Examination of Its Nature, Its Strength, and Its Weakness, with Suggestions for Social Reform*. New York, Crowell, 1894.

Etzler, J. A. *The Paradise Within the Reach of All Men, Without Labor, by Powers of Nature and Machinery*. London, J. Young, 1842.

Evans, John H. *Joseph Smith, an American Prophet*. New York, Macmillan, 1933.

Faulkner, Harold U. *The Decline of Laissez Faire, 1897–1917*. New York, Rinehart, 1951.

———. *Politics, Reform, and Expansion, 1890–1900*. New York, Harper, 1959.

———. *The Quest for Social Justice, 1898–1914*. New York, Macmillan, 1931.

Filler, Louis. *Crusaders for American Liberalism*. New York, Harcourt, Brace, 1939.

Fine, Sidney. *Laissez Faire and the General-Welfare State: A Study of Conflict in American Thought, 1865–1901*. Ann Arbor, University of Michigan Press, 1956.

———. "Richard T. Ely, Forerunner of Progressivism, 1880–1901," *Mississippi Valley Historical Review*, XXXVII (March 1951).

Fish, Carl R. *The Rise of the Common Man, 1830–1850*. New York, Macmillan, 1929.

Flower, Benjamin O. *Progressive Men, Women and Movements of the Past Twenty-Five Years*. Boston, no publisher, 1915.

Fox, Early Lee. *The American Colonization Society, 1817–40*. Johns Hopkins University Studies in Historical and Political Science. Baltimore, Johns Hopkins Press, 1919.

Frothingham, O. B. "Brook Farm: What It Was and What It Aimed To Be," *Christian Register*, LXI (March 9, 1882).

Gabriel, Ralph H. *The Course of American Democratic Thought*. 2d ed. New York, Ronald, 1956.

Gaston, Herbert E. *The Nonpartisan League*. New York, Harcourt, Brace, 1920.

Gilman, Nicholas P. *Socialism and the American Spirit*. Boston, Houghton Mifflin, 1893.

Goldman, Eric F. *The Crucial Decade—and After: America, 1945–1960*. New York, Vintage, 1956.

Green, Evarts B. *The Revolutionary Generation, 1763–1790*. New York, Macmillan, 1943.

Green, Thomas H. *American Social Reform Movements: Their Patterns Since 1865*. New York, Prentice-Hall, 1949.

Greene, William B. *The Incarnation, a Letter to Rev. John Fiske, D.D.* West Brookfield, Mass., Published by the Author, 1848.

———. *Socialistic, Communistic, Mutualistic, and Financial Fragments*. Boston, Lee and Shepard, 1875.

———. *The Sovereignty of the People*. Boston, A. Williams & Co., 1868.

Griffin, Clifford. *Their Brothers' Keepers: Moral Stewardship in the United States, 1800–1865*. New Brunswick, N.J., Rutgers University Press, 1960.

Grossman, Jonathan. *William Sylvis, Pioneer of American Labor: A Study of the Labor Movement During the Era of the Civil War*. New York, Columbia University Press, 1945.

Gunther, John. *Inside U.S.A.* New York, Harper, 1947.

Gunton, George. *Wealth and Progress; A Critical Examination of the Wages Question and Its Economic Relation to Social Reform*. New York, D. Appleton & Co., 1891.

Haller, Mark H. *Eugenics*. New Brunswick, N.J., Rutgers University Press, 1963.

Handlin, Oscar. *The Americans: A New History of the People of the United States*. Boston, Little, Brown, 1963.

Hart, Albert Bushnell. *National Ideals Historically Traced, 1607–1907*. New York, Harper, 1907.

———. *Slavery and Abolition, 1831–1841.* New York, Harper, 1906.
Haynes, Frederick Emory. *James Baird Weaver.* Iowa City, State Historical Society of Iowa, 1919.
———. *Social Politics in the United States.* Boston, Houghton Mifflin, 1924.
———. *Third Party Movements Since the Civil War, with Special Reference to Iowa; A Study in Social Politics.* Iowa City, State Historical Society of Iowa, 1916.
Herron, George D. *The Christian State, A Political Vision of Christ.* New York, 1895.
Hertzka, Theodor. *Freeland; A Social Anticipation.* Trans. Arthur Ransom. New York, D. Appleton & Co., 1891.
Hertzler, Joyce Oramel. *The History of Utopian Thought.* New York, Macmillan, 1926.
Hicks, John D. "The Political Career of Ignatius Donnelly," *Mississippi Valley Historical Review*, VIII (June–September 1928).
———. *The Populist Revolt: A History of the Farmers' Alliance and the People's Party.* Minneapolis, University of Minnesota Press, 1931.
Higginson, Thomas Wentworth. *Cheerful Yesterdays.* Boston, Houghton Mifflin, 1898.
Hillquit, Morris. *History of Socialism in the United States.* New York, Funk & Wagnalls, 1910.
Hinds, William Alfred. *American Communities: Brief Sketches.* Oneida, N.Y., Office of the American Socialist, 1878.
Hine, Robert V. *California's Utopian Colonies.* San Marino, Calif., Huntington Library, 1953.
Hockett, Homer Carey. *Political and Social Growth of the United States, 1492–1852.* New York, Macmillan, 1933.
Hoffer, Eric. *The True Believer: Thoughts on the Nature of Mass Movements.* New York, Harper, 1951.
Hofstadter, Richard. *The American Political Tradition and the Men Who Made It.* New York, Alfred A. Knopf, 1948.
———. *Anti-Intellectualism in American Life.* New York, Alfred A. Knopf, 1964.
———. *The Paranoid Style in American Politics, and Other Essays.* New York, Alfred A. Knopf, 1966.
———. *Social Darwinism in American Thought, 1860–1915.* Philadelphia, University of Pennsylvania Press, 1944.
Holbrook, Stewart H. *Dreamers of the American Dream.* Garden City, Doubleday, 1957.
———. *Lost Men of American History.* New York, Macmillan, 1946.
Hopkins, Charles H. *The Rise of the Social Gospel in American Protestantism, 1865–1915.* New Haven, Yale University Press, 1940.

"If I Were Dictator," *Nation*, November 18, 25; December 9, 23, 1931; January 6, 13, 20, 1932.

Industrial Workers of the World. *Proceedings of the First Convention of the Industrial Workers of the World*. New York, New York Labor News Co., 1905.

Jaher, Frederic Cople. *Doubters and Dissenters: Cataclysmic Thought in America, 1885–1918*. New York, Free Press, 1964.

Jameson, J. Franklin. *The American Revolution Considered as a Social Movement*. Princeton, Princeton University Press, 1940.

Johnson, Julia E. (compiled by). *Capitalism and Its Alternatives*. New York, H. W. Wilson Co., 1933.

Kaplan, Sidney. "Social Engineers as Saviors: Effects of World War I on Some American Liberals," *Journal of the History of Ideas*, XVII (June 1956), 347–69.

Kaufmann, Moritz. *Utopias; or, Schemes of Social Improvement. From Sir Thomas More to Karl Marx*. London, C. K. Paul & Co., 1879.

Kelley, O. H. *Origin and Progress of the Order of the Patrons of Husbandry in the United States*. Philadelphia, J. A. Wagenseller, 1875.

Kendall, Amos. *Autobiography of . . .* Boston, Lee and Shepard, 1872.

Kent, Austin. *Free Love; or, a Philosophical Demonstration of the Non-Exclusive Nature of Connubial Love*. Hopkinton, N.Y., Published by the Author, 1857.

Laidler, Harry W. *Social-Economic Movements*. New York, Crowell, 1947.

Lasch, Christopher. *The New Radicalism in America, 1889–1963*. New York, Alfred A. Knopf, 1965.

Lens, Sidney. *Radicalism in America*. New York, Crowell, 1966.

Lewis, Edward R. *A History of American Political Thought from the Civil War to the World War*. New York, Macmillan, 1937.

Luthin, Reinhard H. *American Demagogues, Twentieth Century*. Boston, Beacon Press, 1954.

McDonald, Fred H. "Series on Planning," *Review of Reviews* (July–October 1932).

McGrady, Thomas. *Beyond the Black Ocean*. Chicago, C. H. Kerr & Co., 1901.

McLuhan, Marshall. *Understanding Media: The Extensions of Man*. New York, McGraw-Hill, 1964.

McPherson, Aimee Semple. *The Story of My Life*. Los Angeles, Echo Park Evangelistic Association, 1951.

Madison, Charles, A. *Critics and Crusaders: A Century of American Protest*. New York, Holt, 1947.

Mann, Arthur. "Frank Parsons: The Professor as Crusader," *Mississippi Valley Historical Review*, XXXVII (December 1950).

———. *Yankee Reformers in the Urban Age*. Cambridge, The Belknap Press of Harvard University Press, 1954.

Mannheim, Karl. *Ideology and Utopia: An Introduction to the Sociology of Knowledge*. New York, Harcourt, Brace, 1936, 1940.
Martin, James J. *Men Against the State: The Expositors of Individualist Anarchism in America, 1827–1908*. DeKalb, Ill., Adrian Allen Associates, 1953.
Masquerier, Lewis. *Sociology; or, The Reconstruction of Society, Government, and Property*. New York, Published by the Author, 1877.
Meredith, Ellis (arranged by). *Democracy at the Crossroad: A Symposium*. New York, Brewer, Warren & Putnam, 1932.
Merriam, Charles Edward, and Harry Elmer Barnes, ed. *A History of Political Theories, Recent Times; Essays on Contemporary Developments in Political Theory*. New York, Macmillan, 1924.
Meyers, Marvin. *The Jacksonian Persuasion: Politics and Belief*. New York, Vintage Books, 1957.
Mitchell, Wesley Clair. *A History of the Greenbacks, with Special Reference to the Economic Consequences of Their Issue: 1862–65*. Chicago, University of Chicago Press, 1903.
"Modern Panacea," *Commonweal*, XV (January 13, 1932).
Moore, David Albert. *The Age of Progress; or, A Panorama of Time*. New York, Sheldon, Blakeman & Co., 1856.
Morgan, Arthur Ernest. *Nowhere Was Somewhere: How History Makes Utopias and How Utopias Make History*. Chapel Hill, University of North Carolina Press, 1946.
Mott, Frank Luther. *Golden Multitudes: The Story of Best Sellers in the United States*. New York, Macmillan, 1947.
Mowry, George E. *The California Progressives*. Paperback ed. Chicago, Quadrangle, 1963.
Mudge, Eugene T. *The Social Philosophy of John Taylor of Caroline: A Study in Jeffersonian Democracy*. New York, Columbia University Press, 1939.
Mumford, Lewis. *The Story of Utopias*. New York, Boni and Liveright, 1922.
Myers, Gustavus. *The History of American Idealism*. New York, Boni and Liveright, 1925.
———. *History of Bigotry in the United States*. New York, Random House, 1943.
Myrdal, Gunnar. *An American Dilemma: The Negro Problem and Modern Democracy*. 2 vols. New York, Harper, 1944.

"National and World Planning," *Annals of the American Academy of Political and Social Science*, CLXII (July 1932).
Negley, Glenn R., and J. Max Patrick. *The Quest for Utopia: An Anthology of Imaginary Societies*. New York, Henry Schumann, 1952.
Nevins, Allan. *The Emergence of Modern America, 1865–1878*. New York, Macmillan, 1927.

Niebuhr, Reinhold. "Modern Utopians; Hypocrisy of the Times and the Utopianism of the Radicals," *Scribner*, C (September 1936).
Nock, A. J. "Thoughts on Utopia," *Atlantic*, CLVI (July 1935).
Nordhoff, Charles. *The Communistic Societies of the United States; From Personal Visit and Observation*. New York, Harper, 1875.
Noto, Cosimo. *The Ideal City*. New York, no publisher, 1903.
Noyes, John Humphrey. *History of American Socialism*. Philadelphia, Lippincott, 1870.

Paine, Thomas. *Agrarian Justice, Opposed to Agrarian Law, and to Agrarian Monopoly. Being a Plan for Meliorating the Condition of Man, by Creating in Every Nation a National Fund*. London, W. T. Sherwin, 1817.
Parrington, Vernon L. *Main Currents in American Thought*. Vol. I, The Colonial Mind, 1620–1800. Vol. II, The Romantic Revolution in America, 1800–1860. Vol. III, The Beginnings of Critical Realism in America, 1860–1920 (completed to 1900 only). New York, Harcourt, Brace, 1927–30.
Parrington, Vernon Louis, Jr. *American Dreams: A Study of American Utopias*. Providence, R.I., Brown University Studies, 1947.
Parsons, Frank. "Great Movements of the Nineteenth Century. I. The Sweep of the Century and Its Meaning," *Arena*, XXVI (July 1901).
———. "The Philosophy of Mutualism," *Arena*, IX (May 1894).
"Patent Five Cent Utopia," *Atlantic*, CLIV (July 1934).
Perry, Arthur Latham. *Elements of Political Economy*. New York, Scribner, Armstrong, & Co., 1874.
Peters, Madison Clinton. *The Panacea for Poverty*. New York, W. B. Ketcham, 1898.
Petersen, Arnold. *Daniel DeLeon: Social Architect*. 2 vols. New York, New York Labor News Co., 1941–53.
Pickering, John. *The Working Man's Political Economy, Founded Upon the Principle of Immutable Justice, and The Inalienable Rights of Man*. Cincinnati, Thomas Varney, 1847.
Podmore, Frank. *Modern Spiritualism: A History and a Criticism*. 2 vols. London, Methuen, 1902.
Principles of the Native American Party. Poughkeepsie, N.Y., no publisher, 1846.
Proudhon, Pierre Joseph. *Solution of the Social Problem*. New York, Vanguard, 1927.

Quint, Howard H. *The Forging of American Socialism: Origins of the Modern Movement*. Columbia, University of South Carolina Press, 1953.

Ratcliffe, S. K. "The New American Demagogues," *Fortnightly Review*, CXLIII (June 1935).

Rauschenbusch, Walter. *Christianizing the Social Order*. New York, Macmillan, 1912.
Raymond, Rossiter W. *Peter Cooper*. New York, Houghton Mifflin, 1901.
Ridge, Martin. *Ignatius Donnelly: Portrait of a Politician*. Chicago, University of Chicago Press, 1962.
Robbins, Elliott. *Panacea for the Healing of the Nation*. New York, Globe Stationery and Printing Co., 1876.
Rocker, Rudolph. *Pioneers of American Freedom*. Los Angeles, Rocker Publications Committee, 1949.
Ross, Edward A. *Social Control: A Survey of the Foundations of Order*. New York, Macmillan, 1901.
Russell, Frances Theresa. *Touring Utopia*. New York, Dial, 1932.

Sachs, Emanie L. *"The Terrible Siren," Victoria Woodhull (1838–1927)*. New York, Harper, 1928.
Schlesinger, Arthur M. *The American as Reformer*. Cambridge, Harvard University Press, 1950.
———. *New Viewpoints in American History*. New York, Macmillan, 1922.
———. *Paths to the Present*. New York, Macmillan, 1949.
———. *The Rise of Modern America, 1865–1951*. 4th ed. New York, Macmillan, 1951.
Schlesinger, Arthur M., Jr. *The Age of Jackson*. Boston, Little, Brown, 1945.
———. *The Coming of the New Deal*. Boston, Houghton Mifflin, 1959.
———. *The Crisis of the Old Order, 1919–1933*. Boston, Houghton Mifflin, 1957.
———. *The Politics of Upheaval*. Boston, Houghton Mifflin, 1960.
——— and Morton White, ed. *Paths of American Thought*. Boston, Houghton Mifflin, 1963.
Schurz, Carl. *Henry Clay*. 2 vols. Boston, Houghton Mifflin, 1899.
Schuster, Eunice Minette. *Native American Anarchism: A Study of Left-Wing American Individualism*. Northampton, Mass., Smith College Studies in History. Vol. XVII, Nos. 1–4 (October 1931–July 1932).
Seitz, Don C. *Uncommon Americans: Pencil Portraits of Men and Women Who Have Broken the Rules*. Indianapolis, Bobbs-Merrill, 1925.
Seldes, Gilbert. *The Stammering Century*. New York, John Day, 1928.
Sherwin, Oscar. *Prophet of Liberty: The Life and Times of Wendell Phillips*. New York, Bookman Associates, 1958.
Simms, Henry H. *Life of John Taylor: The Story of a Brilliant Leader in the Early Virginia State Rights School*. Richmond, William Byrd Press, 1932.
Simons, Algie Martin. *Social Forces in American History*. New York, Macmillan, 1912.
Skidmore, Thomas. *The Rights of Man to Property!* New York, Printed for the Author by A. Ming, Jr., 1829.

Slosson, Preston W. *The Great Crusade and After, 1914–1928*. New York, Macmillan, 1935.

Smith, G. "Prophets of Unrest," *Forum*, IX (August 1890).

Smith, T. V. *The American Philosophy of Equality*. Chicago, University of Chicago Press, 1927.

———. *The Promise of American Politics*. Chicago, University of Chicago Press, 1936.

Sotheran, Charles. *Horace Greeley and Other Pioneers of American Socialism*. New York, Mitchell Kennerley, 1915.

Soule, George. *A Planned Society*. New York, Macmillan, 1932.

———. *Planning U.S.A.: A Concise History of Economic Planning in This Country plus an Authoritative Explanation of What Is Being Done to Meet the Urgent Problems of Today*. New York, Viking, 1966.

Sparks, Edwin E. *The United States of America*. 2 vols. New York, Putnam's, 1904.

Spitz, David. *Patterns of Anti-Democratic Thought: An Analysis and a Criticism, with Special Reference to the American Political Mind in Recent Times*. New York, Macmillan, 1949.

Sprague, Philo W. *Christian Socialism: What and Why*. New York, Dutton, 1891.

Stedman, Laura, and George M. Gould. *Life and Letters of Edmund Clarence Stedman*. 2 vols. New York, Moffat, Yard & Co., 1910.

Sullivan, Mark. *Our Times: The United States, 1900–1925*. Vol. I, The Turn of the Century, 1900–1904. Vol. II, America Finding Herself. Vol. III, Pre-War America. Vol. IV, The War Begins, 1909–1914. Vol. V, Over Here, 1914–1918. Vol. VI, The Twenties. New York, Scribner's, 1926–35.

Sumner, William Graham. *What Social Classes Owe to Each Other*. New Haven, Yale University Press, 1925.

Swartz, Clarence L. *What Is Mutualism?* New York, Vanguard, 1927.

Swing, Raymond G. *Forerunners of American Fascism*. New York, Julian Messner, 1935.

Symes, Lillian, and Travers Clement. *Rebel America: The Story of Social Revolt in the United States*. New York, Harper, 1934.

Taft, Philip. *Movements for Economic Reform*. New York, Rinehart, 1950.

Tarbell, Ida M. *The Nationalizing of Business, 1878–1898*. New York, Macmillan, 1936.

———. "New Dealers of the 'Seventies: Henry George and Edward Bellamy," *Forum*, XCII (September 1934).

Taylor, John. *An Inquiry into the Principles and Policy of the Government of the United States of America*. New ed. New Haven, Yale University Press, 1950.

———. *Tyranny Unmasked*. Washington City, Davis and Force, 1822.

Thistlethwaite, Frank. *The Great Experiment*. Cambridge, Cambridge University Press, 1955.

Thomas, Lately. *The Vanishing Evangelist: The Aimee Semple McPherson Kidnap Case*. New York, Viking, 1959.
Tilton, Theodore. *Victoria C. Woodhull; A Biographical Sketch*. New York, Golden Age, 1871.
Trollope, Frances. *Domestic Manners of the Americans*. London, Printed for Whittaker, Treacher & Co., 1832.
Trowbridge, J. T. "A Reminiscence of the Pentarch," *Independent*, LV (February 26, 1903).
Tucker, Benjamin R. *Instead of a Book by a Man Too Busy to Write One, a Fragmentary Exposition of Philosophical Anarchism*. New York, Benjamin R. Tucker, 1893.
Tyler, Alice. *Freedom's Ferment: Phases of American Social History to 1860*. Minneapolis, University of Minnesota Press, 1944.

Unger, Irwin. *The Greenback Era: A Social and Political History of American Finance, 1865–1879*. Princeton, Princeton University Press, 1964.
"Utopia," *Daedalus*, XCIV (Spring 1965).

Van Deusen, Glyndon G. *Horace Greeley, Nineteenth-Century Crusader*. Philadelphia, University of Pennsylvania Press, 1953.

Wagner, Donald O., ed. *Social Reformers: Adam Smith to John Dewey*. New York, Macmillan, 1934.
Walsh, Chad. *From Utopia to Nightmare*. New York, Harper, 1962.
Ward, Lester F. *Dynamic Sociology, or Applied Social Science*. 2 vols. New York, D. Appleton & Co., 1883.
Wayland, J. A. *Leaves of Life: A Story of Twenty Years of Socialist Agitation*. Girard, Kans., Appeal to Reason, 1912.
Weaver, James B. *A Call to Action: An Interpretation of the Great Uprising, Its Source and Causes*. Des Moines, Iowa Printing Co., 1892.
Wecter, Dixon. *The Age of the Great Depression, 1929–1941*. New York, Macmillan, 1948.
———. *The Hero in America*. New York, Scribner's, 1941.
Weisberger, Bernard A. *They Gathered at the River: The Story of the Great Revivalists and Their Impact Upon Religion in America*. Boston, Little, Brown, 1958.
Welter, Rush. *Popular Education and Democratic Thought in America*. New York, Columbia University Press, 1962.
Wertenbaker, T. J. "Ten Eventful Years in the U.S.," *Current History*, XXXIII (October 1930).
Westmeyer, Russell Eugene. *Modern Economic and Social Systems*. New York, Farrar & Rinehart, 1940.
White, Morton G. *Social Thought in America: The Revolt Against Formalism*. New York, Viking, 1949.

Whiteman, Luther, and Samuel L. Lewis. *Glory Roads: The Psychological State of California*. New York, Crowell, 1936.

Wish, Harvey. *Society and Thought in Early America: A Social and Intellectual History of the American People Through 1865*. 2 vols. New York, Longmans, Green, 1950–52.

Wittke, Carl F. *The Utopian Communist: A Biography of Wilhelm Weitling, Nineteenth-Century Reformer*. Baton Rouge, Louisiana State University Press, 1950.

Woodhull, Victoria C. *A Speech on the Principles of Social Freedom Delivered November 20, 1871*. New York, Woodhull & Claflin, 1874.

Woodward, C. Vann. *Tom Watson, Agrarian Rebel*. New York, Macmillan, 1938.

Wooldridge, Charles William. *Perfecting the Earth: A Piece of Possible History*. Cleveland, Utopia Publishing Co., 1902.

Zinn, Howard, ed. *New Deal Thought*. Indianapolis, Bobbs-Merrill, 1966.

SUSAN B. ANTHONY

Address to the Legislature of New York, adopted by the State Woman's Rights Convention, held at Albany. Tuesday and Wednesday, February 14 and 15, 1854. Prepared by Elizabeth Cody Stanton of Seneca Falls, New York.

Anthony, Katharine. *Susan B. Anthony: Her Personal History and Her Era*. Garden City, Doubleday, 1954.

Anthony, Susan Brownell. *An Account of the Proceedings on the Trial of Susan B. Anthony, on the Charge of Illegal Voting, etc*. Rochester, N.Y., Daily Democrat and Chronicle Book Print, 1874.

Arnold, Marguerite. "Are Women Intelligent?", *Century Magazine*, CI (December 1920).

Dore, Rheta Childe. *Susan B. Anthony: The Woman Who Changed the Mind of a Nation*. New York, Frederick A Stokes, 1928.

Flexner, Eleanor. *Century of Struggle: The Woman's Rights Movement in the United States*. Cambridge, The Belknap Press of Harvard University Press, 1959.

Harper, Ida Husted. "Susan B. Anthony," *Independent*, LX (March 15, 1906.

———. *The Life and Work of Susan B. Anthony, Including Public Addresses, Her Own Letters and Many from her Contemporaries During Fifty Years*. 2 vols. Indianapolis, Bowen-Merrill, 1898.

———. *The Life and Work of Susan B. Anthony, Including the Triumphs of Her Last Years, Account of Her Death and Funeral and Comment*
"Susan B. Anthony," *Harper's Weekly*, L (March 24, 1906).
of the Press. Indianapolis, Hollenbeck Press, 1908.

Lutz, Alma. *Susan B. Anthony: Rebel, Crusader, Humanitarian*. Boston, Beacon Press, 1959.

Villard, Fanny Garrison. "Susan B. Anthony," *The Nation*, CX (February 14, 1920).

EDWARD BELLAMY

Bellamy, Edward. *Equality*. New York, Appleton, 1897.

———. *Looking Backward, 2000–1887*. Boston, Houghton Mifflin, 1889.

———, ed. *The New Nation*. (1891–94).

———. "Progress of Nationalism in the United States," *North American Review*, CLIV (June 1892).

———. *Talks on Nationalism*. Peerage Press, 1938.

Bowman, Sylvia E. *et al. Edward Bellamy Abroad: An American Prophet's Influence*. New York, Twayne, 1962.

———. *The Year 2000: A Critical Biography of Edward Bellamy*. New York, Bookman Associates, 1958.

Franklin, John Hope. "Edward Bellamy and Nationalism," *New England Quarterly*, XI (December 1938).

Gilman, Nicholas P. " 'Nationalism' in the United States," *Quarterly Journal of Economics*, IV (October 1889).

Morgan, Arthur E. *Edward Bellamy*. New York, Columbia University Press, 1944.

Peebles, H. P. "Utopias of the Past Compared with the Theories of Bellamy," *Overland Review*, XV (June 1890).

Roberts, J. W. *Looking Within: The Misleading Tendencies of "Looking Backward" Made Manifest*. New York, A. S. Barnes, 1893.

Sanders, George A. *Reality; or, Law and Order vs. Anarchy and Socialism. A Reply to Edward Bellamy's "Looking Backward" and "Equality."* Cleveland, Burroughs Brothers, 1898.

Walker, Francis A. "Mr. Bellamy and the New Nationalist Party," *Atlantic Monthly*, CXV (February 1890).

Willard, Frances E. "An Interview with Edward Bellamy," *Our Day*, IV (December 1889).

WILLIAM JENNINGS BRYAN

Bryan, William Jennings. *The First Battle: A Story of the Campaign of 1896*. Chicago, W. B. Conkey Co., 1896.

———. *The Great Fight for Free Silver*. Edgewood Publishing Co., 1897.

———. *Speeches . . . Revised and Arranged by Himself*. 2 vols. New York, Funk and Wagnalls, 1909.

——— and Mary Baird. *The Memoirs of William Jennings Bryan*. Chicago, John C. Winston Co., 1925.

Coletta, Paolo E. *William Jennings Bryan*. Vol. I: Political Evangelist,
Glad, Paul W. *The Trumpet Soundeth: William Jennings Bryan and His*
1860–1903. Lincoln, University of Nebraska Press, 1964.
Democracy, 1896–1912. Lincoln, University of Nebraska Press, 1960.

Hibben, Paxton. *The Peerless Leader: William Jennings Bryan*. New York, Farrar and Rinehart, 1929.

Josephson, Matthew. *The Politicos, 1865–1896*. New York, Harcourt, Brace, 1938.

Long, J. C. *Bryan, the Great Commoner*. New York, Appleton, 1928.

Melder, Keith. *Bryan the Campaigner*. Bulletin 241: Contributions from the Museum of History and Technology, Paper 46. Washington, D.C., Smithsonian Institution, 1965.

Norris, George W. "Bryan as a Political Leader," *Current History*, XXII, (September 1925).

Rosser, Charles McDaniel. *The Crusading Commoner: A Close-up of William Jennings Bryan and His Times*. Dallas, Tex., Mathis, Van Nort & Co., 1937.

Shaw, Albert. "William Jennings Bryan," *American Review of Reviews*, LXXII (September 1925).

White, William Allen. "The End of an Epoch," *Scribner's Magazine*, LXXIX (June 1926).

Williams, Wayne C. *William Jennings Bryan: A Study in Political Vindication*. New York, Fleming H. Revell Co., 1923.

Wish, Harvey. "John Peter Altgeld and the Background of the Campaign of 1896," *Mississippi Valley Historical Review*, XXIV (March 1938).

HENRY CLAY

American Colonization Society, A Few Facts Respecting Them. Boston, Peirce and Williams, 1830.

Brown, Isaac V. *Biography of the Rev. Robert Finley, D.D., of Basking Ridge, N.J., with an Account of His Agency as the Author of "The American Colonization Society; also a Sketch of the Slave Trade; a View of Our Industrial Policy and that of Great Britain Towards Liberia and Africa*. Philadelphia, John W. Moore, 1857.

Clay, Henry. *The Works of* . . . Edited by Calvin Colton with an Introduction by Thomas B. Reed and a History of Tariff Legislation, 1812–1896, by William McKinley. New York, G. P. Putnam's Sons, 1904.

Colton, Calvin. *The Life and Times of Henry Clay*. 2 vols. New York, A. S. Barnes, 1846.

A *Defence of Southern Slavery Against the Attacks of Henry Clay and Alex'r Campbell*. By a Southern Clergyman. Hamburg, S.C., Robinson & Carlisle, 1851.

An *Enquiry into the Origin, Plan, and Prospects of the American Colonization Society*. Fredericksburg, The Arena Office, 1829.

Fox, Early Lee. *The American Colonization Society, 1817–1840*. Johns Hopkins University Studies in Historical and Political Science. Baltimore, Johns Hopkins Press, 1919.

Garrison, William Lloyd. *Thoughts on African Colonization; or, An Im-*

partial Exhibition of the Doctrines, Principles and Purposes of the American Colonization Society, etc. Garrison and Knapp, 1832.

Jay, William. *An Inquiry into the Character and Tendency of the American Colonization and American Anti-Slavery Societies.* New York, Leavitt, Lord & Co., 1835.

Morris, Thomas. *In Reply to the Speech of the Hon. Henry Clay.* New York, American Anti-Slavery Society, 1839.

Proceedings, on the Formation of the New York State Colonization Society. Albany, Websters and Skinners, 1829.

Stebbins, G. B. *Facts and Opinions Touching the Real Origin, Character and Influence of the American Colonization Society: Views of Wilberforce, Clarkson, and Others, and Opinions of the Free People of Color of the U.S.* Boston, John P. Jewett & Co., 1853.

Van Deusen, Glyndon G. *The Life of Henry Clay.* Boston, Little, Brown, 1937.

FATHER CHARLES E. COUGHLIN

Coughlin, Rev. Charles Edward. *A Series of Lectures on Social Justice . . .* (broadcast over a national network). Royal Oak, Mich., Radio League of the Little Flower, 1935.

———. *"By the Sweat of Thy Brow"; a Series of Sermons Broadcast . . . from the Shrine of the Little Flower, October 1930–February 1931.* Royal Oak, Mich., Radio League of the Little Flower, 1931.

———. *Driving Out the Money Changers* (broadcast over a national network). Royal Oak, Mich., Radio League of the Little Flower, 1933.

———. *Eight Lectures on Color, Capital, and Justice.* Royal Oak, Mich., Radio League of the Little Flower, 1934.

———. *Money! Questions and Answers.* Royal Oak, Mich., National Union for Social Justice, 1936.

———. *The New Deal in Money.* Royal Oak, Mich., Radio League of the Little Flower, 1933.

Father Coughlin, His "Facts" and Arguments. General Jewish Council, 1939.

Lee, Alfred McClung, and Elizabeth Briant Lee, ed. *The Fine Art of Propaganda: A Study of Father Coughlin's Speeches.* New York, Harcourt, Brace, 1939.

Mugglebee, Ruth. *Father Coughlin: The Radio Priest of the Shrine of the Little Flower.* Garden City, Garden City Publishing Co., 1933.

Shenton, James P. "The Coughlin Movement and the New Deal," *Political Science Quarterly,* LXXXIII (September 1958).

Swing, Raymond G. *Forerunners of American Fascism.* New York, Julian Messner, 1935.

Tull, Charles J. *Father Coughlin and the New Deal.* Syracuse, Syracuse University Press, 1965.

JACOB S. COXEY

Austin, Shirley Plumer. "Coxey's Commonweal Army," *Chautauquan*, XIX (June 1894).
———. "The Downfall of Coxeyism," *Chautauquan*, XIX (July 1894).
Hooper, Osman C. "The Coxey Movement in Ohio," *Ohio Archaeological and Historical Quarterly*, IX (October 1900).
McMurry, Donald L. *Coxey's Army: A Study of the Industrial Army Movement of 1894*. Boston, Little, Brown, 1920.
Stead, W. T. "'Coxeyism': A Character Sketch," *Review of Reviews*, X (July 1894).
Vincent, Henry. *The Story of the Commonweal; Complete and Graphic Narrative of the Origin and Growth of the Movement*. Chicago, W. B. Conkey Co., 1894.

FATHER DIVINE

Boaz, Ruth. "My Thirty Years with Father Divine," *Ebony*, XX (May 1965).
Father Divine: His Words of Spirit, Life and Hope. Edited by St. John Evangelist and James Hope, 1961.
Hosher, John. *God in a Rolls Royce*. New York, Hillman-Curl, 1936.
Lanyon, Walter Clemon. *It Is Wonderful*. London, E. K. Reader, 193?.
———. *Out of the Clouds*. Los Angeles, Bookhaven Press, Kellaway-Ide Co., 1941.
Levick, Lionel. 'Father Divine Is God," *Forum and Century*, XCII (October 1934).
McKelway, S., and A. J. Liebling. "Who Is This King of Glory?" *New Yorker*, June 13, 20, 27, 1936.
The New Day (periodical)
Parker, Robert Allerton. *The Incredible Messiah: The Deification of Father Divine*. Boston, Little, Brown, 1937.
The Spoken Word (periodical)
World Herald (periodical)

GEORGE HENRY EVANS

Commons, John R., *et al.*, ed. *A Documentary History of American Industrial Society*. Vol. VII, VIII, IX. Cleveland, Arthur H. Clark Co., 1910.
Evans, Frederick W. *Autobiography of a Shaker and Revelation of the Apocalypse, with an Appendix*. New York, F. W. Evans, 1869.

MARCUS GARVEY

Cronon, Edmund David. *Black Moses: The Story of Marcus Garvey and the Universal Negro Improvement Association.* Madison, University of Wisconsin Press, 1955.

Garvey, Mrs. Amy Jacques. *Garvey and Garveyism.* Kingston, Jamaica, published by the Author, 1963.

Silberman, Charles E. *Crisis in Black and White.* New York, Random House, 1964.

Streator, George. "Three Men—Napier, Moton, Garvey—Negro Leaders Who Typified an Era for their People," *Commonweal,* XXXII (August 9, 1940).

HENRY GEORGE

Barker, Charles Albro. *Henry George.* New York, Oxford University Press, 1955.

De Mille, Anna George. *Henry George: Citizen of the World.* Chapel Hill, University of North Carolina Press, 1950.

Dixwell, George Basil. "*Progress and Poverty*": *A Review of the Doctrines of Henry George.* Cambridge, J. Wilson & Son, 1882.

George, Henry. *Works of . . .* New York, Doubleday, Page, 1904.

George, Henry, Jr. *The Life of Henry George.* New York, Doubleday & McClure, 1900.

Higgins, Rev. S. J. *The True Philosophy of the Land Question; Fallacies of Henry George Exposed and Refuted.* Cincinnati, Press of Keating & Co., 1887.

Jorgensen, Emil O. *Did Henry George Confuse the Single Tax?* Elkhart, Ind., James A. Bell Co., 1936.

Nock, Albert Jay. *Henry George: An Essay.* New York, William Morrow & Co., 1939.

Post, Louis F. *The Prophet of San Francisco: Personal Memories and Interpretations of Henry George.* New York, Vanguard, 1930.

Young, Arthur Nichols. *The Single Tax Movement in the United States.* Princeton, Princeton University Press, 1916.

WILLIAM HOPE HARVEY

Bliss, H. L. *Coin's Financial Fraud; A Complete and Comprehensive Treatise on the Currency Question, and an Answer to and Complete Refutation of the Advocates of the Free Coinage of Silver.* Chicago, Donohue, Henneberry & Co., 1895.

Harvey, William Hope. *Coin's Financial School.* Chicago, Coin Publishing Co., 1894.

———. *Coin on Money Trusts and Imperialism*. Chicago, Coin Publishing Co., 1899.

Hofstadter, Richard, ed. *Coin's Financial School* (by William Hope Harvey). Cambridge, Belknap Press of Harvard University Press, 1963.

Nichols, Jeannette P. "Bryan's Benefactor: Coin Harvey and His World," *Ohio Historical Quarterly*, LXVII (October 1958).

EDWARD KELLOGG

Destler, Chester McArthur. "The Influence of Edward Kellogg upon American Radicalism, 1865–96," *Journal of Political Economy*, XL (June 1932).

Kellogg, Edward. *A New Monetary System: The Only Means of Securing the Respective Rights of Labor and Property, and of Protecting the Public from Financial Revulsions*. Mary Kellogg Putnam, ed. 2d ed. New York, Rudd & Carleton, 1861.

———. *Currency: The End and the Remedy* (by Godek Gardner, pseud.). 4th ed., improved. New York, no publisher, 1844.

———. *Labor and Capital: A New Monetary System*. Edited by his daughter, Mary Kellogg Putnam. New York, J. W. Lovell Co., 1883.

———. *Labor and Other Capital: The Rights of Each Secured and the Wrongs of Both Eradicated*. New York, Published by the Author, 1849.

———. *Remarks upon Usury and Its Effects: A National Bank a Remedy; In a Letter, etc.* (by Whitehook). New York, Harper, 1841.

BENJAMIN B. LINDSEY

Lindsey, Benjamin B. "What Do You Think?" *Outlook*, CXLVIII (April 25, 1928).

——— with Rube Borough. *The Dangerous Life*. New York, Liveright, 1931.

Steffens, Lincoln. *Upbuilders*. New York, Doubleday, Page, 1909.

Wells, H. G. "Modern Experiment with Marriage," *New York Times*, June 26, 1927.

HUEY LONG

Davis, Forrest. *Huey Long: A Candid Biography with a Digest of the Share-Our-Wealth Principles Prepared by Senator Huey Long*. New York, Dodge Publishing Co., 1935.

Huey Pierce Long: The Martyr of the Age. A publication of the Louisiana State Museum, New Orleans, November 11, 1937.

"Huey Proposes," *New Republic*, LXXXII (March 20, 1935).

Kane, Harnett T. *Louisiana Hayride: The American Rehearsal for Dictatorship, 1928–1940*. New York, William Morrow, 1941.

Long, Huey P. *Every Man a King: The Autobiography of . . .* New Orleans, National Book Co., 1933.
———. *My First Days in the White House*. Harrisburg, Pa., Telegraph Press, 1935.
———. "Share Our Wealth Plan," *Review of Reviews*, XCI (April 1935).
Louisiana Conservation Review Memorial Number (Huey Long), October 1935. Published quarterly by the Department of Conservation. Vol. IV, No. 8.
Sindler, Allan P. *Huey Long's Louisiana State Politics, 1920–1952*. Baltimore, Johns Hopkins Press, 1956.
Sokolsky, George E. "Huey Long," *Atlantic Monthly*, CLVI (November 1935).

CARRY A. NATION

Asbury, Herbert. *Carrie Nation: The Woman with the Hatchet*. New York, Alfred A. Knopf, 1929.
Beals, Carleton. *Cyclone Carry: The Story of Carry Nation*. New York, Chilton, 1962.
Dwyer, James L. "The Lady with the Hatchet," *American Mercury*, VII (March 1926).
Nation, Carry A. *The Use and Need of the Life of . . .* Written by Herself. Topeka, Kans., F. M. Steves & Sons, 1905.
Taylor, Robert Lewis. *Vessel of Wrath: The Life and Times of Carry Nation*. New American Library, 1966.

MORDECAI MANUEL NOAH

Allen, Lewis F. "Founding of the City of Ararat on Grand Island—by Mordecai M. Noah." *Publications of the Buffalo (N.Y.) Historical Society*, I (1879).
———. *The Story of the Tablet of the City of Ararat. Publications of the Buffalo (N.Y.) Historical Society*, XXV (1921), 113–44.
Daly, Charles P. *The Settlements of the Jews in North America*. New York, Philip Cowen, 1893.
"Death of M. M. Noah," *New York Daily Tribune*, March 24, 1851.
Goldberg, Isaac. *Major Noah: American-Jewish Pioneer*. Philadelphia, Jewish Publication Society of America, 1936.
Gordis, Robert. "Mordecai Manuel Noah: A Centenary Evaluation." *Publications of the American Jewish Historical Society*, Vol. XLI, No. 1 (September 1951).
Lebeson, Anita Libman. *Jewish Pioneers in America, 1492–1848*. New York, Brentano's, 1931.
Makover, Abraham B. *Mordecai M. Noah: His Life and Work from the Jewish Viewpoint*. New York, Bloch Publishing Co., 1917.

JOHN HUMPHREY NOYES

The Circular, Devoted to the Sovereignty of Jesus Christ. Oneida, N.Y., Oneida Community, 1855.

Eastman, Rev. Hubbard. *Noyesism Unveiled; A History of the Sect Self-Styled Perfectionists; with a Summary View of Their Leading Doctrines*. Brattleboro, Vt., Published by the Author, 1849.

Edmonds, Walter D. *The First Hundred Years, 1848–1948: 1848—Oneida Community; 1880—Oneida Community, Limited; 1935—Oneida Ltd.* Oneida, N.Y., Oneida, Ltd., 1948.

Estlake, Allan. *The Oneida Community; A Record of an Attempt to Carry Out the Principles of Christian Unselfishness and Scientific Race Improvement*. London, George Redway, 1900.

Handbook of the Oneida Community. Oneida, N.Y., Office of the Oneida *Circular*, 1875.

Newcombe, Patricia Anne. *John Humphrey Noyes: Bible Communism*. M.A. thesis, University of Chicago, June 1958.

Noyes, George Wallingford, ed. *John Humphrey Noyes, the Putney Community*. Oneida, N.Y., 1931.

———. *Religious Experience of John Humphrey Noyes, Founder of the Oneida Community*. New York, Macmillan, 1923.

Noyes, John Humphrey. *History of American Socialism*. Philadelphia, Lippincott, 1870.

Noyes, Pierrepont Noyes. *My Father's House: An Oneida Boyhood*. New York, Farrar & Rinehart, 1937.

Parker, Robert Allerton. *A Yankee Saint: John Humphrey Noyes and the Oneida Community*. New York, G. P. Putnam's Sons, 1935.

ROBERT OWEN

Bestor, Arthur E., Jr., ed. *Education and Reform at New Harmony: Correspondence of William Maclure and Marie Duclos Fretageot, 1820–1833*. Indianapolis, Indiana Historical Society, Vol. 15, No. 3 (1948).

Clayton, Joseph. *Robert Owen: Social Pioneer*. London, A. C. Fifield, 1908.

Cole, G. D. H. *Robert Owen*. London, Ernest Benn, 1925.

Douglas, Paul H. "Some New Material on the Lives of Robert and Robert Dale Owen," February 2, 1942. Typewritten manuscript.

Fisher, W. L. *An Examination of the New System of Society—by Robert Owen*. Philadelphia, John Mortimer, 1826.

Harvey, Rowland H. *Robert Owen: Social Idealist*. Berkeley, University of California Press, 1949.

Holyoake, George Jacob. *Life and Last Days of Robert Owen*. London, John Watts, 1859.

Leopold, Richard William. *Robert Dale Owen: A Biography*. Cambridge, Harvard University Press, 1940.

Lockwood, George B. *The New Harmony Movement*. New York, D. Appleton & Co., 1905.
Owen, Robert. *Discourses on A New System of Society; As Delivered in the Hall of Representatives, In the Presence of the President of the United States, the Ex-President, Heads of Departments, Members of Congress, etc.* Washington, D.C., no publisher, 1825.
———. *New View of Society, No. 11. Mr. Owen's Report to the Committee of the Association for the Relief of the Manufacturing and Laboring Poor; Laid Before the Committee of the House of Commons on the Poor's Laws, in the Session of 1817*. London, R. Watts, 1818.
———. *The Life of . . .* Written by Himself. London, Effingham Wilson, Vol. I, 1857; Vol. Ia, 1858.
———. *Letter to the Senate of the 28th Congress of the United States*. Washington, D.C., Printed at the Globe Office, 1845.
———. *Manifesto*. 6th ed. London, Published at the Social Institution, 1940.
———. *A New View of Society, or, Essays on the Formation of the Human Character*. London, no publisher, 1817.
———. *Threading My Way; Twenty-Seven Years of Autobiography*. London, Trubner & Co., 1874.
Pancoast, Elinor, and Anne E. Lincoln. *The Incorrigible Idealist: Robert Dale Owen in America*. Bloomington, Ind., Principia Press, 1940.
Podmore, Frank. *Robert Owen: A Biography*. 2 vols. London, Hutchinson, 1906.

MARGARET SANGER

Lader, Lawrence. *The Margaret Sanger Story and the Fight for Birth Control*. Garden City, Doubleday, 1955.
Sanger, Margaret. *An Autobiography*. New York, W. W. Norton, 1938.
———. *The Birth Control Review: Dedicated to the Cause of Voluntary Motherhood*. Vol. I (February 1917). New York.
———. *Motherhood in Bondage*. New York, Brentano's, 1928.
———. *My Fight for Birth Control*. New York, Farrar & Rinehart, 1931.
———. *The Pivot of Civilization*. New York, Brentano's, 1922.
———, ed. *Problems of Overpopulation*. New York, American Birth Control League, 1926.
———. *Woman and the New Race*. New York, Eugenics Publishing Co., 1920.

HOWARD SCOTT

Arkwright, Frank. *The ABC of Technocracy*. New York, Harper, 1933.
"A Document on the History and Purpose of Technocracy," *The Northwest Technocrat*, XXVIII (July 1965). Published by Technocracy, Inc., Seattle.

Hazlitt, Henry. "Scrambled Ergs; An Examination of Technocracy," *The Nation*, CXXXVI (February 1, 1933).
MacLeish, Archibald. "Machines and the Future," *The Nation*, CXXXVI (February 8, 1933).
Person, Harlow, and Beulah Amidon. "Economics Makes the Front Page," *Survey Graphic*, XXII (March 1933).
"Portrait of Howard Scott," *Business Week*, January 25, 1933.
Raymond, Allen. *What Is Technocracy?* New York, McGraw-Hill, 1933.
Scott, Howard (and others). *Introduction to Technocracy*. New York, John Day, 1933.
———. *Technocracy: Science vs. Chaos*. New York, Technocracy, Inc., 1933.
———. *The Living Age*. New York, Living Age Co., 1932.
Soule, George. "Technocracy: Good Medicine or a Bedtime Story?", *New Republic*, LXXIII (December 28, 1932).
Technocracy in Plain Terms. New York, Technocracy, Inc., 1939.
Technocracy Study Course. New York, Technocracy, Inc., 1934.
The Technocrat. Los Angeles, Technocracy, Inc.
Ward, Harold. "In Defense of Technocracy," *New Republic*, LXXIII (January 11, 1933).

UPTON SINCLAIR

Sinclair, Upton. *American Outpost: A Book of Reminiscences*. New York, Farrar and Rinehart, 1932.
———. *Autobiography*. New York, Harcourt, Brace & World, 1962.
———. *Candid Reminiscences: My 30 Years*. London, Laurie Ltd., 1932.
———. *Epic Answers: How to End Poverty in California*. Los Angeles, End Poverty League, 1934.
———. *The Epic Plan for California*. New York, Farrar & Rinehart, 1934.
———. *I, Candidate for Governor and How I Ended Poverty*. Los Angeles, Published by the Author, 1933.
——. *I, Candidate for Governor (and How I Got Licked)*. New York, Farrar & Rinehart, 1935.
———. *Immediate Epic*. Los Angeles, End Poverty League, 1934.

IRA STEWARD

Douglas, Dorothy W. "Ira Steward on Consumption and Unemployment," *Journal of Political Economy*, XL (August 1932).
Edlin, William. "The Life and Work of Ira Steward," *The Comrade*, I (December 1901).
Steward, Ira. *The Eight-Hour Movement; A Reduction of Hours Is an Increase of Wages*. An extract of a lecture delivered by Ira Steward. Boston, 1865.

SIMON W. STRAUS

Bexell, J. A. "Waste of Food from the Producer to the Household," *NEA Addresses and Proceedings* (1917).

———. "Thrift and Commercial Supremacy," *Ibid.* (1918).

———. "Thrift and Its Relation to Banking," *Ibid.* (1916).

Blake, Kate Devereux. "Thrift in Relation to the Home," *Ibid.* (1916).

———. "Thrift in the Home," *Ibid.* (1917).

Chamberlain, Arthur H. "Thrift in the Public Schools," *Ibid.* (1918).

———. "Agricultural Preparedness and Food Conservation: A Study in Thrift," *Ibid.* (1917).

Dempsey, C. H. "Adaptation of Courses in Domestic Economy and Industrial Arts to Meet Existing Demands," *Ibid.* (1917).

———. "Thrift in Relation to Industries," *Ibid.* (1916).

"The New American Thrift," *Annals of the American Academy of Political and Social Science,* LXXXVII (January 1920).

Straus, S. W. *History of the Thrift Movement in America.* Philadelphia, Lippincott, 1920.

———. "Thrift: A Patriotic Necessity," *National Education Association Addresses and Proceedings* (1917). Ann Arbor, Mich., Published by the Association, 1917.

———. "Thrift: An Educational Necessity," *NEA Addresses and Proceedings* (1916).

Stuart, M. H. "Thrift in Its Relation to Conservation," *Ibid.* (1916).

Wilson, R. H. "How the School May Help Increase Food Production," *Ibid.* (1917).

———. "Thrift in Its Relation to Country Life," *Ibid.* (1916).

WILLIAM A. (BILLY) SUNDAY

Ellis, William T. *"Billy" Sunday, The Man and His Message. With his own words which have won thousands for Christ.* Authorized Edition. Philadelphia, John C. Winston, 1914.

———. *"Billy Sunday, The Man and His Message, including Mr. Sunday's Autobiography, a Concluding Chapter by Mrs. William A. Sunday, and a Yoke-Fellow's Tribute by Homer A. Rodeheaver.* Philadelphia, John C. Winston, 1936.

McLoughlin, William G., Jr. *Billy Sunday Was His Real Name.* Chicago, University of Chicago Press, 1955.

WALTER C. TEAGLE

Opens "Share-the-Work" Drive, *New York Times,* September 2, 1932, 1:3; Editorial, September 3, 1932, 12:3.

Teagle, Walter C. "Your Job—Will You Share It?" *Review of Reviews and World's Work,* LXXXVI (November 1932).
Walker, L. C. "The Share-the-Work Movement," *Annals of the American Academy of Political and Social Science,* CLXV (January 1933).

DR. FRANCIS E. TOWNSEND

Crowell, C. T. "Townsend Plan," *American Mercury,* XXXIV (April 1935).
Dorman, Morgan. *Age Before Booty: An Explanation of the T Plan.* Foreword by Dr. Francis E. Townsend. New York, G. P. Putnam's Sons, 1936.
Holtzman, Abraham. *The Townsend Movement: A Political Study.* New York, Bookman Associates, 1963.
Huberman, L. "Pulling White Rabbits Out of the Hat; Townsend Plan," *Scholastic,* XXV (December 8, 1934).
"In the Driftway; Townsend Plan," *The Nation,* CXXXIX (November 14, 1934).
Milne, Richard. *That Man Townsend.* Los Angeles, Prosperity Publication Co., 1935.
Swing, Raymond Gram. "Dr. Townsend Solves It All," *The Nation,* CXL (March 6, 1935).
"Townsend Plan," *Christian Century,* LI (December 26, 1934).
"$200 a Month at Sixty; The Townsend Pension Plan," *Forum,* XCII (December 1934).
Wheeler, B. O. "Townsend Plan," *Commonweal,* XXI (February 22, 1935).

JOSIAH WARREN

Bailie, William. *Josiah Warren, the First American Anarchist: A Sociological Study.* Boston, Small, Maynard & Co., 1906.
Conway, Moncure D. *Autobiography—Memories and Experiences.* Boston, Houghton Mifflin, 1904.
———. "Modern Times, New York," *Fortnightly Review,* I (1865).
Warren, Josiah. *Equitable Commerce; A New Development of Principles, for the Harmoneous Adjustment and Regulation of the Pecuniary, Intellectual, and Moral Intercourse of Mankind, Proposed as Elements of New Society.* 2d ed. Utopia, Ohio, A. E. Senter, 1849.
———. *Manifesto.* Berkeley Heights, N.J., Oriole Press, 1952.
———. *True Civilization: An Immediate Necessity and the Last Ground of Hope for Mankind.* Boston, J. Warren, 1863.

FRANCES E. WRIGHT

D'Arusmont, Frances (Wright). *Biography, Notes, and Political Letters of Frances Wright D'Arusmont*. Dundee, Scotland, J. Myles, 1844.

———. *Course of Popular Lectures, Historical and Political*. Philadelphia, Published by the Author, 1836.

———. *A Course of Popular Lectures*. New York, no publisher, 1829.

———. *Views of Society and Manners in America; A Series of Letters from that Country to a Friend in England, During the Years 1818, 1819, and 1820*. By an Englishwoman. London, Longman, Hurst, Rees, Orme, & Brown, 1821.

Everett, L. S. *An Exposure of the Principles of the "Free Inquirers."* Boston, Benjamin B. Mussey, 1831.

Owen, Robert Dale. "Frances Wright, General Lafayette, and Mary Wollstonecraft Shelley," *Atlantic Monthy* (October 1873).

Parks, Edd Winfield. "Dreamer's Vision, Frances Wright at Nashoba (1825–30)," *Tennessee Historical Magazine,* II (January 1932).

Perkins, A. J. G., and Theresa Wolfson. *Frances Wright, Free Enquirer: The Study of a Temperament*. New York, Harper, 1939.

Waterman, William Randall. *Frances Wright*. Studies in History, Economics and Public Law. New York, Columbia University, 1924.

A NOTE ON THE EDITORS

Arthur and Lila Weinberg are best known for their books about Clarence Darrow: *Attorney for the Damned* was Mr. Weinberg's first book; together the Weinbergs edited *Verdicts Out of Court*, a collection of Darrow's writings and speeches. But they have had a continuing concern with reform and reformers in American history, and have also published *The Muckrakers* and *Instead of Violence*, a collection of writings on pacifism. *Passport to Utopia* is their fifth book. The Weinbergs have three daughters and live and work in Chicago.